Jill Liddington was born in Manchester in 1946 and now lives in Halifax, West Yorkshire. Since 1982 she has been a lecturer in Community Adult Education in the Department of External Studies, Leeds University, working mainly in the Bradford area. She is co-author of *One Hand Tied Behind Us: The Rise of the Women's Suffrage Movement*, published by Virago in 1978, a contributor to *Over Our Dead Bodies: Women against the Bomb* (1983), and author of *The Life and Times of a Respectable Rebel: Selina Cooper 1864–1946* (1984), also published by Virago.

In *The Long Road to Greenham*, Jill Liddington draws on handwritten diaries, little-known autobiographies, forgotten minute books, and life-story interviews with peace activists. Her richly researched and readable work disentangles the different and often complex feminist analyses of militarism over the last 170 years, offering the first major reappraisal of the women's peace movement from its beginnings to the present day.

THE LONG ROAD
TO GREENHAM

Feminism and Anti-Militarism in Britain since 1820

Jill Liddington

Published by VIRAGO PRESS Limited 1989
20–23 Mandela Street, Camden Town, London NW1 0HQ

Copyright © Jill Liddington 1989

*A CIP Catalogue record for this book
is available from the British Library*

Photoset by Rowland Phototypesetting Limited
Bury St Edmunds, Suffolk
Printed in Great Britain by
Cox and Wyman Limited, Reading, Berks.

Contents

Acknowledgements

My bulging file of letters written over the last five years testifies to the enormous number of people who have contributed towards the research for this history. It is impossible to thank every one, but I would particularly like to acknowledge:

Godelieve van Heteren for translating substantial sections from Dutch of the *only* history I could trace describing the nineteenth-century women's peace groups; David Doughan at the Fawcett Library and Malcolm Thomas at the Society of Friends' Library for help with sources for this early period; New York Public Library and Edith Wynner for permission to quote from the Rosika Schwimmer papers (see Sources); West Yorkshire Archive Service, Kirklees, for access to Florence Lockwood's manuscript diaries; Audrey Canning at the Scottish Gallacher Memorial Library for extremely generous help with Glasgow Women's Peace Crusade sources; all the women who kindly allowed me to record lengthy interviews with them, especially the two most elderly, Gwen Coleman and Dame Mabel Tylecote, who died during the writing of this book; Freddie Brougham for transcribing some of the longest interviews; and the School of Continuing Education, Leeds University, for a grant towards early research and transcription costs. The tapes and transcripts are now deposited with Calderdale Archives, Halifax.

I would also like to thank Susan Grayzel for material about Frances Hallowes, and Anne Wiltsher for discussions about the women's peace movement between 1915 and 1918; Sonya Leff for showing me the unpublished autobiography of her mother, Vera Leff; Emma Chatterton for her memories of the 1930s Women's Co-operative

Guild; Richenda Barbour for generously lending me the Golders Green Guild branch minute books, and Gill Scott for her scholarly comments upon Guild history; Margot Miller and other WILPF members for help with the post-war women's peace movement; Arthur Goss and Sheila Jones for discussions on the pre-CND peace movement, and Dick Taylor for other CND sources; Diana Shelley, Gay Jones, Meg Beresford, Bridget Robson and Mary Brewer for interviews on the more recent peace movement; Ann Pettitt for access to her collection of Women for Life on Earth papers, now deposited at Glamorgan Archives, Cardiff; Denise Aaron for her Greenham reminiscences; and Lynne Jones, Rebecca Johnson, Meryl Antonelli and Nina Hall for their memories of life at the peace camp.

For comments on sections of the book concerning peace movement history which they lived through or have expert knowledge of, I am particularly grateful to Anne Summers, James Hinton, Gill Scott, Diana Shelley, Sarah Perrigo, Jean McCrindle, Kerry McQuade – and Mary and Alan Betteridge, treasurer of Halifax Women for Peace and Calderdale Archivist respectively. Finally there are four people I particularly want to thank: Ruthie Petrie at Virago, who commented helpfully on the book stage by stage; Julian Harber, peace activist and historian, who shared with me his valuable cache of 1980s CND material and offered his comments chapter by chapter; playwright Frances McNeil, who generously came to my rescue in the final stages of the book, expertly guiding me through the difficult cutting process; and Gillian Beaumont at Virago, who edited the final manuscript with admirable care.

Abbreviations

CND   Campaign for Nuclear Disarmament

ILP   Independent Labour Party

ICW   International Council of Women

IWSA   International Woman Suffrage Alliance

NCANWT   National Council for the Abolition of Nuclear Weapon Tests

NUWSS   National Union of Women's Suffrage Societies

PPU   Peace Pledge Union

UDC   Union of Democratic Control

WIDF   Women's International Democratic Federation

WIL   Women's International League (1915–19)

WILPF   Women's International League for Peace and Freedom (from 1919)

WLM   Women's Liberation Movement

WONT   Women Oppose the Nuclear Threat

WSPU   Women's Social and Political Union

WSF   Workers' Suffrage Federation

Introduction

On Thursday 27 August 1981 a group of thirty-six women set out from Cardiff on a 120-mile walk over the Welsh border into England. They called themselves 'Women for Life on Earth' and their destination was the American base at Greenham Common in Berkshire. Here, ninety-six new nuclear Cruise missiles were to be based. The women arrived ten days later, and demanded a televised debate between themselves and the government on the nuclear issue. Four women chained themselves to the fence around the base to underline their demand. But the government felt able to ignore this eccentric pinprick. No debate took place. Instead, the Women for Life on Earth contingent stayed. The Greenham Common peace camp was born.

In 1982 the camp became women-only. Arrests and imprisonments multiplied; and in the autumn other women were invited by chain letter to come to Greenham on Sunday 12 December to 'embrace the base'. And so they did. Next day, the *Daily Mirror* blazoned across its front page: 'PEACE! The plea by 30,000 women who joined hands in the world's most powerful protest against nuclear war.'[1] Suddenly Greenham was news. The camp became the most powerful symbol of a popular refusal to accept nuclear weapons – anywhere. Greenham's magic was centrifugal, inspiring other camps, other campaigns, and a fresh new style of nonviolent protest linking personal gender politics and global power politics.

The camp survived – despite icy winters, thousands of arrests, repeated evictions, and increasing media silence. Its images and culture provided an icon for the eighties. Over seven years after the walk first arrived at Greenham, women remain – miraculously – camped around the perimeter wire; their refusal to pack up and go away is a vivid reminder of the inventiveness and tenacity of the opposition to nuclear militarism. The late 1980s, its mass peace movement now in decline, offers an opportunity for a reappraisal of Greenham and its history.

The walk for 'Life on Earth' lacked a tidy, easily traced ancestry: it seemed to spring up from nowhere. Certainly, the idea of a semi-permanent women's peace camp around a nuclear missile base was unthinkable before the 1980s. Curiosity about precedents grew. It provoked the question: 'Did women do anything for peace *before* Greenham?' But there was no one accessible account to which the Greenham women could turn.

Yet the history of earlier women's peace campaigns in Britain extends back to 1915 when an International Congress of Women was held at The Hague; and small-scale women's peace groups can even be traced back to 1820 when a handful of 'Female Auxiliary Peace Societies' sprang up in various towns.

Why had all this been forgotten? Partly because a women's peace movement has had a highly cyclical history. This is, of course, also true of the history of the broader women's movement and of the general peace movement. But a women's peace movement is *particularly* marked by dramatic peaks and troughs, with popular support suddenly rising up – as in 1981–82 around Greenham – and then dropping away – as in the late 1980s. At times, its language and imagery has encapsulated prevailing fears about militarism, moving tens of thousands of women to action. This was so around 1930 when a broad coalition of women's groups petitioned the World Disarmament Conference at Geneva; and during the 1917–18 Women's Peace Crusade, when women took to the streets to demand a negotiated peace to end the Great War. More usually, however, a women's peace movement comprised a cluster of smaller campaigning groups. This was the scale of the

Women's International League which sprang from the Hague Congress in 1915. At other times there has been fragmentation. In the late nineteenth century the small women's peace groups were largely cut off from the wider equal-rights changes taking place. And in the wilderness years after the decline of CND (1964–65), only a brave handful of determined peace rebels kept faith.

So when younger women asked the question: 'Did women do anything for peace *before* Greenham?', few could remember the answer. A living oral tradition had grown rusty. My own experience must mirror that of many others, for I just missed being part of the Aldermaston generation, and have only hazy schoolgirl memories of attaching myself to the tail-end of CND's great Easter marches. By the time I became a student in 1964 CND was no longer in vogue and I, a modish eighteen-year-old, drifted away with all the rest. Soon the horrors of Vietnam drained fear about nuclear weapons of real urgency; and with the welling up of a women's liberation movement in 1970, peace fell even lower on my agenda.

During the 1970s, words like 'Hiroshima' and 'radiation' slipped completely from my vocabulary. Certainly, the notion of a women's peace movement was not something I was aware of. In the mid 1970s, when Jill Norris and I delved into the history of the radical suffragists, we kept an eye open for campaigns on equal pay and child allowances – but not peace. Indeed, we originally planned to stop well short of the First World War. Only as we dug deeper into the lives of these remarkable women did we discover their passionate anti-militarism. So our final chapter, 'What did you do in the Great War?', noted a Women's International League (WIL) and even a Women's Peace Crusade.

Later, looking at the life story of one such suffragist, Selina Cooper, I discovered that *her* deep peace convictions lasted a lifetime. In 1926 she helped to organize a women's Peacemakers' Pilgrimage, and in 1934 investigated German Nazism at first hand at the invitation of a Women Against War and Fascism group. 1980, when I was doing this research, was the time when a popular disarmament movement was rising up once more; yet I made few clear connections between these earlier women's campaigns and current peace actions. When the Greenham camp began in 1981, I just observed it as a valuable but distant happening.[2] Only the following year did this women's peace camp really seep into my imagination. The chain letter inviting women to 'embrace the base' criss-crossed the country. I made copies for other women in Halifax, then booked a very *large* coach for 12 December. A women's peace movement had arrived.

But if the volatility of campaigns and fickleness of political memory provide part of the explanation of the 'forgetting', inadequacies of historiography provide the rest; for a women's peace movement has been exceedingly poorly served by historians. Neither the early Female Auxiliary Peace Societies, nor the 'Olive Leaf Circles' of the 1840s, are recorded in the two major nineteenth-century peace movement narratives.[3] The only account is in *Vrouwen Vochten Voor de Vrede* (Women Fought for Peace), available only in Dutch.[4]

Similarly, peace historians writing of the First World War show scant interest in why so energetic a women's peace campaign should rise up, producing first WIL and then the Women's Peace Crusade.[5] Why? Most histories have traditionally focused upon the conflict between peace activists and the military state; their most dramatic moments have been 'personal witness' resistance to conscription by Conscientious Objectors. Enormously brave though these individual protests were, they allowed historians to shift attention away from feminist forms of resistance. Such priorities spilled over into peacetime histories. Thus a major interwar peace history completely omits the pacifist Women's Co-operative Guild; and dismisses WIL as being 'doctrinally too confused ever to become important'.[6] Such accounts add up to a denial of women's peace history.

Similarly, standard women's movement histories have until recently said little about peace campaigns. For instance, the political uproar during the Boer War caused by Emily Hobhouse's investigation into the internment of women and children in south Africa has been largely ignored. The reasons for this silence lie with the politics of these historians, so different from the women who formed WIL in 1915. The classic women's movement history, *The Cause* (1928), was written by Ray Strachey, close friend of Mrs Fawcett. But Fawcett, eminent suffragist and leader of NUWSS, was selected by the government in 1901 to lead an official committee to investigate Hobhouse's claims about the camps in south Africa – and to produce a whitewashing report. Fourteen years later, arch-patriot Fawcett was deeply wounded when leading suffragists resigned from NUWSS over the Hague Congress. It *was* an extremely painful moment: so patriotic Strachey marginalizes those tiresome peace women and omits WIL. Similarly, Sylvia Pankhurst, who had originally supported the Hague plans, later fell out with WIL; so when she came to write her seminal *The Suffragette Movement* (1931) she said little, merely casting a few disparaging remarks about the movement's 'wire-pulling'.[7]

But historians would be remiss to neglect the links between feminism and anti-militarism, stretching back as they do over 170 years. Any history of peace politics which ignores the issue of gender and ignores the powerful language and imagery of women and peace remains inadequate and misleading; so is any history of feminism in Britain which omits peace ideas and campaigns.

Some of these silences have been broken by more recent accounts. During 1983–84 a handful of Greenham books was rapidly published. They recorded the urgency of women's personal commitment and courage at the time – before Cruise arrived in late 1983 – when it still seemed just possible to 'stop the missiles'. But these accounts are necessarily celebratory anthologies rather than critical appraisals.[8] Slightly later, feminist historians were moved to look again at the birth of WIL and to stress the links between women's suffrage and peace campaigns.[9]

But such accounts seldom went back much further than 1915, and none beyond the 1890s and Bertha von Suttner's best-selling peace novel *Lay Down Your Arms*.[10] So I have attempted here to bring together this richness and complexity, and to offer a history of feminism and anti-militarism over the last 170 years in one single accessible volume.

The story focuses on Britain but remains, of course, internationalist: I have assessed influences from Europe, America and elsewhere and have looked broadly at 'anti-militarism' rather than at 'peace' (with its connotations of 'personal witness' pacifism), believing that some things – Nazi genocide, superpower imperialism – are probably *worse* than war.[11] And I have taken a broad definition of feminism.

The 'feminisms' discussed here are complex, and in trying to unravel the tangle I found that there seem to be three traditions. (These constantly overlap, of course; but separating them helps us to understand why the linking of feminism and anti-militarism could appear and reappear in such very different guises at various times.) The oldest strand is a maternalist feminism. It was thought appropriate for Victorian women to undertake quiet peace propaganda, particularly through their influence as *mothers* within their own domestic sphere. From 1820 onwards they formed small women's (though not necessarily feminist) peace groups. By 1914 this maternalist thinking had been broadened by Olive Schreiner, a feminist who argued in *Woman and Labour* that women as mothers 'pay the first cost on all human life' and so are instinctively against war. In the 1930s the Women's Co-operative Guild mounted a poignant 'never again' campaign against any return to military conscription of their sons. In 1945 the atomic bombing of Hiroshima and Nagasaki revealed the genetic damage radiation caused to unborn children; and part of the effectiveness of Greenham actions was the symbolic juxtaposition of diminutive children's clothes dangling from a military fence.

Two problems immediately arise for a feminism rooted in a view of women as primarily nurturers and carers. First, can groups such as the Olive Leaf Circles really be described as 'feminist'? Second, does the very power of maternalist language leave it vulnerable to hijack by less peaceable causes? For instance, the Swedish writer Ellen Key, widely read before the First World War, used a maternalist language whose racism we now find highly distasteful. And in the 1980s the implications of the 'nappies-on-the-fence' imagery has – rightly – been subject to critical reappraisal: Lynne Segal recently pointed out, in *Is The Future Female?*, that 'motherliness' can serve 'as a basis for radical *and* conservative collective endeavours of women'.[12] Yet this powerful maternalist imagery has always been widely appropriated at times of crisis.

The second strand, an equal-rights feminism, is rooted in a recognition of women's traditional exclusion from political power and in the optimistic belief that once this was rectified war would cease – or at least become less likely. This thinking, stemming from the classic Liberalism of John Stuart Mill and his *Subjection of Women*, attracted particularly widespread support during the great pre-war women's suffrage campaign, and helped to shape WIL. But this emphasis on 'equality' is also complex. Premissed on a sense of men's and women's 'sameness', it can lead to an equality trap which, applied to militarism, has to be rebuffed by 'Equality in the Army – No Way!'.[13] For a feminism which merely demands equal power with men is inadequate; equal-rights feminism needs to recognize the differences between male and female, and to demand for women access to the public sphere in order to transform it. The most effective and memorable polemic on women's exclusion from power, and so power-to-transform, is surely Virginia Woolf's *Three Guineas* (1938), with its cry that women are 'outsiders' who 'have no country . . .', whose 'country is the whole world'.[14]

The third (and more recent) radical feminist strand stresses not only gender difference but also male violence. The influential American writer Charlotte Perkins Gilman wrote in *The Man-Made World* (1911) that in warfare 'we find maleness in its absurdest extremes'.[15] It is difficult to trace a continuous line here; but seventy years later this was echoed vividly in some of Greenham's anti-men separatism and in the demand 'Take the toys from the boys'. This 'maleness = violence' strand links military aggression with domestic and sexual violence. But its attack upon men individually and on patriarchy generally, and its failure to acknowledge women's own collusion with militarism, have deprived this strand of popular support, and has at times caused painful controversy.[16]

Much of this book, then, is concerned with the history of ideas and the interconnectedness of these three strands. I have gone back to classic feminist texts. The more popular – *Woman and Labour* and *Three Guineas* – are still accessible; but many are long out of print, including von Suttner's epic novel which so effectively captured the *fin-de-siècle* optimism for international arbitration, and Frances Hallowes's *Women and War* (1914); yet such writings remind us that in 1915 an organized women's peace movement sprang not only from the suffrage movement but also from the maternalist imagery that swathed so much Edwardian feminism.[17]

Studying the history of these ideas helps in assessing continuities and shifts within a women's peace movement in Britain. Changes are certainly very apparent. When WIL rose up it took a very different shape from the smaller women's peace groups of a century earlier; and the 1980s women's peace movement re-emerged very distinct from WIL; yet the three strands remain recognizable intellectual traditions.

There are institutional continuities, too. Three key organizations – the International Council of Women (ICW, formed in 1888), the International Woman Suffrage Alliance (IWSA, 1902) and WIL (1915) – survive still, and each has its own historians. But such chronicles often obscure more than they illuminate. For instance, the ICW history scurries past the Great War in a dozen embarrassed lines; and the IWSA history skips nimbly over its rebels who travelled to The Hague and formed WIL. For such chroniclers have the unenviable job of writing with many an elder stateswoman, who has devoted her long life to the cause, peering over their shoulders. The result can be more of a loyalists' testimonial to a dwindling membership than a robust history.[18]

Institutional histories, along with the biographies and autobiographies of lifelong peace campaigners, overstress the continuities. Surely what particularly characterizes a women's peace movement in Britain is its episodic, cyclical history: women in their thousands became deeply involved for a few years, a few months, or a few weeks, then turned back to more immediate concerns. So to the classic texts and institutional chronicles already mentioned I have added personal testimony, drawing upon handwritten diaries and little-known life stories, and recording twenty-four interviews, both with women whose high profile made headline news and with grass-roots activists. This is crucial; for one of the problems of peace movement histories is their heads-without-bodies feel, with 'leaders' who claim to represent so-and-so million women around the world – but do not. I have tried to ensure a balance between the dedicated few, whose commitment to peace never wavered, and the far larger group whose burst of activity – perhaps triggered by a particular crisis – was much briefer. (This is, of course, particularly important concerning Greenham, where all-embracing claims like 'We're all Greenham women now' belied an enormous range of experiences.) I have also tried to ensure a balance of regions and occupations, so that the voices of working-class women are not silenced. And I have looked for a spread of ages: respondents' birth dates range over eighty years, from 1885 to 1967.[19]

Here, then, is the story of more than four generations of women. However, this book cannot be a definitive history of a women's peace movement in Britain – that has to await the eventual release of the bulging official files. This account is partly celebratory of the legendary Greenham peace camp and the remarkable campaigns that preceded it; but it is also a critical appraisal of earlier 'women-are-for-peace' writings. I hope it will be read by both those who were touched by Greenham's magic in the early 1980s and those who remained resistant to it; by those who believe there is no justification for *any* country to possess nuclear weapons and those who still believe in the right to 'strong national defence'. For this history clearly reveals that whenever militarism – nuclear or otherwise – threatens people's lives, women's imaginative peace actions have greatly alarmed the government of the day, which finds the conjuncture of feminism and anti-militarism peculiarly threatening.

Jill Liddington, Halifax, June 1989

Part I

IDEAS
(1820–1915)

1

The Olive Leaf Women
(1820–70)

Only in the ninth month of the First World War did a women's peace movement emerge as an organized, politically active campaign: in April 1915, despite the fighting raging across Europe, over a thousand women met together at The Hague. From this historic International Congress sprang the Women's International League (WIL), which still survives today.

Before 1915 a women's peace movement was often just a shadowy undercurrent of isolated groupings and minority ideas, easily overtaken by the growing women's suffrage campaign. Certain feminists *did* examine peace issues alongside women's rights; and on the eve of the First World War writers like Olive Schreiner and Charlotte Perkins Gilman found an enthusiastic readership in Britain for their proclamation of women's natural peace instincts and their attack on 'man-made' war. But very few feminists made anti-militarism a higher priority than that one insistent demand: votes for women.

Looking further back, it is even more difficult to glimpse anything recognizable as a continuous women's peace *movement*. Very early feminist peace polemicists – notably Anne Knight – had championed women's rights *and* peace, but by the late nineteenth century there were two distinct strands. The older one, of small Quaker-led women's peace auxiliaries, lay within the maternalist 'separate spheres' view of women's domestic role, emphasizing women's calming influence as wives and mothers, and women's duties – not their rights. The second strand, equal-rights feminism, inspired by John Stuart Mill, flourished from the 1860s onwards, and emerged powerfully around the turn of the century to become effectively *the* women's movement.

From then on the language of suffrage underpinned much of feminist thinking about peace, and shaped the women's peace movement as it emerged at The Hague in 1915.

During the late nineteenth century, however, these two strands remained essentially separate. Few women straddled both peace *and* equal rights; and the emerging feminist movement only rarely – during the 1870s Bulgarian Atrocities agitation and later during the Boer War – concerned itself about international peace. Yet, significantly, Emily Hobhouse's Boer War peace campaign, which helped to polarize suffragists into pro- and anti-war camps, prefigured the emergence of WIL – which split the suffrage movement over the peace issue. These first four chapters, then, describe the different peace languages of maternalism and equal rights, and suggest how the events of 1915 were presaged by women's earlier peace activity.

Anti-war polemicists had long existed in Britain, but remained rather isolated until the formation of the London Peace Society in 1816.[1] Led by prosperous Quakers like the Frys, the Society offered hope after the war-weariness of the Napoleonic era. Although it never represented more than a small minority, even among middle-class Nonconformists, it managed in its first three years to set up ten local auxiliary societies, each with a minimum of forty members.

Many of these early members were women; and by 1820 a handful of Female Auxiliary Peace Societies had sprung up in centres such as Leeds and Tavistock and, by 1823, Huddersfield.[2] The Peace Society, with its Quaker belief in influencing public opinion quietly by distributing anti-war literature, applauded this move. In 1823 its monthly *Herald of Peace* published 'An Appeal to Christian Females, on the Subjects of Peace and War', which particularly recommended to women 'the immediate formation of local female peace associations', for:

There is something exceedingly characteristic and beautiful in the idea, of the Female population of the world, with its bewitching smiles and affectionate importunity, removing from the hand of wrathful man the firebrand of war, and gently substituting the olive-branch of peace.[3]

The Peace Society stressed women's influence as mothers, and encouraged them to write tracts and articles for the *Herald of Peace*. For instance, in 1823 the widely translated *An Examination Of The Principles Which Are Considered to Support The Practice of War, by a Lady*, explained that the 'retiring and unobtrusive character' of women did not 'prohibit them from employing their literary talents in the exposure and condemnation of practices which are subversive of the social and domestic virtues'.[4]

Later, in the 1840s, more women responded by banding together into local 'Olive Leaf Circles', groups of fifteen to twenty, from various Christian denominations, who met in each other's houses every month. They discussed peace ideas in Britain and abroad, corresponded with other Olive Leaf Circles, and helped to write improving tales for children. From 1844 *The Olive Leaf or, Peace Magazine for the Young* published such morally uplifting parables as 'The Two Bullets' (First Bullet – 'Why, brother, I scarcely knew you; how deformed and bruised you are.').[5] By the early 1850s there were 150 local Olive Leaf Circles with an impressive membership of 3,000 in Britain alone. They supported needy circles abroad; well-to-do Quakers like Mrs Fry organized bazaars; Liverpool and Manchester circles supported Danish ones; circles in Yorkshire assisted Spanish groups. More generally, women would insert Olive Leaves (short peace messages) in foreign papers, and even exchange 'Olive Leaf' recipes.[6]

From the 1840s onwards the Peace Society in Britain and its sister societies in America and Europe convened international peace congresses. These were impressive and well organized; among the numerous British delegates were such influential Liberals as Richard Cobden MP, whose boundless enthusiasm for Free Trade was mirrored by a similar enthusiasm for world peace: both would flourish if unfettered by meddling government intervention. But at such congresses only official delegates, selected by peace associations and their affiliates, were allowed to make a speech – and no woman could become an official delegate. Women attended only as wives accompanying their husbands.[7] In this, of course, the peace movement was like other mid-century 'progressive' campaigns such as the Anti-Corn Law League, where segregated seating was the norm. This gained particular notoriety at the 1840 World's Anti-Slavery Convention in London, when four American women delegates were banished into obscurity and not allowed to speak.

This did not go unchallenged. A Quaker tradition of a female ministry had not died out, and among those present in 1840 were two outspoken Quakers, Elizabeth Pease of Darlington and Anne Knight of Chelmsford. Less is known of Pease;[8] but for Knight, best remembered for her fiery championing of women's suffrage and for her Chartist links, this Convention was a turning point.

Anne Knight was born in 1786, daughter of a prosperous wholesale grocer. She dressed in plain Quaker style and remained single, impatient with what she called 'these marriage contrarieties'. Knight travelled widely across Europe by donkey-cart, river-boat, and foot, and by 1830 was deeply involved in the anti-slavery campaign. Her interest in the role of women in such moral reform movements grew; at the 1840 Convention she met Lucretia Mott, Quaker minister and pioneer American feminist; and after the furore over the seating, Knight wrote excitedly to an anti-slavery friend in Boston of 'a new and grand principle launched in our little island'; women will 'no longer "sit by the fire and spin"'.[9]

Women's suffrage became increasingly pressing for Knight; when she attended the 1849 peace congress in Paris she was disturbed to find men like Cobden suspiciously evasive on such matters. She fired off an apocalyptic open letter to him, attacking both the genteel fund-raising of unenfranchised Peace Society women, *and* Britain's all-male 'military despotism':

> Let us not be urged to prick our fingers to the bone in 'sewing circles' for vanity fair, peace bazaars, where health and mind equally suffer in the sedentary 'stitch, stitch, stitch . . .' ever toiling, never to see a Right! . . . amassing names for petitions to men . . . all these underground toils, while our poor brother is groping his way in darkness without the good sense and clear discernment of his sister at his side. . . . Time is it that progress should begin in earnest, and no longer schemes of expediency taking place of JUSTICE! Let us have power for all the adult people, as in Deut. 31, xii, we shall then shake off the monster Moloch, and bid it begone for ever, with its horrible majority of nearly three hundred slaughtermen, from the house of lawmaking.[10]

Knight believed women's suffrage would bring peace. Women would transform Westminster's 'majority of slaughtermen', and 'would soon take the tools of murder from the hands of her brute-force brother and he would learn war no more'. But Knight created her greatest stir at the 1851 London peace congress. She wrote to the Peace Society's conference committee asking if she could attend as a delegate, but was rebuffed by officials.[11] Even among Quakers accustomed to female preachers, women speaking in public contravened hardening notions about female gentility. Although women had begun to take a more public role in the temperance and anti-slavery movements, it would be many years before they spoke at international *peace* congresses.

Anne Knight died in 1862. She had represented a powerful interweaving of equal-rights feminism and anti-militarist convictions. But from the 1850s such connections weakened; the Olive Leaf Circles began to decline; and for at least the next two decades such groups shrank back to a handful of Quaker loyalists.

Why? First, the initial energy of the Peace Society flagged. They became isolated during the Crimean War (1854–56), when Britain, France and Turkey's Ottoman Empire fought Czarist Russia. In the American Civil War (1861–65) the Peace Society grew further distanced from potential sympathizers when it refused to support Abraham Lincoln's Unionists against the Southern states, so seeming to condone slavery. The so-respectable Peace Society, one historian explained, came to lack 'the zeal of the crusader, the prophetic impulse, the ability to issue a clarion call against the behemoth, war'.[12]

The second reason lies with the changing expectations about women's lives. The belief that women rightly occupied a domestic 'separate sphere', distinct and apart from men, became increasingly embedded in middle-class culture.[13] Anything which took women away from their family and out into a more public area threatened the sanctity of the home. During the Crimean War, Swedish philanthropist and feminist Frederika Bremer wrote to *The Times* with an 'Invitation to a Peace Alliance' for women. She wrote, she said, in the 'hope that through woman a peaceful alliance might be concluded embracing the whole earth – an alliance opposing the direful effects of war', and helping to relieve the suffering. But the *Times* editorial dismissed Bremer's proposal as 'the mere illusion of an amiable enthusiast', likely to become bogged down by 'sub-committees of benevolence, by corresponding secretaries, and archives, and muffins, and green tea'. For, after all,

The influence of women is boundless in the world; as mothers, wives, sisters, daughters, we have to thank them for well-nigh every particle of real happiness we enjoy in our passage from the cradle to the grave. . . . But we have a very strong belief . . . that any attempt to drill [a woman] into the measured step of a battalion of charity marching to the relief of the world in general would most signally break down. In benevolence . . . women show to most advantage in the quiet of their own homes. . . . As many as step out of this sacred circle are not altogether so admirable as those who remain within it. . . . Besides, if universal womanhood is to turn itself to the organization of charitable associations, what is to become of our *homes*?[14]

Later, this 'separate spheres' ideology was powerfully codified by the eminent Victorian art critic John Ruskin:

The man's power is active, progressive, defensive. . . . His intellect is for speculation and invention; his energy for adventure, for war, and for conquest. . . . But the woman's power is for rule, not for battle, – and her intellect is not for invention or creation, but for sweet ordering, arrangement, and decision. . . . Within his house, as ruled by her . . . need enter no danger, no temptation, no cause of error or offence. This is the true nature of home – it is the place of Peace.[15]

The Times's condescension and the domestic idyll popularized by Ruskin made it increasingly difficult for Victorian women to follow the anti-militarist path blazed by pioneers like Anne Knight. Indeed, increasingly feminism grew up separate from peace politics. In the 1860s, suffragists campaigned for the freedom to enter the world of male privilege – rather than against the wrongs of war; and Peace Society women quietly tried to persuade people of the evils of war – but seldom demanded rights for themselves. These two groups, though from similar class backgrounds, seemed to coexist largely independently of each other.[16]

The equal-rights movement was in its infancy when in 1867 it was given a historic boost by the Liberal MP John Stuart Mill, who introduced into Parliament an amendment to the

Second Reform Bill to permit suitably qualified women the same suffrage rights as men. It was, of course, defeated; but out of this defeat sprang a vigorous women's rights movement. Already a remarkable *Englishwoman's Journal* had been launched. Then in 1869 *The Subjection of Women* was published reflecting beliefs shared by Mill and his wife Harriet Taylor Mill. It attacked marriage laws: now slavery was ended, only one form of tyranny remained – 'the law of servitude in marriage'. For, Mill wrote, 'marriage is the only actual bondage known to our law. There remain no legal slaves, except the mistress of every house.'[17] Thus inspired, Emily Davies founded a women's college, which moved to Cambridge and became Girton; and young Mrs Fawcett, wife of another leading Liberal MP, made her first public speech, beginning her lifelong commitment to women's suffrage. Equal-rights feminism was now firmly on course.

The isolation of the Peace Society, the power of the 'separate spheres' ideology, and the growth of an equal-rights movement with few real links to peace politics all help to explain the weakness of women's peace groups in the 1860s. But there were also other reasons for the Olive Leaf women to feel demoralized. In a lecture given in 1865 to trainee soldiers, Ruskin attacked European women; they were, he suggested, too often happy to gaze down upon fighting from on high, and to 'draw the curtains of their boxes . . . so that from the pit of the circus of slaughter there may reach them only . . . a murmur as of the wind's sighing, when myriads of souls expire.' Ruskin, who retained a romantic admiration for ancient Greek warriors but disliked modern warfare, rounded upon the women in his audience as the *real* culprits:

And now let me turn for a moment to you, – wives and maidens, who are the souls of soldiers; to you, – mothers, who have devoted your children to the great hierarchy of war. . . .

You may wonder, perhaps, that I have spoken all this

night in praise of war. Yet, truly, if it might be, I for one, would fain join in the cadence of hammer-strokes that should beat swords into ploughshares: and that this cannot be, is not the fault of us men. It is *your* fault. Wholly yours. Only by your command, or by your permission, can any contest take place amongst us. And the real, final reason for all the poverty, misery, and rage of battle throughout Europe, is simply that you women, however good, . . . are too selfish and too thoughtless to take pains for any creature out of your own immediate circles. . . . Now I just tell you this, that if the usual course of war, instead of unroofing peasants' houses, and ravaging peasants' fields, merely broke the china upon your own drawing-room tables, no war in civilized countries would last a week. . . .

Let every lady in the upper classes of civilized Europe simply vow that, while any cruel war proceeds, she will wear *black*; – a mute's black, – with no jewel, no ornament. . . . I tell you again, no war would last a week.[18]

Victorian wives, having made their homes into Ruskin's 'place of Peace', were now, despite their votelessness, held entirely responsible for militarism. Yet this lecture became a popular classic. Certainly the *Herald of Peace* was happy to echo this humbug; and the Peace Society even edited a booklet, *Ruskin on Women*, which remained in circulation a quarter of a century later.[19]

The new generation of equal-rights feminists also had particular reasons to pay little attention to the Peace Society and its women's auxiliaries. Mill, a firm believer in progress, held that a highly civilized nation like Britain had developed *beyond* warfare; now 'the main occupation of society has changed from fighting to business, from military to industrial life'. As more nations became 'civilized' and enjoyed 'free trade', war would become another anachronism. And women, now beginning to occupy themselves beyond their own families, were an important part of that process: 'The influence of women counts for a great deal in . . . its [Europe's] aversion to war.'[20]

Mill's lofty optimism about warfare passing away proved tragically wrong – even in Europe. In 1866, the army of the old Austrian Habsburg Empire faced the rising military might of Bismarck's Prussia. The confrontation was at Königgrätz in northern Bohemia, not far from Prague in present-day Czechoslovakia. The battle was between military styles: Austria's gallant old-world officer caste proved no match for Prussia's conscript army, with its new needle guns. Twenty-four thousand Austrians were killed or wounded and 13,000 were taken prisoner. With corpses strewn across the Bohemian countryside, Königgrätz became the greatest European battle before the mass bombardments of the First World War. Forty thousand were killed; 190,000 soldiers died in the Franco–Prussian War four years later.[21]

While this did not compare to the massive carnage of the Crimean and American Civil Wars, it did clarify certain developments. A new united German Empire under Prussian leadership had changed the face of Europe. In 1871, just two years before Mill's death, the King of Prussia was proclaimed Emperor of Germany. Large-scale warfare had returned, and large armies, spurred on by Prussia's *Landwehr* (literally, territorial reserve) conscription system, became the order of the day. Even Britain, where the last vestiges of a compulsory peacetime militia system had faded out in the 1850s, could call upon an army of over half a million (though of course most of these soldiers were out in India).[22] So, in the 1870s, some of the new generation of feminists began to look more critically at militarism, and to make links with the old-established Peace Society and Olive Leaf women.

2

Lay Down Your Arms
(1871–99)

During the Franco–Prussian War (1870–71) a few of the new equal-rights feminists began to look more critically at war and what it did to women's lives. Mill's thinking here remains unclear; but in 1871 a report in the pro-suffrage *Englishwoman's Review* (now thirteen years old, with a slightly different name) on 'Women and War' suggests that both Mill and some feminists believed not only that industry was now superseding war but also that war had increased the subjection of women:

> There is scope for women in industry, although not in war. Women can work much better than they can fight. . . . Their interests are imperilled by any breach of the peace. . . . By emancipating women we should liberate a great peace-loving power, and enormously strengthen the pacific tendency of commerce. . . . In war they [women] have everything to lose, nothing to gain.[1]

We do not know whether such writers had read Ruskin's lecture; but here was a forceful attack on his humbug proclamation that voteless women were wholly responsible for war. Rather, the new argument ran, future progress lay with industry, women's emancipation, and peace.

Women's peace groups were also given a dramatic – albeit temporary – boost in the early 1870s from America. Julia Ward Howe had been horrified by the Franco–Prussian War and tried to disseminate American peace ideas. She planned an international women's peace congress linked to the old Olive Leaf Circles. But such translations are difficult, and after the war enthusiasm waned. Howe visited Britain in 1872, and the *Englishwoman's Review* reported that since her first plan had failed (because women 'could not leave their homes to attend a distant Congress'), she had selected 2 June as an annual women's international peace day and was advocating local groups linked to a Women's Peace Society. An essay competition, on the subject 'In what ways do wars and military systems affect women . . . ?' was announced; and a petition was circulated for 'signature by ladies for the establishment of a Court of International Arbitration, on the ground not only of the miseries particularly affecting women in war, but also on account of the immorality occasioned by a standing army'.[2]

The idea took hold in Britain. One of Ward Howe's supporters read a paper at a Social Science Congress on the idea for a 'Women's International Peace Society' based upon 'an appeal to justice instead of force; and also of ensuring to women the right to be heard or represented'. It looked to such practical mechanisms as international arbitration (also now taken up by the pacifist Peace Society) and to 'the establishment of a permanent High Court of Arbitration'. The speaker, Mrs E. M. King, added:

> I would end with an appeal to women and for women. Here is work offered to you, sisters, which is altogether beautiful, and which cannot soil the most delicate fingers. To be a bearer of the olive branch involves a labour that can offend no feeling, taste, or sentiment. . . .[3]

What actually emerged, in April 1874, was more modest: a Women's Peace and Arbitration Auxiliary of the Peace Society. Tiny compared to the earlier Olive Leaf Circles, it claimed only 137 members[4] and was quickly almost swamped by much more popular – though transitory – peace protest.

In the 1870s, Britain's growing enthusiasm for imperialism became more visible. The Suez Canal was purchased,

Queen Victoria was proclaimed Empress of India. Between 1873 and 1879 Britain participated in the Ashanti War in west Africa; the Second Afghan War; and in south Africa the annexation of the Transvaal, followed by the Kaffir and Zulu Wars. But the greatest outcry against Britain's military adventures was provoked by the commitment of Disraeli, the Tory Prime Minister, to defending Turkey's decaying Ottoman Empire – ostensibly to protect the liberties of Europe, but, more cynically, to secure Britain's crucial route to India. In 1876 two small Balkan nations declared war on Turkey. Disraeli, with a fleet nearby to support the Sultan, felt smug that he could protect British interests. But he was highly embarrassed when the Turks turned on the rebels, and notorious Muslim mercenary bands, the *bashi-bazouks*, massacred 15,000 unarmed Bulgarians – Christian men, women and children. The killings provoked massive public outcry: particularly quick off the mark was the Peace Society, with a protest deputation to the Foreign Office.

Also quick off the mark was the new Women's Peace and Arbitration Auxiliary, whose protest meeting unanimously carried a resolution deploring the Turkish cruelties; it urged the government to 'exert a prompt decided action . . . to prevent the recurrence of these outrages . . . and to secure for the Christian provinces' freedom from 'the arbitrary control of the Turkish Government' – but reaffirmed the Auxiliary's pacifist optimism that all this could be secured 'by a mutual understanding between the European Powers without recourse to arms'.[5]

The *Englishwoman's Review* reported this meeting and urged more women to join in the public protest; for it too believed that once women's claim to the vote was recognized, 'the horrors of war will be in a great measure averted, and its sufferings alleviated'. And women responded: no fewer than 43,845 signed a petition addressed to Queen Victoria at Balmoral Castle, on behalf of the women of England. (Smaller local petitions included one to the Queen from women in Cambridge; another, to the Foreign

Office, from women in Coventry with well over a hundred pages of signatures, clearly suggested efficient house-to-house canvassing.)[6] At the same time, medical relief for the Bulgarians was organized, with Florence Nightingale, renowned for her Crimean nursing, writing encouragingly from her sickbed.[7]

But amid all the bustle to transport flannel to wrap babies in to Belgrade, the Atrocities agitation quickly ran out of steam. In 1877 Russia declared war on Turkey, which asked Britain for help, and Disraeli despatched the fleet. The following year Britain acquired a new word, 'jingoism', from a music-hall song:

 We don't want to fight, yet by Jingo! if we do,
 We've got the ships, we've got the men, and got the money too.

Yet 1878 seemd to provoke an even more coherent women's peace protest. The *Review* published an article on 'The Peacemakers' which further articulated the equal-rights arguments: women's 'persistent exclusion from any share in political power by the negation of the franchise' weakens 'proportionately the hands of the Peace party in England'. It also described a pamphlet written by a Women's Peace and Arbitration Auxiliary member on 'Women and War', which argued that 'women suffer even more than men from the misery and desolation consequent upon every outbreak of actual warfare'. It also reported women's involvement (including that of suffrage groups) in anti-war actions. Another women's peace memorial to Queen Victoria collected no fewer than 11,955 women's signatures in nine days – including that of Mill's stepdaughter Helen Taylor, (but not of Mrs Fawcett) – and again, local petitions were signed by 3,453 women in Gloucester and 10,076 in Birmingham. And the *Englishwoman's Review* came out unequivocally with equal-rights arguments, reminiscent of Mill, linking feminism and anti-militarism:

 We claim that women should be educated, not, as now, to
 awake into a sudden burning interest in matters wherein

they are powerless to act, but to take a keen, intelligent view
of all the politics of the day, to assist each in her degree in the
selection of competent governors, to be a unit instead of a
cipher in the sum of national efficiency.[8]

But although Britain's imperialist adventures continued,
particularly on the Nile and in Africa's southern cape, little
of this popular peace protest lasted. The Women's Peace
and Arbitration Auxiliary did gain a few additional members, and carried on with fund-raising bazaars and handing
out tracts. But of course, it remained, despite Anne
Knight's earlier attempts, virtually impossible for women
to speak in public about peace. When Julia Ward Howe
visited Britain, she was not allowed to address Peace
Society meetings. Indeed, not until the 1878 peace congress
in Paris did continental and American women speak for the
first time: Howe proclaimed that since peace work was
based on continuous study, women should study the rights
of mankind, for a person who knows no rights knows no
duties. (The Women's Peace and Arbitration Auxiliary
sent its own president, the wife of the secretary of the Peace
Society, but apparently she did not speak.)[9]

Indeed, British women worked more quietly for peace
than their American or European sisters and, except for
periods of crisis, still seemed rather isolated from the
women's rights movement. This began to change in Britain
only in the 1880s. By 1880 membership of the Women's
Auxiliary had risen (though only to 442); and there was
protest both over military drill in schools and over how 'our
own country, the land of the Bible, the land of professed
freedom, was committed to . . . the horrible barbarism of
aggressive warfare'. One of these new members was Helen
Taylor, who by 1881 was invited on to the Women's
Auxiliary platform, seconding the motion that 'the moral
progress of the nineteenth century of the Christian era
demands a more rational settlement of international disputes than the barbaric arbitrament of the sword.' Taylor
was one of the few women to combine her peace and

arbitration commitment with women's suffrage in any sustained way: in 1885 she tried to stand as a parliamentary candidate, but the returning officer refused her nomination.[10]

More usual within the Women's Auxiliary were the Quakers. Their religious approach to peace – distributing tracts and running bazaars – did not challenge the 'separate spheres' framework as Knight had done. They still seemed scarcely interested in equal-rights arguments. To us they may seem quaintly eccentric; but their courageous campaigns tellingly reveal the limits within which the majority of late-Victorian women lived.

Best known was Priscilla Peckover. Born in 1833 into a wealthy Quaker family – her brother, Lord Peckover, was head of an old family banking business and a pillar of the Peace Society – she grew up at Wisbech in the East Anglian Fens, and was much taken up with temperance and phil- anthropy. Not until 1878, when she was in her forties, did Peckover hear that Quaker women would also be asked to testify against war. She joined the Women's Peace and Arbitration Auxiliary: this changed her life. In 1879, with Britain at war with both the Zulus and the Afghans, she became gripped by the vision that 'in our Bible-reading Christian land' there must be many longing for 'a protest against the Spirit of War'. She obtained the approval of the Auxiliary for her proposal: a brief declaration ('I believe all war to be contrary to the mind of Christ ... and am desirous to do what I can to further the cause of Peace'), accompanied by a penny subscription, would be signed by 'women of all ranks'.[11]

Without delay, Peckover went from door to door in her Quaker Bible district. Many signed her pledge and she soon had a long list of 'members'. Before the year was out she called together a Women's Local Peace Association, and soon the Peace Society invited her to address them. Though she had never made a public speech before, she went and explained her remarkable achievement. Peckover now devoted her extraordinary energies to her Local Peace Association (over which she presided for the next half-century), setting up branches around the country. By the mid 1880s she had virtually single-handedly won ten thousand 'members'! Her declaration was translated into French, German, Polish and Russian, and she even had twelve Armenian supporters in Constantinople. In 1882 Peckover began her own sixpenny [2.5p] paper, *Peace and Goodwill, A Sequel to the Olive Leaf*. It propagated her quiet Quaker approach to peace and included uplifting verse for children:

> A little explained, a little endured
> A little forgiven, the quarrel is cured.[12]

Peckover's evangelism might lack a sharp analysis of British imperialism; and her emphasis on duties rather than rights must have distanced her from women like Helen Taylor. But her zeal was unparalleled, with thousands of copies of an 'Earnest Appeal to all Women Everywhere' issued at the time of war in Sudan, and her single-mindedness inspired dedicated followers, giving other women confidence to speak at Peace Society meetings.[13] For instance, a Mrs Auckland told the Peace Society how 'mothers rule as queens in their own households over their children' and urged that 'there should not be the military drum and other military toys in the nursery'.[14] Particularly devoted was Ellen Robinson, a Quaker who helped to form the Liverpool and Birkenhead Ladies' Peace and Arbitration Society; from the late 1880s onwards she wrote peace pamphlets, travelled the country speaking, and worked as Secretary to Peckover's Local Peace Association.[15]

Yet the Peace Society and its Women's Auxiliary were increasingly inappropriate for the 1880s and 1890s. New groups of socialists and feminists, anarchists and free-thinkers, wanted not a religious but a more *political* approach. In 1880 an International Arbitration and Peace Association and later an Inter-Parliamentary Union were formed, both reflecting the hope that such practical mechanisms could prevent war. These hopes spread in the 1890s. By 1900 there were well over four hundred peace organizations around the world – mainly in Scandinavia, but including over forty in Britain and over seventy in Germany.[16]

As this new optimistic internationalism was spreading, the lives of young women growing up in late-Victorian Britain were changing dramatically too. As yet such changes scarcely touched working-class girls: they now had to attend elementary school, but were still permitted by successive Factory Acts to leave full-time education and go out to work at ten.[17] But now a small elite of largely upper-middle-class girls could take advantage of the pioneers' struggle for higher education and training. An influential group of women graduates was emerging from the new colleges: not just from Girton and Newnham at Cambridge, but also now from Lady Margaret Hall and Somerville, from the London colleges and Scottish universities.

However, it was Emily Davies's Girton which remained a crucial seedbed for the new generation who would later become key figures in a women's peace movement. One was Margaret Llewelyn Davies, Emily's niece; after Girton, she became a social worker and in 1887 joined her local branch of the Women's Co-operative Guild, formed four years earlier to give working-class wives a chance to discuss matters beyond narrow domestic confines. Her remarkable talents were recognized, and in 1889 she became General Secretary; the Guild remained her lifetime passion.

Helena Maria Sickert, daughter of a Danish newspaper artist, was born in Munich in 1864. Her family moved to England when she was four, and later the highly intellectual Helena recorded in her autobiography: 'I must have been about fifteen or sixteen when, prowling round the tiny school library, I came across Mill's *Logic* and was enthralled by it.' She went on to read *The Subjection of Women*, delighted to discover that Mill was a feminist: 'it was greatly encouraging to find my own personal inarticulate revolts linked up with what I now recognized as a world-movement.'[18] After a struggle with her mother about the cost, she entered Girton in 1882 to study Moral Sciences, which then included psychology, philosophy, economics and politics. It was still unthinkable to attend mixed lectures in Cambridge unchaperoned; but Sickert thrived on her independence. 'To have a study of my own and to be told that, if I chose to put "Engaged" on my door, no one would so much as knock was in itself so great a privilege as to hinder me from sleep.' She made friendships – with Llewelyn Davies and others – that lasted a lifetime; graduating in 1885, she was appointed a lecturer in psychology at Westfield College. Three years later she married Frederick Swanwick and they moved to Manchester, where he was a lecturer in mathematics.[19]

Helena Maria Swanwick had chafed at being chaperoned, but students enjoyed considerably more personal freedoms than their mothers' generation. Not so the majority of middle-class girls: in the 1880s they remained dependants of fathers, brothers, husbands.

Although she later plunged recklessly into anti-war activity, the life of Emily Hobhouse, daughter of an Anglican archdeacon in Cornwall, suggests how little had changed. Emily was born in 1860 into one of England's leading Liberal families: an uncle and a cousin were West Country Liberal MPs and her younger brother Leonard became a leading Liberal intellectual. Emily's mother died when she was only nineteen; so from then on she shouldered her share of parish duties, distributing food, clothes and literature to the poor. But Archdeacon Hobhouse never permitted his daughter to enter any of the more challenging ecclesiastical spheres; when the Bishop suggested that twenty-four-year-old Emily might lead a women's committee formed to raise money for the local cathedral, her Victorian father vetoed such a wild notion. And when Emily developed feelings for a member of his church choir, whose sister had been a housemaid at the rectory, he again forced his daughter to submit to his iron will.

Eight years passed; in 1892 her father grew ill, resigning his office. So, aged thirty-two and still his dependant, Emily Hobhouse, as one of her biographers put it, 'found herself in charge of a permanent invalid. It was she who took him for drives in the ponycart, she who waited after each service at the vestry door to give him her arm across the road.'[20]

Other young women discovered that their dependence on their fathers was little more than theory: they *had* to earn a living. Luckily, the growth of elementary education and other white-collar jobs opened new opportunities. A particularly important route to financial independence was the pupil-teacher system, which allowed lower-middle-class girls to stay on at school to help with the children in return for a small wage and 'training'. For instance, Annot Wilkie, born in 1874 in Scotland, the daughter of an impoverished draper, worked as a pupil teacher until she was sixteen, then left for teacher training college, and later taught classes of a hundred children in Dundee. The nearby University of St Andrews, though still excluding women from actually attending, did allow them to become external students; at the age of twenty-seven, Annot was finally awarded her degree. Aghast at the poverty of the Dundee miners' families, she became caught up in the new movements: the women's suffrage campaign and the socialism of the new Independent Labour Party (ILP) led by Keir Hardie, Ayrshire Miners' secretary. Later she married Sam Robinson, an ILP activist, and moved to Manchester.[21]

The fifth and final woman whose life can illustrate the wider changes then taking place is Isabella Ford. Born in 1855, daughter of a wealthy Leeds solicitor and landowner, she grew up in an imposing house kept by half a dozen servants. But unlike Emily Hobhouse, Isabella Ford was a

Quaker. Her mother, cousin of Elizabeth Pease, worked against slavery and for women's suffrage, and in the 1870s organized health lectures for working-class women. Isabella also plunged into the new socialist and feminist organizations. From the mid 1880s she was in contact with the Women's Trades Union League, formed to encourage women workers where union organization was weak. Later Ford left the Women's Liberal Association branch she had helped to form, and in 1893 joined the brand-new ILP. By this time she was also active in the revived suffrage movement. But Ford, despite her Quakerism, was not involved in the Peace Society like Priscilla Peckover, but rather with the newer internationalism concerned, for instance, about the rights of small nations.[22]

The regional suffrage societies were reorganized in 1897 and a new umbrella group, the National Union of Women's Suffrage Societies (NUWSS), was formed, giving a new buoyancy to the thirty-year-old movement. Mrs Fawcett, now widowed, became its ladylike and highly respected president; Isabella Ford was a leading member. Suffrage links even began to be made with working-class women through the big cotton trade unions in Lancashire, and through the Guild.[23]

By the late 1890s, such changes touched even Emily Hobhouse in her Cornish rectory. Her father died in 1895; and at the age of thirty-five she was finally free. She had no major financial worries. But what should she *do*? As one biographer put it, Hobhouse 'had passed no examinations, she had obtained no diplomas, and she was untrained to follow any calling.' Suddenly, perhaps impetuously, she took off. Assisted by her friend the Bishop (now, providentially, an archbishop), she became a 'lady missionary' among the miners of Virginia, Minnesota. Accompanied only by her maid, she sailed across the Atlantic and began to tackle the town's drunkenness, prostitution and corruption. Her Virginia Temperance Union and Free Library Association firmly established, Hobhouse left Minnesota after about a year (and a mysterious engagement to the ex-Mayor of Virginia). She travelled south to Mexico City, where she awaited her fiancé.[24]

By the end of the 1890s, then, the lives of all five women – Llewelyn Davies and Swanwick, Robinson, Ford and even Hobhouse – had changed dramatically. The means by which they changed – education, employment, travel – and the new socialist and suffragist organizations through which they worked are amply recorded. But less well known, yet of particular importance here, were the growing *international* organizations. In the late nineteenth century these echoed maternalist values, focusing on women's special moral influence regarding temperance and Christianity. It was just such an impulse that brought European delegates to America in 1888 to form an International Council of Women (ICW). Although the original idea had been for a suffrage organization, this was rejected (because they aimed to bring together *all* women's groups – including temperance, church and child welfare). ICW avoided *any* stance on suffrage, and its final consensus remained heavily Ruskinite: exclusion of women from the male public sphere was less challenged as 'subjection' than celebrated as securing sound domestic foundations against, for instance, drunkenness. As one French delegate put it, women organizing together utilized the 'motherheart of the world', a way of achieving equal 'personal purity and morality for men and women'.

The first National Council to affiliate was the United States' – followed by Canada, Germany and Sweden. Britain eventually formed her own Council in 1895, and it affiliated to ICW in 1898. By 1900 Denmark, Holland, Italy and New Zealand had also joined; and ICW began to hold five-yearly council meetings – the first in Chicago in 1893, followed by London in 1899.[25]

One woman caught up in ICW was Charlotte Perkins Gilman, an American feminist writer born in 1860. She somehow managed to make a living (despite an unhappy

marriage and terrifying personal depressions) by keeping a
boarding-house, becoming an itinerant lecturer – and writing. Her short story 'The Yellow Wallpaper' first appeared
in 1892, and she was warmly received when she visited
England four years later. Her second visit, for ICW's 1899
London meeting, coincided with the English publication of
her best-known book, *Women and Economics*: Gilman argued
that political rights and suffrage were not enough; economic independence was vital, along with co-operative
solutions to free women from the isolated drudgery of
housework.[26]

Amid this bustling internationalism, socialism, and intrepid
women travellers, peace was now visibly on the political
agenda. The abolition of war seemed almost within reach.
Alfred Nobel, the eccentric Swedish inventor of dynamite,
even bequeathed money for a prestigious peace prize. This
end-of-the-century international optimism rose to a vivid
climax in 1898 when, from Russia, Czar Nicholas II's peace
manifesto called for a conference on disarmament at The
Hague the following year.

A call from the ruler of so reactionary a regime had a
mixed reception in Europe. Peace groups, including Peckover's, responded enthusiastically; but many socialists
remained extremely cynical; the Czar's hypocrisy was
damned because 'no strokes of the pen can separate capital-
ism and bloodshed'. And at the International Socialist
Congress in 1900, peace conferences like that at The Hague
were condemned.[27]

Indeed, the militarism debate in Britain had intensified.
The Tories won the 1895 general election and energetic MP
Joseph Chamberlain became Colonial Secretary under
Lord Salisbury. Triumphant Tory imperialism now
gripped Britain. At the same time, a new generation of
Liberal intellectuals joined by socialists like Keir Hardie,
developed a critique of imperialism. Tension mounted in
south Africa, provoking Hardie's prophetic anger at how

working people were being duped into fighting other people's wars: 'They supply the soldiers to be shot and the money for the conflict. . . . Their sons who die on the field of battle will be shovelled into nameless trenches . . .'.[28]

A particularly memorable warning came from southern Africa itself – from Olive Schreiner, born in 1855, whose novel *The Story of an African Farm* was published in 1883 to acclaim. Later, she too responded angrily to the cruelty with which the British imperialist Cecil Rhodes was 'pacifying' the Matabele and Mashona peoples. *Trooper Peter Halket of Mashonaland* was a direct attack on Rhodes's preference for 'land to niggers'. It was addressed to people in Britain, for 'if that public lifts its thumb there is war, and if it turns it down there is peace.' But despite *Trooper Peter* and Schreiner's visit to Britain with her husband, public opinion remained fatally indifferent to pleas for peace.[29]

The international women's movement now joined this new breed of anti-militarist Liberals and socialists. Like them, it had no unified view on imperialism, but by the end of the century 'peace' was certainly very high on ICW's agenda. The 1899 meeting brought to London women from twenty-eight countries, including Gilman from America. The American and Canadian Councils tabled far-reaching arbitration resolutions; ICW agreed to pledge itself to 'take steps in every country to further and advance by every means in their power the movement towards International Arbitration'. A public meeting on arbitration was attended by 4,000; Ellen Robinson spoke and the Hague Conference was heartily welcomed. An ICW Standing Committee on Peace and International Arbitration was formed, with Austria's leading peace propagandist, Bertha von Suttner, as its secretary. Now 'woman will become a true helpmeet to man,' approved Peckover, 'to cut away the roots of the barbaric and unchristian systems of war and militarism.'[30]

Indeed, ICW, still keener to stress Ruskinite duties than Mill's equal rights, remained much more enthusiastic about peace than about votes. In fact, there was a bitter fracas over suffrage. A lengthy session on the subject had been scheduled. Among the participants would be Mrs Fawcett, Susan B. Anthony from America, and Marie Stritt, president of the German National Council of Women. But anti-suffragists also demanded the right to speak. The ICW executive, still not prepared to commit itself, supported them. The organizers of the suffrage session objected. ICW refused to sponsor the session. So Mrs Fawcett's NUWSS had to offer independent sponsorship instead. (The row about women's political rights did not stop there. Suffragists, incensed by the ICW's timidity, decided to form a breakaway organization. A new international women's *suffrage* alliance was planned, separate from the old ICW.)[31]

In 1899 such plans had yet to be fully developed, and the maternalistic values of the various ICW Councils still represented the international voice of women; so any writing popularizing the growing optimism for peace and arbitration was likely to share this point of view. No writer revealed this more effectively than Bertha von Suttner. Her perspective contrasted with Schreiner's, for she was neither a socialist nor a strong feminist; and, unlike Peckover, she was a freethinker. Much more worldly than such Quaker women, von Suttner moved among the politically conservative elite of the International Arbitration and Peace Association; and her novel, *Die Waffen Nieder! (Lay Down Your Arms)*, captured all the 1890s' hopes for the abolition of war.

Baroness Bertha von Suttner, born in Prague in 1843, grew up at the heart of Austria's ramshackle Habsburg Empire. Her father, a count, could trace his line back to twelfth-century Bohemia. After his early death, Bertha's mother gambled their money away. To earn her living, Bertha became governess to a Baron von Suttner's family. She and the Baron's son planned to marry, but his parents disapproved; so in 1876 Bertha fled to Paris, to become Alfred Nobel's secretary. She secretly married the Baron's son, and fled again – this time with her husband – to the Caucasus Mountains. Here they lived as *émigré* intellectuals, reading Darwin on evolution and histories of civilization, and writing novels and stories.

In 1885 they returned to Austria and then to Paris, renewing contact with Nobel, who gave them an *entrée* to key literary and political salons.[32] Here much of the conversation focused on the tension between France and Germany. Amid the chat of peace and war, von Suttner made a discovery that changed her life: the International Arbitration and Peace Association now existed in London. 'I was electrified,' she recorded in her memoirs. She was so enthusiastic that she decided to write a major new book: a melodramatic anti-war novel.[33]

Die Waffen Nieder!, subtitled 'The Autobiography of Martha von Tilling', became a best-seller. It tells the tragic tale of Martha, a contemporary of her creator, born into the ritualized military world of Vienna's aristocracy. Almost all the men in *Lay Down Your Arms* are noble warriors: Martha is wooed by Arno, a dazzlingly handsome count of the hussars. She marries him and a son is born; Arno is killed in battle. Martha retires from society and starts questioning such military slaughter. She reads about Darwin's ideas and is dazzled by a new *History of Civilization in England*, which offers a scientific explanation of society's progress. Martha begins to see that 'the estimation in which the warrior class is held is in inverse ratio to the height of culture which the nation has reached'.[34] Eventually she returns to Vienna and marries Lieutenant-Colonel Baron Frederick Tilling – who, surprisingly, shares her growing anti-militarism. But war breaks out again. 'Lay Down Your Arms, down with them forever!' Martha, now pregnant again, writes passionately in her diary.

Her confinement begins. After a painful parting, Frederick's regiment marches out, banners flying. The baby dies the day it is born. Under such extreme stress, Martha has a long delirious dream, likening her labour pains to the battlefield agonies. She:

fancied that cannon and naked weapons (I distinctly felt the bayonet thrusts) were the instruments of delivery, and that I was lying there the prize contention between two armies rushing on each other. . . . Every moment I was awaiting the bursting shell which was to shatter us all three – Arno, Frederick, and me – to pieces, in order that the child should come into the world. . . .[35]

In 1866 there is further fighting, this time between Austria and Prussia. Frederick is ordered to Bohemia. Martha's soldier-father, disdainful of the Prussian *Landwehr* conscription system, prophesies Austrian victories over the army of impudent 'tailors' apprentices'. But the slaughter of Königgrätz proves him wrong. Martha resolves to visit the battlefield herself, but retreats appalled by the full horror of Königgrätz:

> No more thunder of artillery, no more blaze of trumpets, no more beat of drum; only the low moans of pain and the rattle of death. In the trampled ground some redly-glimmering pools, lakes of blood; all the crops destroyed, only here and there a piece of land left untouched, and still covered with stubble. . . . And on this battle-ground thousands and thousands of men dead and dying – dying without aid. No blossoms of flowers are to be seen on wayside or meadow; but sabres, bayonets, knapsacks. . . . Near the cannon, whose muzzles are black with smoke, the ground is bloodiest. There the greatest number and the most mangled of dead and half-dead men are lying, literally torn to pieces with shot. . . . Many of them are still alive – a pulpy, bleeding mass, but 'still alive'.[36]

Victorious Prussians bring a cholera epidemic. Martha loses her sisters, brother and father. Martha, Frederick and their son flee to Switzerland. The tragedy of the battlefields of Bohemia passes into history. Frederick resigns from military service and plans a 'league of peace': '"I have renounced the trade of war . . . I enter the service of the peace army".'

The novel ends melodramatically. Martha, eventually doubly widowed, feels that her only hope for the future lies with the peace associations springing up across the 'civilized' world, campaigning for arbitration to 'enthrone justice in place of brute force'. The next section is highly autobiographical: Martha enquires about the International Arbitration and Peace Association and receives this reply from London, dated July 1889:

> At no time, perhaps, in the history of the world has the cause of peace and good-will been more hopeful. It seems that, at last, the long night of death and destruction will pass away; and we who are on the mountain-top of humanity think that we see the first streaks of the dawn of the kingdom of Heaven upon earth.

At the end Martha's son, now a young man, reaffirms the optimistic anti-war faith of his mother and Frederick:

> We are already standing at the gate of a new period. Glances are directed forwards. All are pressing on strongly towards another, a higher form. Savagery, with its idols and its weapons [is passing away].[37]

Bertha von Suttner's novel, originally published in German in 1889, sold out quickly. An unofficial English edition was rushed out in America; an authorized translation, *Lay Down Your Arms*, was subsequently published in 1892 at the request of the International Arbitration and Peace Society. French, Spanish, Swedish editions followed. Although hardly a great novel, *Lay Down Your Arms* captures both the naivety and the sophistication of the 1890s optimism. And it proved sensationally successful propaganda. The author's old friend Nobel congratulated her on her 'admirable masterpiece': it helped to persuade him to bequeath his Peace Prize. The Czar was also much moved by the book. Leo Tolstoy likened it to *Uncle Tom's Cabin*: 'The abolition of slavery was preceded by a famous novel. . . . May God grant that the abolition of war will follow on your novel.'[38]

Von Suttner, no feminist, made little theoretical link between anti-militarism and gender. But the sorrowful tale of Martha Tilling introduced readers to three aspects of women's relationship to war that would be further developed in the 1900s. First, it depicted how *women* suffer in war – by bereavement and widowhood, and by epidemics. Second, it described upper-class women's *collusion* in war, rather along the lines of Ruskin: if girls insist on admiring handsome hussars, military virtues will be perpetuated. And third, it drew – briefly – an analogy between women's physical suffering in childbirth and men's agonies on the battlefield, a theme eloquently developed later by Olive Schreiner.

More immediately, von Suttner brilliantly popularized the 1890s peace optimism. She helped to found the Austrian Peace Society in 1891; and, untroubled by socialist carping about blood on his hands, once the Czar issued his manifesto she threw herself wholeheartedly into the campaign. In 1905 she became the first woman to win the Nobel Peace prize (though by then her influence was waning; anti-war suffragists were demanding more radical changes than the bourgeois baroness could offer).

However, the translator explained, *Lay Down Your Arms* helped her British readers to imagine what it was like still to live 'under the grim "shadow of the sword"', and the threat of conscription. England, he blithely explained, pointed the way to the future:

> The dawn of a better day in respect of war is plain enough in our country. We have advanced far indeed from the state of things that existed a century ago. . . . May we not hope that our influence, as that of a nation not implicated in the mad race of armaments, and yet not removed from the area of European war, may avail. . . . HAIL TO THE FUTURE![39]

But within seven years the Boer War had broken out and the English language acquired yet another new word: mafficking.

3

The Brunt of War
(1899–1904)

The Boer War broke out in October 1899 and lasted until May 1902. These years were highly significant to women's peace movement history in Britain, partly because the tensions then within the women's suffrage movement prefigured the much deeper divisions among suffragists in the First World War; partly because of the light they shed upon women's peace groupings at the time.

There were small clusters of activity – around Priscilla Peckover and the Peace Society, around the International Council of Women; and a few individual suffragists, like Isabella Ford, were concerned about the Boers. But there was no coherent, unified strategy or organization. This left something of a vacuum – a vacuum filled by Emily Hobhouse. She had no direct connection with either the Peace Society or NUWSS; but she was indirectly affected by the internationalist optimism for peace and arbitration so effectively captured in *Lay Down Your Arms*. Inspired by such idealism, Hobhouse and her impetuous actions raised issues about women and war which profoundly embarrassed Britain's militarist Tory government. Already, then, we see glimpses of what would later become a movement.

Emily Hobhouse, waiting in Mexico City, bought an estate and learnt the language; but her fiancé never turned up. All her plans foundered; in 1899 she returned to London. She took a flat in Chelsea, not far from her distant relatives and increasingly close friends) Kate Courtney and her husband Leonard, the Liberal MP. Hobhouse decided to throw herself into the Women's Industrial Council, a new organization of Liberal and Fabian women working to improve working women's wages and conditions.[1] She never played a major role, but she took the work seriously and set about studying industrial law, spending much of her time at the British Museum Reading Room. But this newly ordered existence was soon to end dramatically with the declaration of the Boer War[2] – a war against which Hobhouse threw herself impetuously.

Since the mid 1890s tension had been mounting between the stolid Dutch-speaking Boer farmers and the more recent British settlers. In 1897 Colonial Secretary Chamberlain, still hoping to topple the Afrikaaners without resorting to war, despatched Sir Alfred Milner as High Commissioner in South Africa and Governor of Cape Colony. But war seemed unavoidable. In summer 1899 Olive Schreiner produced an impassioned eve-of-war appeal: 'Who gains by war? . . . Not the brave English soldier. There are no laurels for him here. . . . Who gains by war?' Three thousand copies were sold out in five days; she followed it up with cables, protesting against Chamberlain's provocative policy. At the same time a Transvaal Committee, formed by anxious Liberals, held its first public meeting to protest against 'reckless threats of war'.[3]

But in autumn 10,000 extra troops were despatched, and in mid October war came – despite all the arbitration hopes of the Hague Peace Conference. British frontier towns like Mafeking were besieged; even so Britain, with her larger army, still expected it all to be over by Christmas. But they had reckoned without their own poor leadership and the Boers' tenacity, local knowledge and superior weapons. In December a 'Black Week' of defeats plunged British public opinion into gloom. A new commander-in-chief, Lord Roberts, was sent out, with General Kitchener as his chief of staff; this new command met with greater military success. Mafeking was finally relieved – prompting hysterically jingoistic celebrations in Britain – and the Transvaal was annexed. Roberts happily assumed that the war was over and went home, leaving Kitchener to conclude a peace. He was wrong. The Boer farmers refused to accept defeat and turned to guerrilla warfare. Railway lines were blown up, convoys ambushed, outposts raided.

The British retaliated harshly, issuing a series of punitive proclamations. By autumn 1900 a policy was adopted of burning Boers' farmsteads which might shelter guerrillas. Most provocatively, makeshift concentration camps were erected into which troops herded Boer refugees – mainly women and children. In the Khaki Election that autumn, the mafficking craze kept Salisbury, Chamberlain and the Tories in power. But many Liberals and socialists were outraged at the increasingly brutal treatment of the Boers, particularly non-combatants. The debate about women and war, and with it Emily Hobhouse, now swept to centre stage.

For the next two years our story becomes essentially hers. The Peace Society, remembering its futile attempts to halt the Crimean War, kept its head down; the tiny women's peace groupings, led by Quakers like Priscilla Peckover and Ellen Robinson, were likewise too disengaged from the political rough-and-tumble to challenge Salisbury's government head-on. The International Council of Women might have made a recent commitment to peace and arbitration; but with national Councils now in both Britain and Holland it was scarcely eager to take a stand on the Boer War. And Mrs Fawcett's NUWSS was torn. Hobhouse, a courageous maverick, filled this vacuum.

The Liberal Party was divided on the war. Imperialists – Asquith, Grey, Rosebery – felt that it was inevitable; others sat on the fence; but a growing number believed that Britain had behaved disgracefully, and – despite being hounded as 'pro-Boers' – had the courage to say so. Leonard Courtney was among those who bravely denounced jingoism; but when he tried to speak in his Cornish constituency about peaceful arbitration, he was hissed down. When Cronwright Schreiner (husband of Olive, whose name he had adopted) travelled to England to speak against the war, his audience pelted him with fish heads and turf. And when the American anarchist Emma Goldman spoke in London she had to be smuggled into the hall; even then patriots tried to storm the platform.[4]

A newly formed South African Conciliation Committee, with Leonard Courtney as president, held its first public meeting at New Year 1900. Through her friendship with the Courtneys, Emily Hobhouse was involved from the beginning. A Women's Branch was formed, and she became honorary secretary. She organized discussion groups and instruction classes, and a drawing-room meeting given by her aunt, Lady Hobhouse, was arranged for Cronwright Schreiner.[5]

But, as the war dragged on, Hobhouse determined to do more. She conceived the idea that *women* could intervene effectively as conciliators. Years later, she recorded how:

> We longed to protest [against the planned annexation of the Transvaal], and it occurred to me that women, at least, might make a public protest without arousing undue criticism. . . . I, as Honorary Secretary of the Women's Branch of the South African Conciliation Committee, proposed that we, the *women*, should hold a Meeting of Protest. To my great joy, but considerable surprise, Mr Courtney agreed in principle to this proposal. I pressed home the plan. . . . Thus backed, I carried the ideas to our next Women's Committee and urged it there with success. A date, June the 13th [1900], was fixed, and resolving to do it on a large scale as a Demonstration of real importance, the Queen's Hall was secured. From that moment my flat in Chelsea became organizing headquarters. . . . We laboured from 8 a.m. to – often – 11 p.m. for those six weeks. The result was a magnificent assemblage of women.[6]

Hobhouse's roots lay with Liberalism rather than the Peace Society, and most of the women present were linked with the Liberal Party. But the occasion *was* completely new: a major public meeting of women during wartime to protest against government policy and to offer conciliation. Efficiently organized by Hobhouse to stop jingoist hecklers getting in, it was a great success. Four resolutions were passed unanimously, with Hobhouse rather nervously proposing the final one:

Resolution 1

That this meeting of women brought together from all parts of the United Kingdom condemns the unhappy war now raging in South Africa, as mainly due to the bad policy of the Government: a policy which has already cost in killed, wounded and missing over 20,000 of our bravest soldiers. . . .

Resolution 4

That this meeting desired to express its sympathy with the women of the Transvaal and Orange Free State, and begs them to remember that thousands of English women are filled with profound sorrow at the thought of their sufferings.[7]

Proposing this resolution was a pivotal moment for Hobhouse, whose years of subjection to the archdeacon's rule were now well behind her. 'It chimed in with my feelings and formed the keynote of my life and thought for years to come', she wrote later. Buoyed up, she addressed meetings in Leicester and Leeds, Bradford and Manchester. A particularly rowdy public meeting, again organized by the Women's Branch of the Conciliation Committee, was held in Cornwall, near her old home. The speakers were Hobhouse, Ellen Robinson, and Lloyd George, the Welsh MP and rising Liberal Party star. But they could scarcely utter a syllable before the platform was stormed. A local newspaper gave a graphic account of how the two women fearlessly:

took the opportunity of distributing 'Conciliation' leaflets among the people in the front. Many of these were at once torn up and the pieces tossed contemptuously into the air, while 'Britons Never Shall be Slaves' was sung by the storm(ing) party. . . .[8]

Such tumultuous meetings only strengthened Hobhouse in the fervour of her opposition. Soon news of the farm-burning reached England. Those already critical of the war were now outraged at Britain's callous treatment of the Boer families. Hobhouse, deeply affected, switched her protest from condemning the government's general war policy to practical aid for *non*-combatants. Single-handedly, she conceived and founded the South African Women and Children Distress Fund 'to feed, clothe, shelter and rescue women and children . . . rendered destitute and homeless by the destruction of property'. From the outset, of course, she enjoyed influential support: her aunt even obtained Chamberlain's backing for the innocuous-sounding Fund and a promise to communicate with Milner about it. Her list of subscribers was likewise impressive. Money began to arrive – along with anxious enquiries as to *who* would convey the aid to south Africa.

On the face of it, Hobhouse's plan did not seem so very different from the humanitarian relief schemes organized during the Bulgarian Atrocities. But of course, on this occasion Britain's own troops were directly involved in the fighting; the conflict was with other white Anglo-Saxon Christians (an important factor then, though couched in tones whose racism is objectionable now); in addition, as it was a colonial war, it was 'enemy' women and children whose homes had been destroyed, and so the relief would go to *them*. The plan was political dynamite.

But the impetuous Hobhouse was hatching a more dramatic scheme: she herself would sail out to the war zone and personally deliver the funds to needy refugee women and children. The Fund itself was scarcely organized yet, but she already had her plans. She was, as she later recorded:

independent and free and living at that time alone in my Chelsea flat . . . I believed my money would hold out with care. . . . I took a second-class ticket . . . and stayed in England only long enough to be present at the first meeting of the Distress Fund committee when provisional officers were elected. As a nest-egg I was able to hand the Committee the £300 I had collected privately. . . . I sailed on December 7th, going quite alone. . . .[9]

She whiled away the long journey learning as much Boer Dutch as she could.

Hobhouse arrived shortly after Christmas 1900 when the war, now dragging into its second year, was exasperating British politicians. Kitchener, who had succeeded Roberts, requested more troops. Olive Schreiner, who earlier had freely addressed women's congresses against farm-burning, now found her movements limited by martial law: towns were fortified by barbed wire and she needed a permit to burn a light in her bedroom at night.[10] And in Britain, fear that universal conscription might be introduced helped to swell anti-war feeling. Just as Hobhouse was setting off a women's protest meeting was held in Leeds, chaired by Kate Courtney, with speakers including Margaret Llewelyn Davies and local Guildswomen; one woman said:

I have never spoken in a public meeting before; but I can give my heartfelt support to anything which will keep this conscription from us, for I have four sons, and I would never wish that one of them should become a soldier.

Isabella Ford also spoke, explaining that she had recently received a letter from Schreiner, to whom:

and to many other colonists the worst legacy of this war will be their loss of love for England. . . . How can it be otherwise when one sees, as she has done, farms set fire to, homesteads needlessly wrecked, and families, including, of course, the women and the little children, turned into the fields and streets, without food, extra clothing, or shelter?[11]

Certainly when Hobhouse landed in Cape Town, the conflict was intense. As a result of Britain's scorched-earth policy, the number of homeless Boers escalated. To cope with this emergency, two special camps had been set up, supposedly to accommodate refugees who had surrendered voluntarily; but these soon grew into a whole network of concentration camps. Hobhouse, who had not really known of the camps' existence before she arrived, was suddenly confronted with this entirely new situation. She quickly exploited her introductions to Milner, the High Commissioner, and managed to persuade him that 'for the honour of England we ought to mend matters in the camps'. Kitchener, on the other hand, was more sceptical about her mission, but must have realized that it might be impolitic to refuse so well connected an Englishwoman: he agreed that with certain provisos, she could visit the camps and distribute relief.

Hobhouse set out, clutching 'as credentials Milner's letter of Authorization and Kitchener's telegram. . . . My kind Cape friends provided me with a box of food such as should more or less withstand the heat and a kettle lamp for making tea and cocoa, and a few of them saw me off. . . .'[12] Her train took almost two days to cover the five hundred dry, deserted miles to Bloemfontein. Yet what she found when she reached her destination would shock the world.

The wretched conditions endured by the Boer women and children interned at Bloemfontein and the other camps so appalled Hobhouse that she decided she must return to England and arouse public opinion there. She arrived on 24 May 1901. Rapidly, she appealed directly to Brodrick,

Secretary for War, and to other members of the government, to improve the worst aspects of camp life. Certain concessions *were* made, but no substantial improvement. So Hobhouse decided that extracts from the letters she had written from the camps should be published. In June 1901, therefore, the *Report of a Visit to the Camps of Women and Children in the Cape and Orange River Colonies*, addressed to the Committee of the South African Distress Fund, was produced, sold for a penny [½p] a copy, and circulated to Members of Parliament.

The effect was electrifying. Hobhouse's letters describe day-to-day life in the camps using personal language and homely detail with which her English readers could easily identify. She combines this with a direct appeal to England's honour to *do* something about the cruelties perpetrated in her name. Hobhouse tells of the Boer women in Bloemfontein Camp, wrenched from their homes, all their possessions and any news of their husbands; of treeless heat and flies; of row upon row of suffocatingly hot bell tents; and of sickly Boer children, prey to epidemics like typhoid, languishing without proper bedding – and slowly dying. On one occasion she visited:

> a dear little chap of four, and nothing left of him but his great brown eyes and white teeth, from which the lips were drawn back, too thin to close. His body was emaciated. The little fellow had craved for fresh milk; but of course there had been none. . . . I can't describe what it is to see these children lying about in a state of collapse. It's just exactly like faded flowers thrown away.[13]

Hobhouse did win some practical improvements, but pregnant women still lay on the bare ground for lack of mattresses. From Bloemfontein she went on to Springfontein. Here 'the people are poorer and more utterly destitute than any I have yet seen'. In one letter Hobhouse tells how she tried to provide each family with some clothes 'to cover their nakedness', and to give women material 'to make their own boys' clothing, but we are stopped by the utter famine of cotton or thread. Scissors are handed round from tent to tent; thimbles are very few.'[14]

Back at Bloemfontein, Hobhouse found that improvements *had* been made – but the camp's population had doubled to about 4,000 since her departure six weeks earlier. Vital supplies remained pitifully scarce. She believed that once decent people knew what was happening, they would no longer condone the camps. In one letter she writes:

> I call this camp system a wholesale cruelty. It can never be wiped out of the memories of the people. It presses hardest on the children. They droop in the terrible heat. . . . Will you try, somehow, to make the British public understand the position, and force it to ask itself what is going to be done with these people? There must be full 15,000 of them. . . . If only the English people would try to exercise a little imagination – picture the whole miserable scene. Entire villages and districts uprooted and dumped in a strange, bare place. To keep these Camps going is murder to the children.[15]

The time was right for Hobhouse's *Report*. The concentration camps had become intensely embarrassing to Salisbury's government. The Conciliation Committee kept up a barrage of pamphlets on day-to-day Boer life. The Stop the War Committee announced that the war 'has now degenerated into a campaign of extermination', and that only the Turkish Atrocities in Bulgaria were comparable: for 'never before have we waged unrelenting war upon the women and children of brave men whom we are unable to subdue in battle'. 'Friends of Peace' groups formed up and down the country. Liberal MPs asked persistent questions in the Commons. And Sir Henry Campbell-Bannerman, Liberal Party leader, damned British tactics as 'methods of barbarism'. This influential speech decisively tilted the

Liberal scales against the war. In the critical battle for credibility that summer, the government seemed unable to shake off its growing 'atrocities' reputation.[16]

So Hobhouse's *Report* had a ready-made readership. The day after it came out Lloyd George spoke at a key public meeting, likening the government to Herod, who crushed 'a little race by killing all the young children'. Hobhouse quickly became the subject of heated controversy. *The Times*'s letters included one from a member of the 'Guild of Loyal Women' in South Africa, outraged by her lack of patriotism. As the turbulent summer wore on she continued, against heckling and obstruction, to tell the truth about the camps. Her *Report* also won important support abroad; French, German and Dutch versions appeared. Swiss women even published an open letter to the women of England, and some Americans spoke out against the British 'Death Camps'.[17]

The government found itself deeper and deeper in the mire. The cost of the war escalated. And, given the government's racist perspective, the question of the concentration camps remained doubly awkward: *this* conflict was between *white* troops and other *white* troops, with Christian Anglo-Saxon women and children being subjected to British 'methods of barbarism'. The government's only way out was to confront its critics on their own terms: to despatch an official hand-picked Committee of Ladies to investigate, to report back – and to discredit Hobhouse's account. Fortunately for the government, it did not have far to look for suitable women. Mrs Fawcett of NUWSS was a staunch Liberal imperialist – and unwavering in her support of the war.

Isabella Ford wrote afterwards how Mrs Fawcett was 'most unspeakable during the Boer War – till she went to the Camps'.[18] Certainly Fawcett, like so many other suffrage campaigners, saw no connection whatsoever between feminism and anti-militarism. Indeed, such suffragists based part of their equal-rights claim on the argument that women were *just* as dedicated and courageous as men in the patriotic defence of Britain and her Empire. So it was not surprising that Fawcett should see the causes of the Boer War not as Rhodes's imperialist ambitions or the Boers' grievances but along official lines: that the Boers had refused to admit the British and other 'Uitlanders' to citizenship. And after war began, when criticisms arose, Fawcett, according to her biographer Ray Strachey, impetuously 'sprang into the opposite camp'. Passionate about defending the Empire (she had already written a eulogistic biography of Queen Victoria), she was in touch, through an organization of women Liberal imperialists, with the pro-British Guild of Loyal Women of South Africa.[19]

Naturally feeling ran high at NUWSS meetings, where 'jingoes' like Fawcett confronted 'pro-Boers' like Ford. Indeed, suffrage had to be virtually suspended during the war. Even the discreetly coded NUWSS minutes reveal that it became virtually impossible to find speakers, 'considering the state of political feeling'. Fawcett herself withdrew from executive meetings for the *whole* final year of the war. (Her own autobiography is characteristically discreet here: but Strachey, less restrained, described Hobhouse as 'a violent pro-Boer' who was 'easily deceived by agitators and impostors', sending home accounts weighted with 'excessive bias' which were 'little short of blood-curdling'.[20]

Predictably, Fawcett was quick to defend the concentration camps publicly as 'part of the fortune of war'. So when, in mid July, she received the War Office invitation to lead the official Committee of Ladies, she did not hesitate. Within a month she and five hand-picked experts were on their way to Cape Town. Their four-month investigation, unlike Hobhouse's, was supplied with a special train fitted with berths, a saloon car and a travelling kitchen staffed by a Portuguese cook and a young batman. They conscientiously visited no fewer than thirty-three camps to investigate mortality rates and funeral arrangements, education and sanitary provision.[21]

Although dubbed the 'Whitewashing Commission' by Boers, the women were not uncritical of slipshod camp officials, poor hygiene and inadequate accommodation. But Hobhouse distrusted the Committee; she resented the fact that Fawcett had not contacted her before setting out; and she believed that action, not investigation, was now urgently needed. 'Why enquire into something that the whole world already knows about?' she demanded. She herself wanted to return to south Africa to continue her relief work; but Brodrick – unsurprisingly – refused permission. Hobhouse wrote him a heated open letter, published in *The Times* in September 1901, damning the inhumanity of his refusal:

> Will nothing be done? Will no prompt measure be taken to deal with this terrible evil? . . . Instead [of agreeing to my request], we had to wait a month while six ladies were chosen. During that month 576 children died. The preparation and journey of these ladies occupied yet another month, and in that interval 1,124 children succumbed. . . .
>
> In the name of the little children whom I have watched suffer and die, . . . I make bold to plead with you once more. . . . I urge that immediate steps may be taken . . . lest one day we are bowed down by the humiliating and grievous thought that we have sat still and watched calmly the extermination of a race brave and strong enough to have kept the British Empire at bay for two long years.[22]

From then until the Boers finally surrendered in spring 1902, Hobhouse's one-woman war continued its individualistic course. In October she defiantly sailed for Cape Town; on arrival she was arrested on board ship, refused permission to land, bodily removed to another ship, and deported back to England.

The official *Report on the Concentration Camps in South Africa* was eventually published in spring 1902 and sold at 1s. 8d.

[10p – twenty times the cost of Hobhouse's *Report*]. This official document, a voluminous recital of dry fact, *was* occasionally critical of British maladministration, though it tended to give a favourable overall impression. In the most contested area, mortality statistics, it was exceedingly vague about how far camp death rates had risen and the precise causes of that rise, even placing some blame on the camp dwellers themselves. (The Conciliation Committee calculated that the mortality rate for children had risen to a horrifying fourteen times that of English cities. Certainly, it seems likely that at least 20,000 people died in the British concentration camps.)[23]

In May 1902 a peace treaty was signed. Fawcett re-appeared at NUWSS meetings and the bitter tension of the previous two years abated – for a while. Women's suffrage now emerged as a major force in Edwardian politics. Women textile workers in Lancashire had already pre-sented an enormous suffrage petition to Parliament. In 1903 Mrs Pankhurst formed the Women's Social and Poli-tical Union (WSPU), whose supporters soon became known as suffragettes; and NUWSS received a report of a very successful international suffrage convention held in Washington DC in 1902, at which exciting proposals for the new International Woman Suffrage Alliance had been made. This new organization soon took shape, and planned its first meeting in Berlin for 1904.[24]

The Peace Society emerged a little battered after the war. A co-ordinating National Peace Council was formed in 1904, with a congress in Manchester presided over by Leonard Courtney and attended by representatives of ninety-two peace groups (including the Liverpool and Birkenhead Women's Peace and Arbitration Association, a Manchester Women's Peace Association, Peckover and Robinson).[25]

But shadows of the bitter Boer conflict remained. There was official concern that Britain's poor military perform-ance had been partly caused by soldiers' low standard of physical 'efficiency', and this was linked to mothers'

responsibility to care for their babies adequately. It became
a political priority to prevent further deterioration of the
imperial 'race', so that British soldiers could fight future
wars more effectively.

But while militarists were already planning the *next* war,
Hobhouse returned to south Africa in 1903, staying for a
time with Olive Schreiner and helping Boer families to cope
with the post-war devastation. She faded from the political
limelight as meteorically as she had sprung up. But Hobhouse went out in style. Just as the peace was being signed,
she put the finishing touches on her own exposé of the
effects of militarism. *The Brunt of War and Where It Fell* (1902)
lacked the homely immediacy of her *Report* or the sen-
timental appeal of von Suttner's novel. But it did begin to
draw together, for the first time, some key ideas about
women and war which prefigured later women's peace
movement debates.

The book is dedicated 'To The Women of South Africa'
whose dignity and patience had so impressed Hobhouse.
Then she went straight to the nub:

> This book is designed to give an outline of the recent war,
> from the standpoint of the women and children. . . . On
> them fell the brunt of the war. More adult Boers perished in
> the camps than fell in the field of battle, and over four times
> as many children. . . .

Like von Suttner, Hobhouse still shared an optimistic belief
in progress:

> . . . it seems as though in war an arbitrary line is drawn, one
> side of which is counted barbarism, the other civilization,
> May it not be that, in reality, all war is barbarous, varying
> only in degree? . . . None of us can claim to be wholly
> civilized till we have drawn the line above war itself and
> established universal arbitration in place of universal
> armaments.[26]

Her account is all the more effective for the photographs of Boer children. One picture of a half-starved baby is entitled 'Feeling the Brunt of War'.

Hobhouse's book articulated more explicitly the ideas already alluded to in *Lay Down Your Arms*: that the cost of war cannot be counted only on the battlefield, but falls most heavily on *non*-combatants: women and children. She also indicated how relief of this distress can quickly become a highly charged, politicizing act – particularly when the recipients are from the 'enemy' side and are 'respectable' white Christian housewives. She showed that women conciliators and relief missions could be easily organized and, by highlighting *gender*, could make it difficult for politicians to object to women's physical intervention in the war. She also began to argue that militarism *is* the enemy, not just of civilization, but also of women generally. All these ideas re-emerged dramatically in the First World War.

Hobhouse may well not have called herself a feminist. But, casting frosty glances in Fawcett's direction, she would have noticed that the women's movement was *not* united against the war. She had no illusions about women's collusion with militarism and their enthusiasm for fighting wars – by proxy. Towards the end of *The Brunt of War* Hobhouse chides her English women readers: as 'described by Ruskin, they "shut out the death cries, and are happy and talk wittily among themselves . . ."'; they are reached 'only at intervals by a half-heard cry and a murmur as of the wind's sighing when myriads of souls expire'.[27]

The new International Woman Suffrage Alliance now began to take the debate begun by Ruskin, von Suttner and Hobhouse right into the new century.

4

Sisterhood is International
(1911–14)

The last three years of peace and the first few months of war in 1914 reveal the extent to which militarism became entrenched in British culture after the Boer war. The peace movement – the old Peace Society, radicals within the Liberal Party, or socialists within the Labour Party – remained small and weak by comparison. At the same time, women who had been bravely outspoken about peace during the Boer War now found the suffrage campaign absorbed all their political energies. Outside Britain, the International Woman Suffrage Alliance and writers like Charlotte Perkins Gilman and Olive Schreiner did highlight the links between feminism and anti-militarism. But in Britain the clash between suffragists, suffragettes and the Liberal government meant that when fighting broke out in 1914, the women's movement was extremely ill prepared. Along with the Peace Society and the socialist Second International, the women's movement opposition to militarism collapsed in a rush of patriotism and jingoism.

The Boer War left a sense of crisis in Britain. Militarists, shocked that the army had been so ill equipped, argued that both Britain and her Empire must be more effectively defended in future. This was the era of 'leagues', many demanding greater defence expenditure, some opposing spiralling militarism, all engaged in an epic battle for the hearts and minds of British people. And in the decade leading up to 1914, these arguments were hammered out most crucially within Liberalism.

From the start, it was the militarists who captured the

commanding heights of the Party. In 1902 influential Liberal imperialists (or 'Limps') formed themselves into a Liberal League. Once the Liberals swung into power in 1905 and had this confirmed by the 1906 general election, the League could claim not only Haldane as Secretary for War, but also Grey as Foreign Secretary; and when Asquith became Prime Minister in 1908 the 'Limps' were truly in the ascendant. One historian who later asked what had happened to the League was told: 'the Liberal League did not vanish. What happened is simply that in 1905 it absorbed the Liberal Government. That is why we went to war in 1914.'[1]

Others wanted to go further and introduce conscription. A National Service League urged compulsory military training for men; using a wide range of propaganda techniques, by 1914 it could claim 220,000 supporters. It never made much political headway over peacetime conscription; but behind this smokescreen, Haldane's War Office proceeded with more moderate army reforms. There was also great debate about naval expenditure. In the 1909 naval scare, with leaks about how Germany was accelerating the building of its Dreadnought ships, the press whipped up speculation about Germany's imperial ambitions and German spies in Britain.

With fears of war fanned by the Tory press, both the National Service League and its sister Navy League formed strong women's sections. They did not, of course, suggest that women should fight, for popular militarism was premissed upon a 'separate spheres' view; rather, they urged women to help with fund-raising. A British Women's Patriotic League was formed in 1909, with the aim of recruiting over a million for the Territorial Army. At the same time, the Territorials were recruiting nurses from civilian hospitals. The enthusiasm for military nursing was such that in 1909 the government decided to organize a 'Voluntary Aid Detachments' scheme. Within five years, no fewer than 50,000 women had flocked to become VAD members.[2] So by 1914 for many, many women the prospect of war seemed to offer an irresistible opportunity for excitement, travel *and* dedicated patriotic service.

How many women thought along anti-militarist lines is less clear; certainly they were far fewer and far less organized. Helena Maria Swanwick was one. She too had become sucked into the suffrage campaign, was now on the NUWSS executive and edited its new weekly paper, *Common Cause*. Like other suffragists, she grew impatient with Asquith's government. She also moved in circles increasingly critical of the Liberal leadership's narrow nationalism. Leagues being so much in vogue, these critics formed a League of Liberals against Aggression and Militarism. Its executive included two of Swanwick's friends: C. P. Scott, editor of the *Manchester Guardian*, and H. N. Brailsford, another influential journalist.

There were other sources of opposition to Haldane, Grey and Asquith. Hardie's ILP could sometimes exert influence on the new Labour Party; for instance all Labour MPs, fearful of any whiff of conscription, voted against Haldane's Forces Bill; significantly, though, the trade unions raised scarcely a whisper of protest; and generally Labour MPs with dockyard and arsenal constituencies were reluctant to cut army and navy expenditure. The Labour Party was officially linked to continental socialists; but, as one recent history suggests, 'most trade unionists were undoubtedly quite unaware that . . . they had become enrolled in something called the Second International.'[3]

Indeed, anti-militarism was decidedly thin during these difficult years – despite the hopes of the new National Peace Council. A second Hague Peace Conference was held in 1907; Bertha von Suttner was among those who enjoyed the lavish hospitality of such occasions. But as Britain and Germany refused to compromise, the conference seemed to make little progress on arms limitation. Yet in 1909 Norman Angell's *The Great Illusion*, which argued that war, rather than giving nations economic advantage, was 'bad for business', quickly became a best-seller, going through dozens of reprints and foreign-language editions.

It seemed that people wanted Britain to regain her pre-Boer War dignity – but without going to war. This *did* appear possible: after all, there had been the 1908 war scare when Austria seized Bosnia and Herzegovina in the Balkans, and the 1909 Anglo–German naval crisis – both of which had been settled without war. So, in summer 1911, attention was elsewhere when the Agadir Crisis erupted. Suffrage optimism was at its height. WSPU organized a 'Women's Coronation Procession': 40,000 suffragists and suffragettes walked in an impressive seven-mile procession that took three hours to pass. Yet what started as a minor tension in Morocco quickly blew up into a major Anglo–German confrontation. Lloyd George, onetime anti-war rebel, publicly proclaimed that Britain, a great nation 'by centuries of heroism and achievement', could not be treated 'as if she were of no account in the Cabinet of Nations . . . peace at that price would be a humiliation intolerable for a great country like ours to endure.'[4] Germany felt that Britain was yet again thwarting her rightful claims. Talk of war was in the air. Asquith, Grey, Haldane and Lloyd George secretly planned moving the Expeditionary Force across the Channel should hostilities break out.

In the end, Britain did not go to war in autumn 1911, but anti-militarists were furious. The National Peace Council protested. The campaigning journalist E. D. Morel fiercely denounced secret diplomacy. About eighty Liberal MPs formed a Foreign Affairs group to keep a sharp eye on their Foreign Secretary. C. P. Scott, Brailsford, Leonard Hobhouse, Lord Courtney and the young Bertrand Russell all tried to shift government policy away from secret treaties. But their influence was – sadly – paltry.

Against this background of combustible Anglo–German naval rivalry, the most effective way in which Edwardian feminists forged links with their European sisters was through the International Woman Suffrage Alliance. Since its first meeting in Berlin in 1904 the flourishing IWSA had obviously met the needs of a new generation of highly educated suffragists, grown impatient with the International Council of Women's shilly-shallying over equal rights.[5] Among those who travelled to Berlin in 1904 with Mrs Fawcett was a twenty-two-year-old Newnham graduate, Margery Ashby, who was so profoundly moved by this meeting of suffrage pioneers that she dedicated her life to IWSA. Margery Corbett Ashby (she married in 1910) found that it fitted her orthodox Liberalism like a glove: over the next seventy years she attended all but one of the IWSA congresses.

But to others, these congresses were less welcoming. At the 1906 Copenhagen Congress, IWSA (now led by another American, Carrie Chapman Catt), considered WSPU's membership application; but this was opposed by Fawcett, IWSA vice-president, on the grounds of Pankhurst militancy. So the suffragettes were banned from the world's suffrage meetings for the next seven years. Unperturbed, IWSA continued to flower: it began its own monthly journal, *Jus Suffragii*, to enable voteless women around the world to communicate more rapidly. Later, at the 1908 congress in Amsterdam, Finnish and Norwegian women were congratulated on winning the vote (and, in Finland, electing nineteen women to Parliament). And by the 1909 congress in London (now acknowledged as the suffrage movement's storm centre) the number of countries affiliated to IWSA had risen to twenty-one.

But perhaps the price paid for this expansion was *genuine* internationalism; for at the London Congress it was agreed that IWSA was 'pledged to observe absolute neutrality on all questions that are strictly national'.[6] In other words, it was really just a loose federation. Its sixth congress was held in June 1911 in Stockholm (the British delegates included loyal Liberals like Fawcett and Corbett Ashby; Ethel Snowden, wife of ILP MP Philip Snowden; Chrystal Macmillan from Scotland; and Catherine Marshall, a young suffragist from the Lakes). Swanwick published a lengthy report on the congress in *Common Cause*; but it focused on the Fredrika Bremer Association in Sweden and on defending 'the mothers of our race' – *not* on the current Anglo–German threat to world peace. Only months later did *Common Cause* carry an article on 'Women and War' which began to explore links between feminism and anti-militarism:

> All the women in the world . . . , who have no voice in deciding whether war shall be made or peace maintained, . . . are certainly those who suffer most if war does break out. The pain and injury which war brings to a race are inevitably felt most by the mothers of the race. . . . If the statesmen of Europe really care for peace, let them enfranchise those whose function it is to preserve life in the race. . . . In the freedom of women lies our strong hope of future peace.[7]

In Britain, such discussion of maternalist and equal-rights arguments against militarism remained rare. The struggle for the vote still predominated in feminists' minds. But beyond Britain the debate about women's suffrage and 'the mothers of our race' *did* dovetail into anti-militarism; for by 1911 discussion about votes for women and motherhood was raising a very wide range of issues.

Official concern remained strong about the next generation of soldiers' health. The Women's Co-operative Guild and Women's Labour League (as the women's section of the Labour Party was then known) also campaigned for mother and baby clinics. But discussion went beyond concern for infant mortality. There was debate about whether motherhood *was* women's supreme and sacred duty – or could women freely chose to 'shirk' it, or combine it with a paid job? And if motherhood *was* women's supreme and sacred duty, should they be guaranteed maintenance by the state? Indeed, how should a nation best ensure the healthy future of its 'race'? This last question surfaced partly through the vogue for eugenics: should eugenic concerns be women's primary goal in life, overriding any notion of, say, equal rights to education?

Ideas about warfare deepened this complex debate. Bertha von Suttner and others had already presaged a time when whole nations, even 'regiments of women', might fight; and modern weaponry meant the numbers of dead and wounded could rise horrifically. (In 1912, von Suttner even wrote a pamphlet, *Barbarity in the Skies*, warning of aeroplanes in war.[8]) Was this – the reproduction of fodder for gun and cannon and aerial attack – really the end to which women's lives should be dedicated?

It was difficult for British women, immersed in the day-to-day struggle for the vote, to unpick all the skeins of the debate on women's suffrage, motherhood and warfare. But then into the suffrage maelstrom came influential writers from abroad like Gilman and Schreiner, each with a significant following in Britain. Their ideas, combined with the organizational weight of NUWSS and IWSA, underpinned the beginnings of an organized women's peace movement in 1915.

Charlotte Perkins Gilman's British readership widened in 1909 when she began her monthly magazine, *The Forerunner*.[9] It sold at a dollar a year; this brought it within the reach of, for instance, suffragettes in the Rochdale WSPU, who acquired bound annual volumes.[10] Similarly, one young working-class woman from Manchester, who used to attend an ILP adult class, remembers the effect Gilman's ideas on women's economic independence had on her, and how her group used to import the magazine: 'I got my name on this list. . . . We passed it round. We read it, and it was a circle.'[11] In 1909–10 *The Forerunner* also serialized Gilman's *The Man-Made World*, published in book form in 1911.

In *The Man-Made World*, Gilman emphasized sexual difference, women's moral superiority, a concern for childcare and, sharing the current enthusiasm for eugenics, racial improvement. Gilman's own harsh 'uncuddled childhood' and chequered experience of motherhood stripped her views on the family of any romanticism. Subtitled 'Our Androcentric Culture', her book attacks both 'that primal altar, the cook-stove' and the 'sacred selfishness of the home'.[12] It opens with a critique of the way patriarchal society still anachronistically imprisoned women:

> The domestic industries, in the hands of women, constitute a survival of our remotest past. . . . The man-made family has resulted in arresting the development of half the world. We have a world wherein men, industrially, live in the twentieth century; and women, industrially, live in the first. This abnormal restriction of women has necessarily injured motherhood. . . .[13]

Gilman added: 'We have cut off half the race from the strengthening influence of natural selection, and so lowered our race standards.' She believed that childcare was so important that it should be the responsibility of trained specialists rather than automatically the biological mother. For her, equal-rights feminism was mixed with eugenics.

Gilman argued that 'our progress is . . . seriously impeded by . . . the masculine tradition. . . . Man, as a sex, has quite naturally deified his own qualities rather than those of his opposite.'[14] This was demonstrated most dramatically in politics – originally unconnected with warfare but now marred 'by the constant obtrusion of an ultra-masculine tendency':

> In warfare, *per se*, we find maleness in its absurdest extremes. Here is to be studied the whole gamut of basic masculinity, from the initial instinct of combat, through every form of glorious ostentation, with the loudest possible accompaniment of noise.[15]

Gilman asserted that 'primitive warfare had for its climax the possession of the primitive prize, the female'; she described 'the proud bellowing of the conquering stag, as he ... returned to his home, with victim chained to his chariot wheels, and trumpets braying'. But, importantly, while primitive combat used to make good eugenic sense, this was no longer so:

> Combat is ... purely masculine, intended to improve the species by the elimination of the unfit. Amusingly enough, or absurdly enough, when applied to society, it eliminates the fit, and leaves the unfit to perpetuate the race ... The pick of the country, physically, is sent off to oppose the pick of another country, and kill – kill – kill!

Writing four years before the outbreak of war, Gilman was chillingly prophetic about where militarism would lead. 'Our whole culture is still hag-ridden by military ideas', she lamented; peace congresses might meet, but 'the tin soldier remains a popular toy. We do not see boxes of tin carpenters by any chance; tin farmers, weavers, shoe-makers.'[16] But in trying to understand the causes, Gilman at least offered hope. Men, responsible for war, might have turned politics 'into an ultra-masculine performance'; but once women became economically independent, freed from the private drudgery of housework and free to select men fit to be fathers, a new womanhood would emerge. 'And these New Mothers will say:

> 'We are tired of men's wars. We are tired of men's quarrels. We are tired of men's competition. We are tired of men's crimes and vices and the diseases they bring upon us, of this whole world full of noise, confusion, enmity and bloodshed.'

Gilman optimistically believed that through eugenics and the power of love women would create a new world without war, in which destructive male qualities were bred out. Although her later authoritarianism and racism were already beginning to show, Gilman's was a fresh new utopian vision.[17]

As an American, Gilman had seen war only at a distance. In southern Africa Olive Schreiner had experienced the Boer War at first hand; and the emotional power of her essay on 'Women and War', published in *Woman and Labour* in 1911, gives it lasting impact. Schreiner gave classic eloquence to the maternalist argument that women were naturally anti-war – because they were mothers.

Schreiner knew about infant mortality: she was one of twelve children, of whom five died young. Then, in 1895, a year after she married, when she was forty, Schreiner gave birth to a baby who scarcely lived a day. At least four miscarriages followed. Schreiner might call Hobhouse imperious but she shared her belief that women bore the brunt of war; and in about 1903, when Hobhouse stayed with her, Schreiner was mulling over the ideas for *Woman and Labour*. Its strength springs largely from the turmoil of personal experience poured into it.[18]

Woman and Labour is best remembered for its battle-cry '*Give us labour and the training which fits for labour! We demand this, not for ourselves alone, but for the race.*' Schreiner, like Gilman, demands that women should have the right to share in useful, satisfying work. But if 'for the present our cry is, "*We take all labour for our province!*"' – should that include war-fighting as well? Schreiner's unequivocal answer was: NO! She too stressed sexual difference, echoing *Lay Down Your Arms* and *The Brunt of War*, but adding a new, more powerful level of argument by specifically comparing women's agony in childbirth to men's suffering on the battlefield:

> We have always borne part of the weight of war, and the major part. . . . We have in all ages produced, at enormous cost, the primal munition of war, without which no other would exist. There is no battlefield on earth, nor ever has been, howsoever covered with slain, which it has not cost the women of the race more in actual bloodshed and anguish to supply, than it has cost the men who lie there. *We pay the first cost on all human life.*

In the long years of childcare 'the women of the race go through a long, patiently endured strain which no knap-sacked soldier on his longest march has ever more than equalled.' Because of this:

> There is, perhaps, no woman, whether she have borne children, or be merely potentially a child-bearer, who could look down upon a battlefield covered with slain, but the thought would rise in her, 'So many mothers' sons! ... So many months of weariness and pain while bones and muscles were shaped within . . . ; – all this, that men might lie with glazed eyeballs, and swollen bodies, and fixed, blue, unclosed mouths. . . .
>
> And we cry, 'Without an inexorable cause, this should not be!' No woman who is a woman says of a human body, 'It is nothing!'[19]

Stressing sexual difference ('she knows the history of human flesh; she knows its cost; he does not'), Schreiner carefully avoids suggesting that women are morally superior to men, or that eugenics will lead to a future without war. Rather, linking her maternalist feminism to her strong equal rights commitment, she envisions a highly optimistic future of peace, premissed upon women's suffrage:

> On that day, when the woman takes her place beside the man in the governance . . . of her race will also be that day that heralds the death of war as a means of arranging human differences. . . . It is especially in the domain of war that we, the bearers of men's bodies, who . . . alone, with a three-in-the-morning courage, shed our blood and face death that the battle-field may have its food . . . ; it is we especially, who in the domain of war, have our word to say, a word no man can say for us.[20]

Schreiner's ideas had tremendous impact. Among the suffragists stirred by her words was Gwen Chambers, then a twenty-one-year-old NUWSS organizer. Over seventy years later she could still recall:

> I was always against any violence. Always for peace. Even at school. I remember having arguments about it. . . . The book I think so much of and have urged women to read, is Olive Schreiner's *Woman and Labour*, which I think is the absolute classic for women. . . .[21]

Other writers also made an impact. Rosa Mayreder, born in 1858, was actively involved in the Austrian peace movement. In her *A Survey of the Woman Problem*, published in English in 1913, Mayreder saw war as the epitome of masculine values: only when women were given a voice in politics would there be any hope for peace.[22] More controversial was Ellen Key, born in 1849 into a wealthy Swedish family, whose idiosyncratic views on 'motherliness' as women's supreme duty, inside or outside marriage, provoked accusations of 'immorality' *and* betraying the equal-rights campaign. But Key was unrepentant; she wrote prolifically and between 1909 and 1916 English editions of six of her books appeared, often with introductions by Havelock Ellis, pioneer of sex psychology. Key's writing is rambling; but, insisted Ellis, her ideas were central to the current feminist debate: 'Here, at the spot where she stands, the nature and direction of the Woman's Movement of the future must be determined.'[23]

Key had libertarian ideas about the upbringing of children, the hope for the future. But she argued that women should undergo a compulsory 'period of training . . . devoting themselves to the care of children, hygiene, and sick nursing', just as 'men serve their years of military service'.[24] By 1912, when an English edition of Key's *The Woman Movement* was published, the growing rigidity of her thinking was becoming clear. No suffragist, she lambasted 'progress-impeding emancipation women' and those who did not agree that '*the work of the mother outside the home* in and for itself is an evil'. Increasingly, she held that the future needs of the race alone must determine women's lives, with the state intervening to assist this eugenic programme. She wanted 'a paternity assessment upon society as a contribution to the maintenance of children and a compensation of motherhood by the state'. Young girls were beginning to see that their worth 'depends essentially upon their value for the propagation of mankind' (i.e. 'the European-American people'); and this was right – if they were 'young, sound, pure-minded, and loving', not 'degenerate, uneducated, decrepit'. She ended her controversial book by suggesting that 'the higher cultivation of the race is the social-political end, and that for this *the service of the mother* must receive the honour and oblation that the state now gives to *military service*.'[25] Key, particularly influential in Germany, gave Ruskin's separate spheres maternalism a new authoritarian twist.

Sweden was at the forefront of the international peace movement, boasting seventy-nine organizations at the turn of the century. A Swedish Women's Peace Movement had flourished since its formation in Stockholm in 1898.[26] Although she did not attend an international peace congress until 1910, Key was sympathetic to anti-militarism, opposing conscription because it risked the healthiest young lives. Already she identified the link between women and peace as racial and eugenicist rather than connected to women's lack of equality and the vote.

Meanwhile, in Britain, the suffrage campaign escalated. ILP suffragists like Keir Hardie and Annot Robinson helped to move the Labour Party into an alliance with NUWSS. In 1912 Swanwick, particularly intolerant of WSPU suffragettes' militancy, resigned the editorship of *Common Cause* over her right to attack them publicly.[27] She began to write *The Future of the Women's Movement*, a summation of what feminism meant to *her*; and in June 1913 she travelled across Europe for the IWSA Congress in Budapest. For Swanwick was now one of those feminists belonging to the international unenfranchised sisterhood, all united around their equal-rights demands. In Britain this sisterhood was now beginning to burst beyond a small elite of Oxbridge intellectuals, reaching out to touch women who, a decade earlier, would have been untroubled by either suffragism or internationalism. It was now possible to perceive, in these crucial eve-of-war years, not just national leaders but also women who, rooted in their own communities, put their international ideals into local practice. The diaries of such women offer a valuable new perspective on the organized women's peace movement which was to spring up so dramatically in 1915.

In Linthwaite, a tiny Pennines textile hamlet in Yorkshire, lived Florence Lockwood, wife of Josiah, a manufacturer. An art student before her marriage, she was now intent on being accepted by Josiah's family but remained acutely aware how stiflingly parochial was much of local 'society' chatter about servants, 'trade' and, above all, the Liberal Party.[28] Then, during a heated local by-election, she heard Mrs Pankhurst. 'That was a psychological moment. . . . What she said was new and inspiring to me. Why should women be political nonentities indeed?' She joined the active Huddersfield NUWSS branch, meeting other women 'awake to the new order of things'. Josiah took an affectionate interest in the suffrage meetings his wife spoke at, and 'would wave his red pocket handkerchief from the audience as a signal of distress. "Thou hast done well, love! Give up".'[29]

Lockwood also joined the Linthwaite Women's Liberal Association, naively believing that it campaigned for the vote, and later became president of the local Colne Valley group. Then in May 1913, the post unexpectedly brought a notice about the IWSA congress in Budapest:

> I was not much interested and certainly had no desire to go, though an ardent upholder of the Cause. . . . I am so firmly

rooted at home that the idea seems impossible – like leaving a fortress. My head is so mazy and muddled. . . . But today I have been studying the hand-bills because Josiah says 'Why not go?' . . . Having made my decision, I hastily made expeditions into Huddersfield on a wild dash for some suitable clothes.[30]

In fact Lockwood, a provincial lady, soon found much that was new once she met the thirty other suffragists. 'As we travelled to Folkestone I felt a sense of ease to be a dwarf among these women, instead of standing out as something exceptional and eccentric, as I appear at home,' she confided to her diary. 'One refined, delicate-looking woman, who had not spoken much, gave me a shock by beginning her contribution to the conversation with: "When I was in prison".' From Vienna they took a steamer down the Danube and were welcomed to Budapest by hundreds of Hungarian suffragists. 'My life at Linthwaite seemed a far-off dream difficult to remember.'[31]

Largely responsible for organizing the congress was Hungarian suffragist Rosika Schwimmer, from a free-thinking middle-class Jewish family: one of her uncles, founder of the Hungarian Peace Society, had worked with Bertha von Suttner. But unlike von Suttner, Schwimmer believed in energetic socialist reform. She had formed a pro-suffragist Hungarian Feminist Association, translated Gilman's *Woman and Economics* from German, and now edited the Hungarian feminist-pacifist magazine, *A Nö*.

Thanks to such organizing skills, women crossed the world to reach Budapest. From America came the widely translated Gilman; Jane Addams, well known for her Hull House Settlement for newly arrived immigrants in Chicago and for books like *Newer Ideals of Peace*; and, of course, Carrie Chapman Catt. From Munich came Lida Gustava Heymann – and Anita Augspurg, President of the German Union for Women's Suffrage. Aletta Jacobs, president of the Dutch suffrage association, also attended; she was Holland's first woman doctor, opened the first birth control clinic in 1881, and translated *Woman and Economics* into Dutch.[32] British delegates included Swanwick, Chrystal Macmillan, and Maude Royden, now *Common Cause* editor. Altogether nearly 400 delegates assembled from two dozen countries, representing twenty-two languages. IWSA now even had affiliation from China.[33]

Two particular concerns were voiced: suffragettes and peace. Sympathy for the brave WSPU militants, long excluded from IWSA, was widespread. Catt argued that it was *suffragette* sufferings that had aroused international interest in the vote. She persuaded the IWSA executive to accept a special resolution supporting the Pankhursts (though this can hardly have found favour with Swanwick and Fawcett). Then the congress looked at the changes that would come about when women got the vote – including peace. 'The continental delegates', Swanwick recalled,

> laid great stress on the enfranchisement of women as a bulwark against war. Maria Vérone, the French barrister, made an impassioned oration, ending with the appeal to us all to wage '*La guerre contre la guerre*'. The English delegates were surprised at this, and one of the most distinguished of them said to me, 'I wonder why they all talk so much about war. There will never be another European war.'[34]

It seems that most British suffragists, still so caught up in dramatic battles with the Liberal government, were much less conscious of war and peace as feminist issues than, say, the French women haunted by memories of the Franco–Prussian War, or Hungarian suffragists, so near the current Balkan conflicts. So Lockwood was not the only British woman who naively found it eye-opening to hear women demanding political freedom in order to work for *peace*. 'Several meetings dealt solely with the question of disarmament and pacifism generally', she noted in her diary. 'These last topics seemed too abstract to enthral me. It was the first time I had heard the words pacifism and pacifist.'

The congress was a magnificent celebration. Lifelong friendships were formed. European women met the legendary Jane Addams; Lockwood got to know Swanwick and a Hungarian teacher, Anna Ehrsam. But at last it drew to a close with a farewell dinner. 'We dined, eight hundred strong, in a big hall,' Lockwood jotted down, 'and nearly all of us made speeches. The roar was deafening, and the band played national airs. It seemed as if we should never finish.'[35]

Budapest reaffirmed the strength of international sisterhood. It took British women beyond their narrow struggle with Asquith, and thrust them into the heart of transEuropean feminism. Suffragist Mary Sheepshanks took on an exciting job: IWSA secretary. This entailed running the new headquarters in London and editing *Jus Suffragii*, previously published in Holland. Before long she was appealing for Czech, Polish, Icelandic, Norwegian and Danish translators. Rosika Schwimmer also brought a new cosmopolitan dynamism to London when she moved there in 1914 to work as international press secretary.[36] And the inspiration of Budapest was felt beyond London, in towns where suffrage was strong; Lockwood even managed to persuade Huddersfield's newspaper to run a regular column, 'Suffrage in Many Lands'. Its readers had to adjust to talk of the Swedish Women's Peace Association and headlines such as 'Good News from Denmark'.[37]

Swanwick finished *The Future of the Women's Movement* later that year. The book is drenched with the internationalist spirit of Budapest – and with suffragists' impatience with the Liberals. Swanwick castigated their current hypocrisy for using 'all the old catch-words of the democratic party, [yet] refusing to apply their Liberalism to women'. But, very much an equal-rights feminist, she also directed her anger at Key's rigid maternalism; and as a

rationalist she turned upon the suffragettes, arguing that
'for women to invite physical force against themselves is to
provoke all the forces of reaction . . . so that . . . all women
are once more in danger of violence from men.' Like
Schreiner, she argued: 'Men who go to war have the honour
and the glory, the bands and the banners. . . . Women die,
and see their babies die, but theirs is no glory; nothing but
horror and shame unspeakable, the slaying of those for
whom they willingly risked their lives . . .'.[38] Swanwick's
own optimism for the future lay in her classic Liberal belief
in progress and civilization: men were beginning to find
outlets other than warfare for their energies, 'and the
women's movement, in part the cause, is also in great
measure the effect of the disappearance of barbarism.'[39]

Indeed, there were signs that the 'rule of force' so despised by Liberal idealists was disappearing. Bertha von
Suttner toured America in 1912 at the invitation of the
Federation of Women's Clubs; she met Catt and Addams,
and spoke on 'women's role in improving world peace'.[40]

In summer 1914 Florence Lockwood heard that her friend
Anna Ehrsam was visiting England, and invited her to
Linthwaite. It was a busy time: the Huddersfield NUWSS
branch had started an 'Active Service League', canvassing
door-to-door and signing up supporters. The death of von
Suttner on 21 June, and the assassination of Archduke
Franz Ferdinand in Sarajevo on the 28th, caused scarcely a
ripple. Ireland and Mrs Pankhurst's arrest loomed larger.
Lockwood was preoccupied with arranging for Rosika
Schwimmer to come up and speak at the local NUWSS
annual garden party on 18 July.

This was a sunny, spacious Edwardian affair, the epitome of middle-class Liberalism, hoping for change – so long
as nothing rocked the boat. The two Hungarian women,
already involved in arranging the next IWSA congress in
Berlin, focused on peace. Suffragists, Ehrsam said, encouraged people in different countries to get to know each other,

which 'is another step towards universal peace'. 'We hate violence and are determined not to resort to it', added Schwimmer.

There was news of shots fired between Serbia and Austria. But only at the very end of July did it dawn on the Lockwood household that war was possible. They scanned the papers anxiously. On Sunday 2 August, Ehrsam packed her bags. 'Progress will be put back one hundred years,' she lamented. 'Men's passions will rise.' On Tuesday 4 August, the Lockwoods waved her goodbye at Huddersfield station. They never saw her again.[41]

Rosika Schwimmer, back at the IWSA office in London, was particularly sensitive to the tensions between the small Balkan nations and even tried – unsuccessfully – to warn Lloyd George about how Austria might react.[42] She was busy, with Catherine Marshall and Emily Leaf from NUWSS, trying to ensure good newspaper publicity – which did not focus only on suffragette violence. She felt she alone was horrified by the war news, for, 'with excusable ignorance about East-European affairs, these young suffragists did not realize the danger of a vast conflagration.'

But as soon as fighting began, most pacifists just gave up. Schwimmer was cynical about the older international organizations. 'All the chirping peace voices', she wrote melodramatically, 'were drowned by the deafening thunder clap of the first shot. . . . It shattered the sleuces [*sic*] and opened the gate for the deluge of fire and blood.'[43] She and others turned to the IWSA: Schwimmer met Fawcett, Macmillan and Sheepshanks to draw up a powerful and moving mediation appeal:

> We, the women of the world, view with apprehension and dismay the present situation in Europe, which threatens to involve one continent if not the whole world, in the disasters and horrors of war. In this terrible hour, when the fate of Europe depends on decisions which women have no power

to shape, we, realizing our responsibilities as the mothers of the race, cannot stand passively by. Powerless though we are politically, we call upon the governments and powers of our several countries to avert the threatened unparalleled disaster. . . .

We women of twenty-six countries, . . . appeal to you to leave untried no method of conciliation or arbitration for arranging international differences which may help to avert deluging half the civilized world in blood.

Millicent Garrett Fawcett
Chrystal Macmillan[44]

This carefully worded manifesto, signed on behalf of no fewer than twelve million women, was delivered to the Foreign Office and to the London embassies on Friday 31 July. Meanwhile, Russia, Germany and France began mobilizing. Desperate attempts were made to halt the war fever and to preserve British neutrality. On Sunday 2 August, Keir Hardie addressed the Second International's anti-war rally in Trafalgar Square. A major women's anti-war rally was planned for the evening of Tuesday the 4th in Kingsway Hall.

But even during the planning there were tensions. Schwimmer, at one extreme, wanted to include the militant suffragettes; Fawcett, at the other, refused. She also opposed Schwimmer's suggestion that Olive Schreiner be invited – but was outvoted. In the event, the crowded and excited Kingsway Hall meeting represented the great breadth and strength of the Edwardian women's movement (except the Pankhursts' WSPU). There was, Schwimmer wrote, 'nothing like it in all the history of pacifism or the women's movement'. On the platform were Mrs Despard of the Women's Freedom League and Emmeline Pethick Lawrence, both rebel suffragettes who had broken with WSPU; Mrs Fawcett in the chair and, despite her objections, Olive Schreiner; Eleanor Barton, president of the Women's Co-operative Guild; Mary Macarthur of the National Federation of Women Workers; Marion Phillips of the Women's Labour League; the president of the National Council of Women, Elizabeth Cadbury, convenor of the ICW peace committee (though ICW was already distancing itself fast from calls for peace); and Helena Swanwick for NUWSS.[45]

Schwimmer, a moving speaker, lamented the certain martyrdom of her country. But, Swanwick later recalled, the die was already cast against peace – and so against the international sisterhood celebrated in 1913:

> The resolution which had been drafted had to be scrapped. . . . It was not a 'Stop the War' meeting. . . . Mrs Fawcett . . . had very grave doubts in her mind. . . . The audience was extremely serious, sad, and anxious to find some effective peace policy. When one speaker cried, 'What can we women do?' a cry arose, 'Down tools! Down tools!' But how can women – the mass of women, mothers and housewives – down tools?[46]

They could not – nor could the Second International. The Peace Society was paralysed. It was all too late. Resolutions from Kingsway Hall were delivered to Downing Street. But within an hour Britain's ultimatum to Germany had expired and the country was at war.

Gwen Chambers, still working as an NUWSS organizer, remembered that moment clearly seventy years later:

> When the war broke out, I and a colleague were addressing an audience on Salisbury Plain, of all places. And one of the soldiers – there were a lot of soldiers, of course – he called out and said, 'If war is declared tonight, what will the women of England do?' And my colleague said, 'I shall work for the victory of my country'. And I said, 'I shall be neither pro-British nor pro-German. I shall work for peace.' . . . But of course very few who were for peace. And you couldn't talk peace then. The country was war-mad.[47]

Women who had met at Budapest only a year before were now hurled away on contradictory trajectories. 'Women, your country needs you,' Mrs Fawcett wrote. 'LET US SHOW OURSELVES WORTHY OF CITIZENSHIP.'[48] Schwimmer, now an 'enemy alien', resigned her IWSA job and threw herself with characteristic verve into a personal crusade for neutral mediation to end the war. In despair, she likened the pacifists' timid surrender to 'a general laying down, like the grass on a gale-swept cornfield'. In a 'man-made world,' Schwimmer held, 'women's passion for peace seemed to me the only hope left.' Jobless and running out of money, she despaired of British women who would not support her plans for a 'Foreign Legion for Immediate Mediation'. Now even Hobhouse preached caution. But Schwimmer was already in contact with Jacobs in Holland, Catt in America – hoping to persuade neutral governments to mediate. On 25 August she sailed to America to rally support there.

What particularly irked the impatient Schwimmer was how complacently even the most internationalist women sank into mindless 'relief' work, which, she believed, 'unfortunately narcotises so many good people'.[49] Margery Corbett Ashby, whose husband joined his regiment when war was declared, worked in a hospital and later on a farm. Radical suffragists like Selina Cooper, who had been campaigning on behalf of labour-suffrage at by-elections, returned home to work on local relief committees. Even Swanwick 'thought it merely futile to try and start a doomed "Stop the War" movement'; instead, she followed the NUWSS directive that, with suffrage now suspended, members devote themselves to relief. (However, she had to resign from her London day nursery for working mothers when the medical officer discovered she favoured a negotiated peace.)[50]

In smaller communities, there was immense pressure on women to busy themselves 'relieving' the effects of war. Florence Lockwood naturally found herself on the Linthwaite War Distress Committee; when Antwerp fell to the

Germans in October she secured accommodation for thirty bedraggled Belgian refugees. But privately she despised women who unthinkingly colluded in the war effort. The pressure to conform mounted. The early battles – Marne in in September and the first battle of Ypres in October – began to devour young men. Who better to assist the war effort than the local employer's wife? Lockwood jotted a despairing note about a recruiting meeting in the mill yard: 'I was chairman but had no chance of protesting at their advocation of war as a redeeming feature for our degenerate age, and National Service being a primal duty . . .'.[51] Everything closed in. To raise money for soldiers' comforts, Lockwood wrote, 'knitting needles clicked. Knitting teas were the order of the day.' Women were to knit – not think.[52]

Women like Swanwick and Lockwood found one slender lifeline in these months. It was the Union of Democratic Control (UDC), a small Liberal intellectual elite which had the courage to question how Britain had been dragged into war. Its secretary was E. D. Morel, indefatigable pamphleteer against secret diplomacy. On the day war broke out he resigned his parliamentary candidature for the Liberals, arguing that 'the time will come when the country will ask those in authority this question: "What did you do to *prevent* that outrage?"'[53] Other founders included Ramsay MacDonald, who resigned the chair of the parliamentary Labour Party over the war; and Norman Angell, the *Great Illusion* peace publicist. The UDC sprang from pre-war Liberalism, attracting Brailsford and intellectuals like Bertrand Russell (though he compared UDC ambitions to '8 fleas talking of building a pyramid'). It was indeed top-heavy, with Morel and MacDonald likened to 'two prize bulls in one three-acre lot'. However, by November the eight fleas and two bulls had grown into a respectable organization with seven branches and an eighteen-strong committee.[54]

Women who had previously been far too immersed in suffrage to become involved with Morel's crusades now welcomed UDC. It made no mention of women's suffrage, true; but its stress on democratic control of foreign policy and international organization after the war naturally appealed to women steeped in internationalism and committed to a 'democracy' based on reason, not force. Morel, however, was rather more instrumentalist, seeing 'women' as a useful source of support. In September he contacted Maude Royden and suggested a separate UDC women's committee; shortly afterwards he wrote to Swanwick, who advised against any such separate organization. Two days later she met Morel: 'He radiated energy and passion . . . I was delighted by his instant question "What can you *do*?"' Swanwick soon found herself elected to the UDC executive.[55]

That autumn there was discussion among some NUWSS members desperately searching for something beyond just 'relief work' about building UDC links. Some suffragists were extremely wary of such male-led groups: Isabella Ford wrote to Catherine Marshall warning that 'we women must not combine with Morel & Co yet'. Yet for others, UDC offered the *only* base to stop them pliantly bending to jingoism 'like the grass on a gale-swept cornfield'.[56]

One such was Mabel Phythian, daughter of a Liberal extra-mural lecturer who had become 'quite outraged on finding he's been led into a war without having any chance to say anything about it'. Through him, she too became quickly caught up in Manchester's UDC, which 'came into particularly lively action immediately after war was declared'. Eighteen-year-old Phythian and a friend, hearing that a UDC meeting banned by the police had moved to a secret venue, were instructed 'that we must take at least three trams – get on and get off, and get on and get off – in order to prevent our being followed'. This they successfully did, and about twenty people arrived at the banned meeting.[57] In summer 1915 the Manchester police even raided UDC's printer, seizing samples of pamphlets, while in London the police took hundreds of its pamphlets including copies of Morel's *Ten Years of Secret Diplomacy*.[58]

Florence Lockwood also clutched at the lifeline offered by UDC. She later recalled how she 'was thankfully caught and rescued from the raging torrent of madness which war engenders, and landed on a small island of sanity'. In early 1915 she plucked up courage (her nephews were now in khaki, and Josiah remained a loyal Liberal) and went along to her first meeting, for she 'had been bombarded of late by their pamphlets'. As president of the Colne Valley Women Liberals, Lockwood was certainly a catch. This UDC branch, Lockwood wrote, 'was only a small island [of sanity], but we were never overwhelmed'.[59] Indeed, by summer 1915 there were nearly fifty branches and about 6,000 members, with financial help coming from wealthy Quaker families and supporters like the Pethick Lawrences. It was strong in the West Riding, the North-East, Manchester and Lancashire and London. Less well documented, though, is how many suffragists, frustrated by relief work, joined.[60]

By spring 1915 it was clear that the war was going extremely badly. Heavy fighting to capture a few yards of enemy territory meant mounting casualty figures. In March news of enormous losses at Neuve Chapelle began to seep through, 'elaborated', as one historian put it, 'by horrifying tales of men hung up like washing on German barbed wire which faulty British shells had failed to cut'. Women at home 'read of the lane of dead at Neuve Chapelle, and how soldiers had wept to see it'.[61] Vera Brittain, whose fiancé Roland was just leaving for the Front, tried desperately to concentrate on when – not if – he would return. But with 'the persistent demoralizing rumour that owing to a miscalculation in time thousands of our men had been shot down by our own guns . . . [i]t was not an encouraging moment for bidding farewell to a lover.'[62]

Yet it was exactly at this moment, when hope was diminishing, that the 1913 spirit of Budapest bubbled up again – and finally exploded into an organized women's peace movement.

Part II

MOVEMENTS
(1915–70)

5

War, Motherhood and The Hague
(1914–15)

In the first months of the Great War, links between feminism and anti-miltarism, so vivid in pre-war writings and
congresses, were muted. UDC, which (with ILP) now led
anti-war feeling, operated for a full six months before
nodding in the direction of equal rights for women. NUWSS
was still headed by patriotic Mrs Fawcett; IWSA by Carrie
Chapman Catt, who would not pronounce decisively on the
war; and WSPU by Mrs Pankhurst and Christabel, now
arch-patriots and – ironically – happy to lend their names
to the government's recruiting campaign.

It was also virtually impossible for individual women in
Britain to criticize the war. So many of the young men they
were close to had enlisted: Mabel Phythian's brother;
Florence Lockwood's nephews; Vera Brittain's fiancé and
her brother Edward. With men either away at the Front or
spurned by jingoistic women 'refusing to be seen in public'
with them, it was hardly the right moment to question such
idealistic patriotic sacrifices on grounds of *gender*. Brittain,
a student at Somerville, tried to forget the war but,
as the young men marched away, found she 'was suffering, like so many women in 1914, from an inferiority
complex'.[1]

Brittain and Phythian were both eighteen. But for the
older women who had devoted the last decade of their life to
suffrage, the feminist jack-in-the-box could not be shut
away. They had seen too much, done too much, learnt too
much. A series of passionate individual anti-war polemics
burst forth. In the jingoism-drenched first months of war,
their anger welled up so fiercely that their unpolished
words jump abruptly from the page, showing every sign of
being written against the clock. Certainly, considerations of

theory and consistency were thrown to the winds in an effort to reach and win an anti-war readership.

These writings are rooted in the three strands of anti-militarist feminism; and it is particularly difficult to disentangle the separate skeins: maternalism, equal rights, and maleness = violence. Each jostles for space, for the power to energize women into *doing* something. The writers frantically snatch at the most persuasive ideas, particularly Schreiner's language about motherhood and warfare. However, in the end it was the equal-rights tradition and the rebel IWSA suffragists who emerged to take *effective* action. This chapter discusses these urgent ideas, and the proposals for action – practical and otherwise – that sprang from them.

Gilman's proclamation that 'in warfare, *per se*, we find maleness in its absurdest extremes' inspired some women at the outbreak of war. Schwimmer wrote in *Jus Suffragii* on 'The Bankruptcy of the Man-made World-War'.[2] Similarly, some WSPU suffragettes now resigned, aghast at the betrayal of their anti-government stance.[3] One such rebel voice came from a dressmaker in north-east Lancashire; a week after war began Harriette Beanland despatched a furious letter to the local paper, denouncing:

> the erroneous impression that this and other countries are at war with one another. They are not. Their governments, composed of men and responsible only to the men of each country, and backed by the majority of men who have caught the war and glory fever, have declared war on one another. The women of all these countries have not been consulted as to whether they would have war or not. . . . If they [men] deliberately shut out women, the peace-loving sex, from their rightful share in ruling their countries and Churches, then all the appeals and sentiments and prayers will be of no avail in preventing hostilities. . . .

> Yours, etc. . . .
> H. M. BEANLAND[4]

But at a time of white feathers and mounting death tolls, a philosophy of women as 'the peace-loving sex' and men as overblown bullies found little toehold. However, in neutral America, Gilman's novel *Herland* (published in 1915) imagined a utopian world without men. (Yet when America eventually entered the war, Gilman sided with the anti-German patriots – and, increasingly racist, drops out of this history.[5])

More influential was the maternalist strand. This had many facets: from Hobhouse (and von Suttner before her) came the notion that as non-combatants women bear the brunt of suffering during war; from Schreiner the idea that women 'pay the first cost on all human life' and so are instinctively against war; and from Gilman and Key the notion that wartime conscription made bad eugenic sense, for it 'eliminates the fit, and leaves the unfit to perpetuate the race'.[6]

This strand of maternalist feminism placed varying emphases on women as sufferers and as nurturers (occasionally shading, via eugenics, into racism). It was a powerful and emotive language that could be appropriated to underpin less popular anti-war arguments. Even IWSA's eve-of-war manifesto said that women must act 'realizing our responsibilities as the mothers of the race'. Similarly, in her East London Federation of Suffragettes, Sylvia Pankhurst (who, as an anti-war socialist, moved yet further away from her mother and sister) stressed in her *Women's Dreadnought* the needs of women, 'always the heaviest sufferers by every war', and organized practical welfare for local mothers and children. Another socialist, speaking out in her local trades council against workers' fighting capitalist wars, borrowed eugenicist arguments to oppose the recruitment drive: for 'the biggest and strongest men lose their lives in war, leaving the mentally unfit to propagate the race.'[7] And Schreiner's plea for women's instinctive pacifism was given a further boost in October 1914 when her influential 'Women and War' section of *Woman and Labour* was reprinted as a pamphlet.

But significantly, the worldwide organization that might be expected to do something about the war on behalf of mothers – the International Council of Women – kept its head down. Since 1899 ICW had boasted a Standing Committee on Peace and International Arbitration. In May 1914 the ICW meeting in Rome put peace at the top of its agenda, 'protesting vehemently against the odious wrongs of which women are the victims in time of war'. And in June the British section formed a Peace Committee, with Elizabeth Cadbury as its convenor. Yet when war broke out – nothing happened. The history of the ICW devotes a dozen lines to the Great War.[8]

But not every member was satisfied. Frances Hallowes, impressed by the Rome peace resolution, was aghast at ICW inaction. She lived in northern India, probably as a missionary's wife, and was president of a local Indian women's suffrage society. Hallowes had links with the Peace Society, and her novels – including tales of the Boer War – were advertised in Peckover's *Peace and Goodwill*.[9]

Even before war broke out in Britain, Hallowes sent *Jus Suffragii* a long and passionate anti-war article, which Sheepshanks printed in September. About the same time it was also published as a twopenny pamphlet, Hallowes's *Women and War: An Appeal to the Women of All Nations* (perhaps modelled on the 'Earnest Appeal to all Women Everywhere' of the Peckover era). She argued that 'woman bears the brunt of war'; but, voteless, is neither responsible for war nor benefits from it: 'Whatever there is of glory, it is for *man*. The fascinations of war, its pomp and pride of uniforms, gold lace, medals and pensions are for *men*.' The Church colludes in war; women, who comprise two-thirds of its membership, must therefore appeal to the Church to work 'hand in hand with the mothers of mankind in this crusade against war'. The 'Appeal' ends: 'Christianity demands of women this crusade of peace! . . . Mothers, wives, daughters, sisters! Go forward – . . . "God wills it".'[10]

But autumn 1914 was hardly an auspicious time to call to women via the Church, and Hallowes's 'Appeal' fell on stony ground. The same issue of *Jus* carried 'A Manifesto To Women Of Every Land' by a Swiss woman, Lucy Thoumaian. She proposed '*weekly women's meetings*, which will go on till we have secured peace'. The meetings would start with prayer, and exhort God and governments 'to shorten the *intolerable evil and sin*, and to resort to *arbitration*. . . . We will do so as mothers of humanity – as sisters of the whole human race.'[11]

A more radical idea came from Dorothea Hollins, a wealthy member of the Women's Labour League. She proposed a Women's Peace Expeditionary Force, at least a thousand strong, to go to the Front and place itself between the contending armies in the trenches. In October she wrote to *Women's Dreadnought*:

> Let this unarmed force . . . attempt to cross Europe in the teeth of the guns . . . dressed in a quiet grey uniform, and carrying a white banner whose symbol should be a dove. . . .
>
> When thousands of men are dying for their country in a cause they understand little of, . . . cannot we women lay down our lives for a mighty cause? . . . The Women's Crusade must be *international* . . . Let us get French, Belgian, American and even German women to join us if we can.[12]

Hollins's Chelsea address was subsequently listed as headquarters of 'the Women's International Peace Crusade'; but again nothing immediately seems to have come of her imaginative proposal.[13]

Within a few weeks, news came through of the disastrous First Battle of Ypres. Hallowes began to write again; but by spring 1915, when she finished, Neuve Chapelle and the Second Battle of Ypres had shocked the world. Such sustained warfare persuaded her to produce a more substantial polemic: her 130-page book *Mothers of Men and Militarism*, 'dedicated to the Mothers of all Nations', was eventually published around mid-1915.

Her argument was partly pro-suffrage, because if the vote is a reward for readiness to endure physically, then mothers have an equal claim with men, as 'there is no national service which involves greater suffering'. She also attacks 'militarism – a masculine invention' and the patriarchal institutions – religion, statesmen and education – in which women put their faith, only to be betrayed. But while Hallowes borrows the imagery of equal rights and Gilmanite feminism, she was at heart a maternalist. She believed that anti-militarism was far wider than suffrage, for warfare damages motherhood.[14] Hallowes, plagiarizing Schreiner ('She knows the history of his flesh'), demands passionately: 'Shall the mothers of men continue to bear and rear boys, to toil and moil for their food, clothing and education, that in the flower of their youthful manhood they may go and feed the huge machine of militarism?' But her views are also based upon the eugenics of Gilman and Key:

> The way of militarism is the way of *Race Suicide*, and as mothers of the race, women have a perfect right to interfere. . . . Eugenics tell her [the mother] that the effect of war upon the nation is to spoil the breed. . . . Militarism says to the strong, '*You go and die for your country – the unfit will build up the new civilization.*'[15]

Hallowes ends – in the name of Julia Ward Howe, Bertha von Suttner, Ellen Robinson – on 'The Solidarity of Motherhood':

> Mothers must seek to create an *international* solidarity which shall be as widespread as the telephone and telegraph. . . . Now is the opportunity to act. . . . All successful movements are organized. Nations organize for war; let women organize for peace.

And finally she lists 'Practical suggestions', starting with forming 'a World's League of Women', a petition to world governments protesting 'against further gigantic

Armaments and Militarism', with a postcard canvass for signatures to be drawn up by an International Council of Women.[16]

But in 1915 such maternalist appeals to action were already growing unfashionable in Britain. Hallowes's book had only limited impact.[17] In Germany and in Sweden, however, the links between ICW maternalist feminism and peace remained strong. This was made clear in Ellen Key's *War, Peace and the Future: A Consideration of Nationalism and Internationalism, and the Relation of Women to War*, published in 1916. It is as rambling as its predecessors; but twenty months of warfare had forced Key to change some of her ideas. War represented barbarism, the victory of might over right, and so she now saw suffrage as essential for enabling women 'to attain a collective influence in order to lift the race out of the stage of the beast of prey'.[18]

Yet Key also recognized women's own strong nationalism; they were as passionately convinced as men that it was a fight to the finish. ICW, she saw, 'has hardly been able to hold together'. Yet she believed that 'The only gleam of hope for the future that, so far, I can discover . . . [is] my faith in the inmost strength of woman's nature' and that 'the motherliness of woman', so incensed by this war, would lead to a mass uprising. This was not because war led to the subjection of women; nor because, unenfranchised, they had not been consulted; nor because they were instinctively more pacifist; but because continued fighting would eugenically damage the 'race': 'as war spills the best blood, it lowers the national standard'.[19] Like Hallowes, Key saw war and conscription as 'the survival of the defective'. Women should do a year's compulsory domestic state service. 'The idea that I have so long advocated that *mothers should be considered the servants of the State*', Key blithely enthused, 'has already been taken up in Germany. And they make no difference between married or unmarried mothers.' Women who 'are opposed to war and are friends of peace . . . are the forerunner of the host', because 'it is to the *race* that woman's self-sacrifice has been devoted.'[20]

War, Peace and the Future was republished in English in 1922; but as Key's ideas came to underpin the proto-Fascist maternalism of post-war Germany, we will follow her no further.[21]

Such appeals to mothers to rise up bore little fruit in Britain – unlike equal-rights arguments about women and war. Less anguished cries bursting forth in the first few months of war, they emerged slowly and were written by well-known suffragists conscious that their every word carried considerable weight. Such women – Helena Swanwick, Mary Sheepshanks, Catherine Marshall, Maude Royden – wrote as eminent members of both Fawcett's NUWSS and of Catt's IWSA.

To Swanwick, reared on Mill and a belief in benevolent progress, war was an anachronistic relic of the rule of physical force. Women involved in relief work, she wrote in September's *Jus Suffragii*, must 'try and save some of the harvest from the trampling hoofs of barbarism'; for relief work offered 'endless opportunities . . . of holding up Suffragist ideals – ideals of civilization and liberty'.[22] Suffragists like Sheepshanks echoed her UDC-like feeling that 'women must use not only their hands to bind [the wounds men have made], they must also use their brains to understand the causes of the European frenzy.' Swanwick, of course, among the suffragists, was particulary close to UDC; but most anti-war suffrage energy, especially at an international level, was going into proposals for specifically women-only action. In November's *Jus*, Aletta Jacobs appealed for 'mothers of all nations . . . [to] work together to make future wars impossible'.[23]

But elsewhere the spirit of Budapest was taking an enormous battering; in the December issue Marie Stritt, president of the German Union for Women Suffrage and speaking for the more nationalist German women, wrote regretfully cancelling the 1915 IWSA congress planned for Berlin. Catt in New York accepted that the Congress was impossible. But the same issue of *Jus* also made peace history. On behalf of Dutch suffragists, Jacobs daringly proposed, instead of Berlin, 'an international business meeting of the Alliance in one of the neutral countries', and offered Holland as the venue. An open letter to Catt from Anita Augspurg, Lida Gustava Heymann and other anti-war German suffragists stretched 'out our hand to our sisterwomen . . . above the war of the nations.' And from Britain, Swanwick wrote: 'Women fight no one – neither man nor woman. Women have no women-enemies.'[24]

By the end of 1914, then, it was clear that IWSA was divided: on one side were staunch patriots like Stritt and Fawcett, while on the other were the internationalists: Jacobs, Augspurg, Heymann, Swanwick, Sheepshanks and others. In Britain, tension within the NUWSS executive intensified. Conciliation became impossible. January's *Jus* included messages from Stritt, Catt and Fawcett, alongside a historic 'Open Christmas Letter' addressed 'To the Women of Germany and Austria':

Sisters, –

Some of us wish to send you a word at this sad Christmastide, though we can but speak through the Press. . . . Do not let us forget that our very anguish unites us. . . .

As we saw in South Africa and the Balkan States, the brunt of modern war falls upon non-combatants, and the conscience of the world cannot bear the sight.

Is it not our mission to preserve life? Do not humanity and common sense alike prompt us to join hands with the women of neutral countries . . . ?

We must all urge that peace be made . . . to save the womanhood and childhood as well as the manhood of Europe.

We are yours in this sisterhood of sorrow.

This was signed by no fewer than one hundred British women. An impressively wide range of women had been approached (though some, mindful that 'the brunt of war' now fell upon the young men in the trenches, must have refused to sign). Emily Hobhouse headed the list; there were suffragists like Swanwick, Royden, Ford and Councillor Margaret Ashton from Manchester; Labour and ILP signatories included Margaret Bondfield, Dorothea Hollins, Marion Phillips and Annot Robinson; there was Margaret Llewelyn Davies of the Guild; suffragettes included Sylvia Pankhurst; even Peace Society supporters like eighty-one-year-old Priscilla Peckover signed; the wives of UDC and Liberal leaders included Mary Morel; Eva Gore-Booth and Esther Roper, who had worked with the radical suffragists in Lancashire; some Quakers; and, more intriguingly, Mrs M. K. Gandhi.[25]

Back in the spring came 'warm sisterly greetings' signed by 155 German and Austrian women – including Heymann, Augspurg and Rosa Mayreder. In America, Schwimmer had been joined by Pethick Lawrence, and together they helped to stir up a women's peace movement there. Eventually, Catt agreed to ask Jane Addams to send out joint invitations to a great Women's Peace Congress in January 1915. Three thousand women packed into a Washington hotel, and the Women's Peace Party was formed.[26]

Increasingly, events now focused around the specific proposal for an IWSA meeting in neutral Holland. Fawcett, appalled at the idea, wrote to Catt to dissuade her from backing it. At a NUWSS council meeting in early February the issue was discussed – rather inconclusively. But at a public meeting afterwards, Fawcett stated that until German troops were driven back it was '*akin to treason to talk of peace*'.[27] Listening suffragists were utterly dismayed that *this* should publicly represent NUWSS policy. Already Chrystal Macmillan had circulated proposals for the shape the IWSA meeting should take: since they lacked official sanction, a meeting of women as individuals seemed best. In answer to an invitation from Jacobs to join her in Amsterdam in mid February, Macmillan therefore left for Holland, along with Catherine Marshall, NUWSS secretary Kathleen Courtney, Emily Leaf, and a Quaker writer called Theodora Wilson

Wilson. They were joined by Augspurg and Heymann, with other German, Dutch and Belgian suffragists. Out of this small planning meeting came the momentous call for an international congress of women to gather at The Hague on 28 April – in less than three months' time.

The five British women returned home enthusiastic and organized a women-only meeting in Caxton Hall for 26 February. They were committed to making the Hague congress a great success, whatever the dangers or cost.[28] The immediate cost was the offices they held within NUWSS. Courtney and Marshall resigned as secretaries and Royden as editor of *Common Cause*. NUWSS had survived intact since 1897. It was a highly charged and painful moment, both for the younger women resigning and for Fawcett. But the older woman's talk of 'treason' was too bitter to swallow. Swanwick entertained her to tea in March. It was a sticky occasion, especially when Swanwick said that she too intended to resign from the NUWSS executive. Fawcett 'just flushed & blinked & rambled away . . .' Swanwick reported. 'She is very miserable about it all but quite dreadfully embittered & unjust.'[29]

More resignations followed, as the controversy reached anxious NUWSS members up and down the country. There was noisy protest when they learnt that they could not send delegates to The Hague; but many groups seemed genuinely confused or uninterested in this internal strife. Certainly, with the war seven months old and young men dying in the trenches, to speak out against a 'fight to the finish' took exceptional courage; and to propose to cross the Channel to meet 'enemy' women must have seemed unbelievably provocative.

For what was to take place at The Hague was the first major international meeting since the outbreak of war. There had already been smaller-scale meetings: of an *Anti-Oorlog Raad* (Dutch Anti-War Council); and of the International Socialist Women's Conference which Clara Zetkin, the German socialist, convened in Berne in March (attended by Marion Phillips, Margaret Bondfield and two others from Britain).[30] But in determining to undertake this daring venture, Marshall, Royden, Courtney and the others were now sustained by a new leap in feminist thinking on militarism which helped to transform the impossibly perilous into the politically imperative.

On 19 April, at breakneck speed, Allen & Unwin published *Militarism versus Feminism: An Enquiry and a Policy Demonstrating that Militarism Involves the Subjection of Women.* Priced modestly at sixpence, it argued from history and anthropology that the level of militarism in any society affected the liberty that its women might enjoy. It was perhaps predictable that in the middle of the most devastating war the world had ever known, such a challenging feminist polemic would not meet the popular readership of *Lay Down Your Arms* or *Woman and Labour.* For *Militarism versus Feminism* is rooted in all the tensions and apprehensions of those first eight months of war, when the pile of wounded and slain mounted remorselessly.

The book was anonymous, but it is clear from sections published earlier in *Common Cause* and *Jus Suffragii* that one of the authors was Charles Ogden, friend of Bertrand Russell and editor of the anti-militarist *Cambridge Magazine.* The other known author was Mary Sargant, a talented muralist; her sister Ethel, a botanist, had become friends with Swanwick at Girton. Mary married an American musician, Henry Florence; when she was widowed she returned to England with her two children and joined the Women's Freedom League.[31] Whether anyone else collaborated is unclear; certainly Royden and Swanwick shared similar views. What is certain is that Ogden and Sargant Florence – like Swanwick – sprang from the equal-rights feminist tradition which owed so much to Mill, to Liberalism, and to Cambridge – especially Girton. They opened their book with panache. Recent propaganda for suffrage and equality had helped to obscure gender differences, but militarism raised different issues:

For Feminism history has only one message on the question of war, and it is this:

Militarism has been the curse of women, as women, from the first dawn of social life. . . . Violence at home, violence abroad; . . . violence between man and woman; *this it is which, more than all other influences, has prevented the voice of woman being heard in public affairs until almost yesterday*. . . . War has engendered and perpetuated that dominance of man as a military animal which has pervaded every social institution from *Parliament* downwards. In War man alone rules: when War is over, man does not surrender his privileges . . . War, and the fear of War, has kept woman in perpetual subjection, making it her chief duty to exhaust all her faculties in the ceaseless production of children that nations might have the warriors needed for aggression or defence. . . . War, which the influence of women alone might have prevented, was used as the main argument against enfranchisement. . . .

War, Militarism, Imperialism; in every form they have proved her undoing.[32]

Already we are in new territory. While keenly pro-suffrage, the emphasis is on gender difference rather than equality; but this 'gender difference' has much more in common with Gilman's attack on patriarchal institutions ('our whole culture is still hag-ridden by military ideas') than with the relentless maternalism of Key and Hallowes. Indeed, seeing childbearing and child-rearing as women's noblest function has, the authors argue, been part of the problem rather than part of the solution.

No writer had stated so succinctly before that war perpetuates the subjection of women. For the authors' indictment is not of men but of militarism and of how, historically, battling 'barbarian' hordes meant that 'every forward movement among women had to contend . . . with the patriarchal system of marriage prescribed by the militaristic legislators of the Old Testament.' More recently the same pattern prevailed, 'until in countries where the din of battle was no longer heard, . . . woman as woman dared to claim a share in directing those social affairs which concerned her.' The authors turn to mid-nineteenth-century Britain. The modern women's movement was born in peace in 1865, 'when John Stuart Mill gave adequate expression to the murmurings of the centuries'. Since then the movement had gathered impetus but not realized its suffrage aims. Why not? The authors suggest that the seeming 'peace' was only wafer-thin; for Britain's industrialization 'had temporarily obscured the militaristic basis of social organization'. In reality, Britain had sustained a regular army and regular 'small wars with uncivilized tribes'. Indeed, the women's movement arose while imperialism meant that Europe 'slumbered in apparent security'.[33]

So Mill was too uncritical of the growth of British imperialism. Ogden and Sargant Florence also offer a critique of those feminist writers who underestimated militarism's subjection of women, and finally return to their starting point: '*in war time only men matter*. . . . Women in war time are a negligible factor. They just lapse.' (The wartime push for women to work in munitions and take over men's jobs had not yet accelerated.) But being marginalized may give women's protest a powerful platform; and, borrowing from the maternalist language they had previously avoided:

> She has neither part nor share in the slaughter of humanity, and *she* may speak where *man* dare not. . . . That is the cry that women may take up: the cry that men will not and dare not hear. . . . Woman, because to her has fallen the task of bringing into the world those human souls and bodies which in war are but food for cannon, is able to realize what man is not able. . . .
>
> 'Women of all nations unite!'; that should be the new cry – not 'Woman has *no* country!' but 'Woman must have every country!'. . . .

By spring 1915 it was clear that 'Labour has failed. Christianity has worse than failed: it has denied itself.'

But that silent half of humanity, permanently non-combatant, on whom the horrors of war fall with equal severity in all nations alike, . . . may through these very sorrows and sufferings find a new and real bond of unity. . . . In them is the hope of man.[34]

Events now moved swiftly. Plans for the Hague Congress took rapid shape. On 13 April, just six days before *Militarism and Feminism* was published, forty-seven American women – including Jane Addams, accompanied by Emmeline Pethick Lawrence but not Carrie Chapman Catt – sailed from New York. In London, an office was opened and applications for The Hague were invited. On 14 April a 'National Conference of Women to discuss the basis of a permanent peace settlement' was convened at Central Hall, 'at the suggestion of the Union of Democratic Control'.[35] The organizing committee for this conference again reads like a roll call of contemporary radical women: Sargant Florence, of course; NUWSS rebels Swanwick, Royden, Courtney, Ford and Ashton; Labour women including Bondfield and Phillips, Ethel Snowden and Mary Macarthur; Guild leaders Eleanor Barton and Llewelyn Davies; suffragettes Mrs Despard and Muriel Matters (who acted as organizing secretary); Peace Society women; those linked to UDC such as Mary Morel; Elizabeth Cadbury of ICW; and Sarah Reddish, a radical suffragist from Bolton.[36]

The movement was growing: committees were formed in Manchester, Newcastle, Birmingham, Edinburgh and Liverpool, with an Irish committee in Dublin. Speakers were in demand. No fewer than 180 women said they wanted to go to The Hague. In addition to the familiar names, the list now included Marshall and Sheepshanks, Gore Booth and Roper, Schreiner and Sylvia Pankhurst, Theodora Wilson Wilson, and Sarah Dickinson, a trade unionist from Manchester.[37]

But the government became edgy at the idea of so many

women travelling to the war-strewn continent. On 16 April, when some of them had already obtained passports, the organizers learnt that the Permit Office refused permission because 'there is much inconvenience in holding large meetings of a political character so close to the seat of war.' Marshall immediately approached the Home Office. Permits were promised for twenty-four selected women. But then the Admiralty – by strange coincidence – closed the North Sea to shipping. The women heard that one more boat was going across the following day, from Tilbury. Telegrams were sent to all those on the list. There was a great rush to get them to London in time: Ashton and Royden arrived from remote parts of the country at dawn. But there were still endless delays: the permits were slow to arrive, and then no boat was available. Deeply disappointed, the women took lodgings at an old hotel near the Tilbury dockside. They waited anxiously for ten days, until the historic congress was over. Then, despite their firm resolve to get to Holland, they made their tragic way home.[38]

Three British women *were* present at the congress: Macmillan and Courtney were already in Holland, and Pethick Lawrence arrived, despite danger and delay, with the forty-seven-strong American contingent. (Schwimmer travelled independently via Scandinavia.) These women were joined by about 1,200 others from a dozen countries. The Dutch predominated, of course. German suffragists had been stopped at the border, and only twenty-eight got through.[39] A dozen women managed to make their way from both Sweden and Norway, nine from Hungary, six from both Austria and Denmark, two from Canada, and one from Italy. No French or Russian woman was able to attend. (The very last to arrive were five Belgians, who had had to travel part of their journey on foot. When they were invited up on to the platform, the whole congress rose to its feet and cheered.)[40]

Aletta Jacobs opened the congress, welcoming all who had braved dangers and difficulties to attend. Using the powerful imagery of maternalism, she said: 'We women judge [the cost of] war differently from men. . . . We women consider above all the damage to the race resulting from war.' With the Second Battle of Ypres, just a hundred miles to the south, bringing home the unfamiliar horrors of gas attacks, it was not the moment for cool theorizing along *Militarism versus Feminism* lines.

Indeed, the fact that the Hague Congress happened at all, in the eighth month of the Great War, was extraordinary. That its four days' deliberations, presided over by the legendary Jane Addams, were conducted peaceably was a magnificent tribute to the organizational expertise and sisterly solidarity experienced at Budapest in 1913. For in the spirit of this internationalism it was agreed to rule out of order any discussion of the relative responsibility for the war and the rules by which war should be conducted. Instead, resolutions focused on practical matters – the democratic control of foreign policy, women's suffrage, and a peace settlement. Schwimmer, seconded by a Norwegian, urged 'the governments of the world to put an end to this bloodshed, and to begin peace negotiations', demanding that 'the peace which follows shall be permanent and therefore based on principles of justice' – wording that satisfied the women from occupied Belgium. Moving this resolution, Schwimmer also proposed a pause for meditation for those fallen in battle and, impressively, the whole congress rose in response.

But the most dramatic moment occurred on the final day, 1 May. Schwimmer proposed that the congress, rather than just making paper promises, should elect envoys who would personally take the resolutions to the heads of both belligerent and neutral countries; and then report back 'the result of their missions to the International Women's Committee for Constructive Peace as a basis for further action'. Understandably, she encountered strong resistance; but in a last-minute appeal, Schwimmer borrowed emotive rhetoric to win support. 'If brains have brought us to what we are in now,' she cried to the assembled delegates, 'I think it is time to allow also our hearts to speak. When our sons are killed by millions, let us, mothers, only try to do good by going to kings and emperors.'[41]

Schwimmer won her vote on the second count. So from May onwards, two envoy groups visited the governments of Europe and America. 'Surely,' Marshall remarked, 'surely never since Mary Fisher, the Quakeress, set out on her mission to preach Christianity to the Grand Turk, was such an adventure undertaken by women!'[42] Addams and Jacobs led one group. The other, led by Schwimmer and Macmillan, interviewed the Swedish Foreign Minister and was informed that Sweden would be willing to host a mediating conference if the women brought him a note from two governments, one on either side, saying that such an initiative would not be unacceptable. For an exhilarating moment during this semi-official diplomacy, with German and British Foreign Ministers agreeing not to oppose such a conference, the women's aim seemed within their grasp. But in wartime, communication was fraught with difficulty. It seemed that Jacobs had doubts, while Addams had already sailed back to the States. Schwimmer was furious. 'Today I loathe the neutrals more than the others', she confessed privately, '. . . In the meantime, the world perishes.'[43]

She too now returned to America. President Wilson did eventually see them: the congress resolutions, he apparently declared, were 'by far the best formulation which up to the moment has been put out by anybody'. By autumn the envoys, now gathered safely in New York, could report that they had been heard with respect by both the President and European heads of state. Their powerful optimism remained. 'Women will soon have political power,' Jacobs told an American journalist. 'Woman suffrage and permanent peace will go together.'[44] But even though the envoys came so near to success, no statesman dared to grasp the women's challenge and call a conference of neutral nations to offer immediate and continuous mediation as a means to end the fighting. That particular hope died.[45]

So what *did* the Hague Congress achieve? Certainly, it is difficult to detract from its symbolic importance. It was the first major international gathering in Europe since the outbreak of war; and it was, contrary to the predictions of its many detractors (*Daily Express*: 'Pro-Hun Peacettes'), notable for its dignified internationalist calm.[46] And although the envoys did not themselves succeed, they were an important part of a wider wartime revival of a peace movement. (From mid 1915 Charles Roden Buxton, a UDC member, began to put forward peace proposals, and despite opposition, within a year his Peace Negotiations Committee was born.) Linked to this, the congress also helped to create the principles of a future peace settlement and the idea of a possible 'League of Nations' to settle future disputes. But most importantly here, from the feminist enthusiasm generated by the Hague Congress sprang the organized international women's peace movement which still survives today.

In Britain, news from Holland was difficult to get: but the tantalizing silence was eventually broken by a telegram from Courtney announcing that – despite the absent 180 British women – the congress had been an enormous success. There was eagerness for information after all the tragic frustrations of Tilbury. On 11 May a conference was arranged in Central Hall, chaired by Marshall. Women hurried to London from all parts of the country eager to hear the story of The Hague direct from Courtney and Addams. All those present were keen for an organization to be formed; and, on a proposal by Bondfield, plans for a draft constitution were enthusiastically agreed. Two days later, a public meeting with a crowded platform, chaired by Swanwick and addressed by Addams and Courtney, confirmed this success, and a stirring record of the Hague Congress was rushed out by the British Committee of the

Women's International Congress. Called *Towards Permanent Peace*, it listed a 155-strong committee. Within a year 2,500 copies had been sold.

The organization took impressive shape. At its first annual general meeting in Britain in autumn 1915, the title 'Women's International League' was adopted; and the first WIL annual report proclaimed the urgency of:

> linking together two movements felt to be vitally connected: the Women's Movement and the Pacifist Movement. The first has been recognized as one of the greatest of world movements towards liberation: it is time the second should be recognized as another. Only free women can build up the peace which is to be, themselves understanding the eternal strife engendered by domination.[47]

WIL, born out of an equal-rights optimism that votes for women *would* bring peace, was of course led by suffragists. Swanwick, already a towering figure, became chair, with Royden, Ashton and Courtney as vice-chairs. The executive committee included Ford and Marshall. But the movement cast its net wider than the NUWSS rebels. Pethick Lawrence became treasurer and Despard an executive member, as were Bondfield, Barton, and Lady Courtney. Within a year WIL could boast 2,458 members in thirty-four branches; twelve months later this had risen to an impressive 3,576 members and forty-two branches.

By 1916, then, WIL had become such a recognizable part of the British anti-war culture and political landscape that Rose Macaulay's novel *Non-Combatants and Others* could offer a gentle and affectionate fictional parody of a WIL woman: Daphne Sandomir, a composite figure, drawn mainly from Mary Sargant Florence, but also perhaps from Maude Royden and Mary Sheepshanks.[48]

6

The Women's Peace Crusade
(1916–18)

Until 1916, Daphne Sandomir, a bishop's daughter 'lately
. . . gone down from Newnham', could well serve an up-
and-coming novelist trying to capture the spirit of the
women's peace movement, for the movement remained
predominantly middle-class. Very few working women
were involved. Energy came from the top down, rather than
from the bottom up; and the women's peace movement
sprang from the constitutional reformist Liberalism of
NUWSS and UDC. It remained within the law even when
sorely provoked by the state: when the North Sea was
suddenly closed to shipping, no illicit commandeering of
vessels was recorded.

In 1916, however, the introduction of military conscription – albeit with an exemption clause for Conscientious
Objectors (COs) – thrust the tentacles of state compulsion
deep into every home, into the 'private' family sphere, and
so directly into many women's lives. Opposition to the war
could no longer remain a matter of cool intellectual convic-
tion. The class base of the anti-war movement now widened
dramatically.

More and more young men were conscripted. The No
Conscription Fellowship (NCF), originally formed in
November 1914, stepped forward to help COs. Tribunals
began hearing the cases of those who objected to military
service on grounds of conscience. 'What crime have I
committed to be here?' cried one CO, a labourer and ILP
activist. 'Is it because I won't murder? I won't murder any
man, neither for you nor for anybody else.'[1] Sometimes
supporters listening to the tribunal proceedings in the gal-
lery sang 'The Red Flag' to keep up the defiant young men's
spirits. COs who failed to report for military duty were

'escorted' from their home towns by police and soldiers in khaki. However, by summer 1916 reports of tribunals were edged out of local newspapers by countless pages describing dead and wounded soldiers. On 1 July alone, the first day of the Battle of the Somme, nearly 20,000 British soldiers were killed.

Alongside these military horrors, the government used successive Defence of the Realm Act (DORA) rulings to clamp down on peace activity. Anti-conscription meetings were attacked, offices raided and troublesome individuals prosecuted. In March 1916 Nellie Best, a member of Sylvia Pankhurst's Workers' Suffrage Federation was sentenced to six months' imprisonment for making statements prejudicial to recruiting.[2] In May two detectives served a summons on Bertrand Russell for writing a leaflet about a CO sentenced to two years' hard labour. Russell was fined £100; his appeal was rejected and his goods were auctioned. The NCF office was raided: police took away copies of its paper *The Tribunal*, membership records and accounts.[3] Catherine Marshall, who became closely involved in running NCF as so many of the young men of military age were imprisoned, calculated that so frequently had she flouted the law to aid COs, she was liable for 2,000 years in prison![4]

There were also profound changes in working women's lives, though these were less sensationally dramatic. When war broke out many women in service industries and luxury trades were dismissed or put on short time. Then in May 1916, in response to a scandal over the shortage of shells for soldiers on the Western Front, a new Ministry of Munitions was set up, headed by Lloyd George. (Two months later Mrs Pankhurst led a 'Women's Right to Serve' march, urging women into the mushrooming munitions factories.) This opening up of new, better-paid jobs for women was, of course, accelerated by the spread of male conscription. Married women returned to paid employment; others moved out of their traditional low-paid occupations and into jobs vacated by men – trams and railways, banking and government service. By the end of 1916 on Clydeside 6,196 of the 11,000 workers employed in shell production in Glasgow's big engineering factories were women. (But skilled men in the local engineering union saw this 'dilution' as a very real threat: they objected to women and unskilled workers undermining their hard-won trade union rules and customs. For women workers in Glasgow were generally low-paid and not well organized in stable unions.)[5]

Ironically, then, this disastrous war was opening up new opportunities for working women. The shell crisis, combined with conscription, offered them a revolutionary new range of better-paid and higher-status jobs. While it lasted, it was as far-reaching a change for working-class women as the earlier opening up of new educational and white-collar opportunities for middle-class women. But whereas it is possible to trace the 1915 Hague Congress and WIL back to these late-Victorian changes, the link between working women's growing economic strength and their peace activity between 1916 and 1918 is more indirect. It is easier to point to a general growing self-confidence than, say, to individual munitions workers' anti-war activities.

In fact, this new peace activity seemed to spring from *pre*-war socialist and feminist networks. From 1916 onwards there was an upsurge of deep anger against conscription and military tribunals; against the mounting death toll, rising food prices and lengthy queuing; and against the DORA attacks on personal liberties. This anger became widespread among working women. To begin with, they were small, isolated rebel groupings which could be easily identified by police spies. But from summer 1917 and for the next eighteen months until Armistice, a Women's Peace Crusade spread like wildfire across the country, giving voice to this rising anger. The Crusade was characteristically rooted in local communities, varying between regions, depending on local political traditions. Often activity stemmed from pre-war suffragette or suffragist groups, now linked to rebel militants, whether anti-conscriptionist or industrial. Very sharp confrontation with the state certainly escalated, as bulging Home Office files testify.

The Women's Peace Crusade captured the war-weary, dissident spirit of 1917–18. It was not an organization in the style of WIL: no membership lists were compiled, no neat annual reports were printed. What follows is therefore a story of a handful óf known women peace rebels and their particular communities, and how these women managed to win impressively broad support during the last eighteen months of the war – from labour, co-operative, religious and union movements.

In Glasgow there was a highly unusual mix of politics which in summer 1916 gave birth to the Women's Peace Crusade. The Glasgow WSPU branch, formed in 1906, had become extremely militant: local suffragettes began pillar-box attacks and window-smashing in 1912, escalating to arson and bombing of empty properties in 1913. But – significantly and unusually – the branch always retained both middle-class *and* working-class members right up to the war. Equally untypically, WSPU worked closely and harmoniously with Glasgow's giant ILP; some young women had joint membership. The city's ILP weekly, *Forward*, even gave WSPU its own propaganda page, 'Our Suffrage Columns', and described women's suffrage as 'another Chartist revival'.[6]

Equally important was the richness of the neighbourhood-based political culture created by Glasgow women. Only 39 per cent, most of them unmarried, were in paid employment. Of those with jobs, the vast majority were low-paid: 18 per cent domestic servants and charwomen; 15 per cent dressmakers and tailoresses; and the rest commercial clerks, textile workers, teachers, nurses, bookbinders, and in jam and carpet factories. With under 6 per cent of Glasgow's married women recorded as 'occupied', and with two-thirds of its population living crammed into one- or two-roomed households, rent rises and housing conditions were naturally a political priority.[7]

Housing was also a key issue in Glasgow's municipal politics; largely through ILP's Housing Committee and the Women's Labour League, a Glasgow Women's Housing Association was formed shortly before the war. By the end of 1914 it had branches throughout the city. There were also over 12,000 Scottish Guildswomen, many of them in Glasgow; and three branches of the Women's Labour League in the city. According to local memory, each Glasgow ILP branch had its own 'women's group', with weekly meetings and usually a speaker; perhaps, one woman recalled, 'local gossip was their main topic', but 'there were, of course, many women who knew what they were talking about – knew their socialism.'[8]

Profiles of three socialist suffragettes dramatically show how different the women's movement was in Clydeside from England. Agnes Muir was born in 1887, one of a black-smith's eleven children. She left elementary school at eleven and worked in a factory and then as a telephone operator. Appalled by the long hours and meagre wages, she became involved with Mary Macarthur in the uphill struggle to organize women post-office workers into a single trade union. At about eighteen Agnes joined ILP and later WSPU. Through local socialist friendship networks she met the journalist Patrick Dollan, then working on *Forward*, and they married in 1912. Their son was born in 1913, and Agnes Dollan probably left her job at about this time. So when the Glasgow Women's Housing Association was formed the following year, her office experience must have qualified her well to be treasurer.[9]

Jessie Stephen, born in 1894, was also one of eleven children. Her father, a skilled tailor, was an ILP member. Jessie did well at school, won a scholarship and became a pupil teacher. 'Unfortunately for my dreams,' she recalled later, 'unemployment became worse so there was nothing for it but to leave school' – and go into service. Finding how exploited girls like her were, Stephen became involved in a Domestic Workers' Federation in Scotland. The weekly subscription was three halfpence [1p]: 'I used to go round the back doors of big houses, getting the girls to join the union'. Following in her father's socialist footsteps, she began selling *Labour Woman* and became vice-chair of her local ILP branch at sixteen. She also joined WSPU in Glasgow, and was soon caught up in local militancy. 'I was able to drop acid into the postal pillar boxes without being suspected,' she reminisced laconically, 'because I walked down from where I was employed in my cap and apron, you know, muslin apron, black frock, nobody would ever suspect me of dropping acid through the box.'[10] Unsurprisingly, she found Glasgow employers reluctant to take on a militant trade unionist; she left for London shortly before the war.

The eldest of these suffragettes, Helen Jack, was born in 1877. She came from a lower-middle-class family: her father was a prosperous master baker with two shops, and Helen stayed on at school until she was seventeen. Her parents were fervently religious anti-Catholic Tories, and Helen attended Evangelical Sunday School, where she met the Reverend Crawfurd; they married when she was twenty. Her husband's parish was right by the Clyde. 'Coming there, into contact with Dockland life – and human misery indescribable,' Crawfurd recalled later, 'I used to listen to open-air speakers – and would feel they were speaking the truth – but if the word socialism was used I walked away. This was of the Devil.'

Women's rights were less wicked. In about 1900 she 'entered the Woman's Suffrage Movement, feeling that if the mothers of the Race had some say – then things would be changed.' However, it was Crawfurd herself who changed – rapidly. She met the woman who ran Glasgow's radical bookshop, who 'plied me with literature – somewhat a mixed grill'. Crawfurd read American revolutionary syndicalists from the Industrial Workers of the World (IWW) and other pamphlets that 'showed me the cloak for capitalist exploitation of the human Race'. For a Tory master baker's daughter and minister's wife it was, she noted euphemistically, 'extremely difficult for me in those days of awakening'.[11]

Crawfurd joined wspu in 1910. Her first militant act was to break the windows of the Minister of Education; she was sentenced to a month in Holloway. In 1913 she was arrested twice for trying to protect Mrs Pankhurst from police brutality in Glasgow and, significantly, for breaking the windows of the Army Recruiting offices. By the time war broke out, Crawfurd, a talented and popular speaker, had endured four imprisonments and three hunger strikes.[12]

Crawfurd became secretary of the Women's Housing Association. There was, of course, some local tension between the labour movement and militant suffragettes; and between 'skilled' men and women in so-called 'unskilled' jobs.[13] But in Glasgow, on the eve of war, the remarkable day-to-day links between feminism and socialism, and between ilp, wspu and neighbourhood campaigns, provided a unique seedbed for a popular women's anti-war protest.

When war began, twenty-year-old Jessie Stephen returned home; like so many other domestic workers, she now found jobs were open to her which had previously been regarded as men's. Agnes Dollan was twenty-six; her son was a toddler. And thirty-six-year-old Helen Crawfurd was deep in suffragette militancy. (During the summer she was arrested, but released after a five-day hunger strike; shortly afterwards she was blamed for a bomb explosion and imprisoned again.) The war must have been a deep shock to her; she felt so betrayed by Emmeline and Christabel Pankhurst's *volte-face* concerning Asquith's Liberal government that she left wspu shortly after war broke out and about the same time joined ilp.

Housing now became a yet more urgent issue in

Glasgow. In its first wartime issue *Forward* called for a government moratorium on rents. Then, as the munitions industry expanded, workers flooded into the city to take up the new jobs: from early 1915 an already acute housing shortage worsened and prices rose. At the same time the first stirrings of industrial resistance to wartime dilution began; from this the Clyde Workers' Committee emerged in October. Against this background, the landlords imposed another wartime rent increase in mid 1915. A strike movement began. Dollan, Crawfurd, a housewife called Mary Barbour and other Women's Housing Association members moved into action, liaising with shop stewards, holding kitchen meetings and urging tenants to withhold increased rents. By October 25,000 tenants were on strike; in November 15,000 demonstrated, with wider industrial unrest threatened. In such a situation 'legal niceties tumbled before the blast', wrote one historian. The next day the government announced a Bill to peg rents.[14]

Wartime Glasgow established itself as the leading militant city. It was also quick off the mark in *peace* activity. In the first wartime 'Our Suffrage Columns', Crawfurd reprinted the IWSA manifesto, and on 9 August ILP and the Glasgow branch of the Peace Society organized a 5,000-strong anti-war demonstration on Glasgow Green. Dollan and Crawfurd were involved, but Crawfurd seems to have taken a low profile during winter 1914–15, probably for personal reasons.[15]

When Crawfurd reappeared in late 1915 she had shed much of her earlier evangelical clutter, and in the aftermath of the Berne and Hague meetings, anti-war commitment among socialists was more buoyant. Quick off the mark, she and Dollan set up a Glasgow branch of WIL in November. Within a year they had recruited eighty-three members. In December she chaired an ILP meeting where Emmeline Pethick Lawrence spoke on 'Can Women Bring Peace?' And in spring 1916, as conscription bit, Crawfurd appeared in court for taking part in a demonstration against the deportation of leading Clydeside shop stewards.[16]

But WIL's UDC links and middle-class Liberalism irked Crawfurd. She needed to be able to forge a more militant, socialist opposition to militarism, so she formed a Women's Peace Crusade. Its precise origins remain cloudy,[17] but in May 1916 a letter appeared in the ILP's *Labour Leader* from an S. Cahill, lamenting that 'the Socialist women of Britain' had not yet mounted 'one public demonstration against this wholesale slaughter of our menfolk'.[18] This letter seems to have energized the ILP women in Glasgow – particularly Crawfurd. Within a fortnight *Forward* announced a 'Great Women's Peace Conference' on 10 June, with tickets available from Crawfurd as organizer.

The appeal to women socialists worked: two hundred delegates from sixteen organizations attended. Speakers included Swanwick for WIL, Dollan for the Women's Labour League, and Emma Boyce from London for the Workers' Suffrage Federation (WSF). Chiming in with Charles Roden Buxton's new Peace Negotiations Committee, the cumbersome title 'Women's Peace Negotiations Crusade' was chosen. Crawfurd became secretary and Dollan chair.[19]

Meanwhile, Jessie Stephen heard that Sylvia Pankhurst was coming to Glasgow to organize a WSF branch. Stephen had met her before in WSPU, and introduced herself at the end of the meeting. Pankhurst asked what she was doing, then suddenly said: 'How would you like to come and work for me?' Stephen was keen; her mother secretly lent her the fare – and she travelled down to rouse London.[20]

Meanwhile, Crawfurd and the others held open-air meetings around Clydeside and Edinburgh in the run-up to a big Women's Peace Crusade demonstration on 23 July. (It was the beginning of the Somme, and when she spoke Crawfurd was careful to point out that although she had a tremendous sympathy for the CO, she wanted to stop the war not for his sake, but for the sake of men in the trenches.) Afterwards, *Forward* jubilantly reported:

> For the past month a vigorous campaign on 'Peace by
> Negotiation' has been conducted in and around Glasgow.
> Large crowds have attended the meetings. . . . The cam-
> paign was brought to a close in Glasgow on Sunday week
> last, when a crowd of 5,000 listened.

Speakers included Dollan, Crawfurd, Margaret Ashton,
Theodora Wilson Wilson and Muriel Matters. Resolutions
on adult suffrage and peace by negotiation were carried
unanimously, despite harassment by 'patriots', and it was
promised that the campaign would reopen in September.[21]

In fact, the Crusade seemed to shrink away during
winter 1916–17. One possible reason was that on 1 November Crawfurd was appointed WIL's Scottish organizer; WIL
had doubtless been impressed by this first showing of a *mass*
women's peace movement. There were already three
branches in Scotland with a total membership of 145, and it
was presumably hoped that Crawfurd could build on this.
Wary WIL, probably hoping to curb her more revolutionary
excesses, stated curtly that Crawfurd 'works under the
direction of the Glasgow Branch'. She certainly kept busy.
She worked at two by-elections at which Peace by Negotiation candidates stood. During her first year Aberdeen
formed a WIL branch and the Scottish membership
doubled, with Glasgow WIL expanding to an impressive
150.[22]

The Women's Peace Crusade, although still rather a
Scottish flash in the pan, had shown itself to be a remarkable political mix. It was obviously closely linked to WIL
and to the Peace Negotiations Committee (which was busy
collecting signatures on a Memorial, organized by Gwen
Chambers amongst others). Thus a report in the *Dreadnought* wrote of the Crusade in the language of Liberalism,
reminiscent of *Militarism versus Feminism*:

> War is the enthronement of force and the dethronement of
> reason, and the history of women's progress makes it plain
> that women have everything to gain by the dominance of

reason, just as they have everything to lose by the domination of force. . . . Militarism means the subjection of women.

The Crusade was also a grass-roots socialist movement. It gave popular voice to resentment against conscription, and moved the anti-war agitation out beyond the earlier small-scale, narrowly based groups. It made effective links with working women in Lowland Scotland – not just with committed socialists but with a broader range of women concerned about the war's effect on their families, their homes and their jobs. Thus the same *Dreadnought* article noted that warfare, rather than liberating women, exploited them:

> Women have only been allowed into industry in great numbers because their labour is necessary to militarism, and not because of any desire on the part of the State, built up by force, to recognize the right of women to earn their own maintenance.[23]

The Crusade also maintained its links with Mary Barbour and the Glasgow Women's Housing Association, holding 'women-only' meetings at 3 p.m. on weekdays and street-corner meetings in working-class communities. Its aim was not genteel lobbying but persuading thousands of women out of their houses and on to the streets for popular open-air rallies to confront the militarist government.[24]

Glasgow was remarkably active; but by far the largest WIL branch was Manchester. Within the first year it recruited no fewer than 393 members, and by autumn 1917 this had mushroomed to 573, almost a quarter of WIL branch membership in Britain. According to undergraduate Mabel Phythian, the strong NUWSS branch led by Ashton had virtually decamped to WIL in 1915. Unlike Glasgow, it was a predominantly middle-class branch with strong links to Manchester University. Phythian's own pocket diary for

1916 is crammed with notes of the peace meetings she attended: Swanwick on WIL, Ashton on 'Militarism and Feminism', and WIL garden parties. By the autumn, entries about Bertrand Russell multiply. He had been banned by the War Office from entering prohibited areas of the country (particularly seaports), but through NCF he had planned a series of political philosophy lectures in six major cities. His Glasgow lecture was cancelled due to the ban but he still gave the first, in Manchester, on 16 October.[25] Phythian's job was to meet Russell at the station and to act as steward at the meetings; seventy years later she still retained the lecture programme and could recall the tension:

> I remember the police raiding Bertrand Russell's lectures. . . . Margaret Ashton was there again, presiding. And Bertie gave six lectures, subsequently published as 'Political Ideals', and banned by the police. And on at least two occasions during those lectures they came in to collect Conscientious Objectors, of which there were a number in the audience. And I remember Margaret Ashton getting up and saying there was to be no resistance or any kind of unpleasantness. 'The police must do their duty, as they had been instructed, and we wouldn't prevent what they had to do.' And she stood all the time on the platform in silent protest. And they led off the people whose papers weren't satisfactory.[26]

Now even the very respectable Phythian became drawn further and further into such confrontations with the state. Certainly Ashton had been spied on by informers for well over a year.[27]

WIL's headquarters were in London. Here there were a dozen branches, with meetings attracting a glittering array of speakers. In December 1915 at a public meeting, chaired by Swanwick, 'To Present the Women's Case against

Conscription', speakers included Barton, Bondfield, Despard, Marshall, Royden and Pethick Lawrence. Four months later there was a three-day conference on 'The Terms of a European Settlement' with, additionally, Charles Roden Buxton, Russell and Brailsford. And – in contrast to Glasgow's noisier rallies – at smaller London meetings, philosophical issues were debated. Royden and Sylvia Pankhurst led a discussion on 'What has Investment of Money to do with War and Peace?' and Royden and Marshall on 'What has the Woman's Movement to do with Foreign Policy?' WIL still placed its traditional Liberal stress on Free Trade, democratic control of foreign policy, and defending personal liberty; so the resolution on conscription spoke of this 'gravest infringement of the rights of conscience and of the liberty of the subject'. And WIL echoed earlier feminist thinking on militarism, protesting at the devastation continued war heaped upon *women* in Belgium, Serbia and Poland:

> We speak of them in particular, not because we overlook or belittle the sufferings and sacrifices of men, but because it is clear that, in invaded countries, the women suffer more than the men, yet in the diplomacy which led to or prolongs the War, they have no share.

Within these traditional terms, WIL made a very successful start. It was linked to the International Committee of Women for Permanent Peace, which now had sixteen affiliated nations, and supported campaigns led by America, Sweden and Holland for a mediation conference of neutral nations. Thus its impressive first *Annual Report* ended defiantly:

> To some of us, in our despondent moods, it may seem as if little or nothing has been done. Conscription is a hideous institution now riveted on what once were free men. . . . Is it a little thing to have the comradeship and the sympathy of those like-minded with ourselves? Have we no strength, no

comfort, in these dark days in the knowledge that, when it was most unpopular, a handful of British women were ready to declare the rooted comradeship of all?[28]

Others, however, felt that the desperate situation demanded more direct confrontation with the increasingly repressive militaristic state. (Early in 1916 Swanwick had ruled that there was no need for WIL to state formally that it would work within the law, since it could be assumed that it would do that anyway unless otherwise stated.) But there *was* growing provocation to be more militant – particularly in London, where peace meetings were rarely reported due to a press boycott, and some papers even helped to harass peace activists. If there was no advance publicity, open-air meetings could still be held; but increasingly WIL was forced to abandon public meetings in London for private ones.[29]

WIL members might prefer to avoid confronting the jingoists and police spies who now accompanied public events – others did not. Pankhurst's WSF became impatient with WIL's caution: Nellie Best's six-month imprisonment in March 1916 had galvanized it into a more radical anti-war mood. Although little more than isolated individuals and small groups, it now spread from its east London base into north London and beyond. Emma Boyce from Hackney, mother of twelve children, became a roving WSF organizer, speaking at Crawfurd's peace meeting in June. She was joined by Jessie Stephen, whose first task was to organize a Hackney branch, learning open-air speaking the hard way. 'After half an hour throwing my voice into space, slowly, very slowly, passers-by came closer to the platform, usually a chair or box borrowed from a shopkeeper.' Then, when 'Sylvia thought I had gained enough experience she sent me off into the provinces.' Armed only with a few survival tips from Boyce, she set off for Sheffield. Other West Riding towns followed, and by May 1917 Stephen crossed the Pennines to set up a WSF branch in

Nelson. But hecklers and stone-throwers made it hard going, for the police just stood by. Stephen grew quite blasée about the constant surveillance: 'Detectives attended all meetings and took shorthand notes of the speeches. . . . One of them always approached the speaker to ask for one's name and address and permanent place of abode.' (However, she soon left her WSF job to work as an ILP organizer in east London.)[30]

Files on anti-war agitators began to bulge. Outside London there might be less harassment, but local police fed secret intelligence back to the Home Secretary. Ethel Snowden and her husband were of particular interest to the Home Office. She undertook a speaking tour of South Wales in December 1916, telling her audiences, amid applause, 'I represent a large and growing number of women . . . and . . . we are going from this time on to altogether refuse to be made the excuse for men cutting one another's throats.' Glamorganshire's zealous Chief Constable had Snowden's every word taken down; but he was cautioned that prosecution would do more harm than good.[31]

Particularly dramatic was the story of Alice Wheeldon, a second-hand clothes dealer in Derby. She and her daughter Hettie, a teacher, had been in WSPU. They were anti-war socialist rebel members of ILP, with personal links to Red Clydeside. Hettie was secretary of Derby NCF, but grew impatient with its moderate pacifism; the Wheeldons were drawn into a shadowy semi-legal network helping fugitive COs to escape. This was an impoverished world: dread of being hunted down was intensified by poverty, helplessness and fear of government informers. 'Mac is terrified. Sticks in all day and only emerges at night', Hettie reported to Alice.[32]

The Wheeldons and their comrades corresponded in code, changing it every so often to confuse the informers, but the authorities seemed determined to get a prosecution. In January 1917 a bizarre 'plot' to kill Lloyd George was supposedly decoded. Alice and Hettie were arrested, with four others. Hettie was found not guilty; but Alice, cross-examined by the Attorney-General, was found guilty of conspiring to kill, and sentenced to ten years.[33]

The Wheeldon story was unusually dramatic; but Dollan and Crawfurd in Glasgow, and Boyce and Stephen as itinerant organizers, all operated at the very edge of the law. Although such women tell us little about how feminist ideas dovetailed into anti-militarist thinking, they tell us a great deal about how such small local groups of socialist suffragettes challenged the state, and about the links and tensions between the anti-war groups. Outside Clydeside, these networks remained small-scale and isolated: individuals could still easily be picked off.

Police surveillance and brutal treatment of COs, casualty lists and long queues all made for harsh and distressing times. Then into this gloom, in spring 1917, came news of a revolution in Russia. It ended Czarist tyranny and also offered an end to the war. WIL sent joyful greeting to Russia's provisional government. 'The exciting days we live in!' marvelled Lockwood, also involved in WIL. 'My sisters,' declared Despard in an open letter to Russian women, 'I cannot use the ordinary commonplaces. To say I congratulate you would be out of place. Rather – I am with you – we are one.' The conference held in Leeds in June to honour the Revolution included organizations like WIL, the Women's Labour League and the Guild.[34]

It gave a tremendous boost to the Women's Peace Crusade. Precisely how the Crusade was resurrected on Clydeside is unclear. Crawfurd remained WIL's Scottish organizer, and seems to have kept at least a skeleton Crusade organization over the winter. There was considerable anti-war activity in spring 1917, organized through the growing anti-war movement: ILP, UDC, WIL and a Glasgow Peace Negotiations Joint Committee. Certainly the news from Russia was welcomed with great enthusiasm: *Forward* claimed 100,000 assembled on Glasgow Green for May

Day. But perhaps what prompted Crawfurd to throw her energies into a renewed Women's Peace Crusade was hearing that Mrs Pankhurst was to visit Russia, supposedly representing British women. (WIL *tried* – unsuccessfully – to organize a 'delegation more truly representative of the democratic women of this country': Despard, Snowden, Bondfield and Pethick Lawrence.) Crawfurd drafted an angry letter, full of rhetorical socialist flourishes, published in *Forward* and headed 'Mrs Pankhurst: Whom Does She Represent?'

> Sir, Mrs Pankhurst has asked for a passport for Russia and it has been granted her. She goes forward to speak for the women of Britain!
> ... Does Mrs Pankhurst speak for us? Has her voice ever been raised since this war started on behalf of the workers of this country against the profiteers or exploiters ... ?
> ... SHALL WE NOT SPEAK FOR OURSELVES? The people of Russia, through their leaders have appealed to the common people of every country to let their voices be heard demanding peace.

The letter ended: 'The Women's Peace Crusade started on Sunday 1st. A huge meeting was held. ... Women, come and support us', and was signed by Crawfurd as Crusade secretary.[35]

It was indeed a bold leap by Helen Crawfurd to link the Russian Revolution and Mrs Pankhurst's visit with the earlier Women's Peace Crusade – and to decide to resurrect it. But it was the right moment – and the right place – to appeal to war-weary women, and her hunch paid off. The imaginative use of symbolic colour and imagery (notably a Women's Peace Crusade badge) reminiscent of suffrage was highly successful. Crawfurd wrote to ILP branches; they helped by chalking the pavements to publicize local open-air meetings at which Crawfurd, Dollan, Barbour and others spoke; and a monster demonstration was announced for Sunday 8 July.

The socialist *Herald* reported the event ecstatically:

> Sunday was a day of triumph for the Women Peace Cru-
> saders. From two sides of the City great processions came
> with music and floating banners, and as they neared
> Glasgow Green they merged into one – a symbol of their
> unity of purpose and resolve. . . . Some 12 to 14,000 men
> and women formed the permanent auditors.

'Though the webs of appeal and argument were varied in
workmanship and in design,' added *Labour Leader*, equally
enthusiastically, 'there were ever present the golden threads
of Peace! Peace! Peace!' Speakers included Crawfurd,
Dollan, Swanwick, Snowden and Matters, and greetings
from Despard and Sylvia Pankhurst were read. Resolutions
congratulating 'the Russian Revolutionary Government',
and on immediate peace negotiations, were carried
unanimously.[36]

The next areas touched by the Crusade magic were
Lancashire, the West Riding and the Midlands. Three days
after the Glasgow demonstration a public meeting was
called in Nelson, an anti-war stronghold, by Gertrude
Ingham, a founder-member of the local ILP and mother of a
CO, a young weaver imprisoned after his military tribunal.
An August demonstration was planned and advertised in
the local paper: 'Nelson Women's Peace Crusade . . .
Mothers, Wives, Sisters and Sweethearts are earnestly
invited to join in the Procession.'

Labour Leader reported that it had received so many
requests for advice that an 'acting committee of ILP women'
– Bondfield, Snowden, and Katharine Bruce Glasier – had
drawn up guidelines on how to form a Crusade committee,
canvass house-to-house, make banners and flags. WIL
also urged *its* branches to take up the Peace Crusade.[37]
Birmingham held a Women's Peace Demonstration on 29
July, with Crawfurd speaking; although their banner was

torn up, 300 came. There was also a mass meeting in Manchester, organized by over a hundred ILP women; the National Labour Press rushed out special Women's Peace Crusade leaflets, 'A Call to Socialist and Labour Women' and 'Questions to Clergymen and Ministers'.[38] For part of the Crusade's success was that it spoke the moral language of Nonconformist Christianity.

In Nelson on 11 August Gertrude Ingham, joined by Selina Cooper, led a procession of over a thousand women through hostile onlookers shouting 'Traitors! Murderers!' When they reached the meeting ground, the menacing crowd had swollen to 15,000. Earth, lumps of grass and even a clinker were thrown, and the speakers were completely drowned in the uproar.[39] Such jingoistic opposition was fomented by the press, and DORA regulations made peace protest increasingly dangerous. The police seized a Women's Peace Crusade leaflet, 'Casualties'. Mabel Phythian also found herself drawn more deeply into semilegal activities:

> What I remember very clearly was being in the WIL office . . . it looks right on to the [Manchester] Town Hall. . . . And on one occasion we – I was in the office for some reason, and the police raided it. We had some pamphlets which were being banned. And they came to collect them. . . . I know that the Salford police didn't ban, and the Manchester police did ban, a list of casualties. And we had a great time going just over the Manchester boundary and handing out the casualty lists for Manchester people crossing the Salford boundary.[40]

Despite harassment and surveillance, the Crusade still spread like wildfire. Three thousand listened to an all-woman platform in Leicester marketplace. 'Everywhere we meet with eager sympathy', reported Ford from Leeds. 'The women are sick of this continued slaughter.' There was such a run on free leaflets that an appeal had to be made to pay for extra printing.[41]

In September improved organization helped to cope with this flood of support. Ethel Snowden announced a new twopenny Women's Peace Crusade button – significantly, suffragist red-on-white rather than Crawfurd's suffragette purple-on-white. Three thousand women marched through Bradford, banners flying and bands playing. 'The Bradford women are splendid', enthused *Labour Leader*. 'They attribute their great success on Sunday chiefly to their open-air meetings at street corners. They have held three of these every week since June.' Local press headlined 'Fights at a Peace meeting', but any disturbances in the Bradford crowd had been small and isolated. The next evening at Cowling, a tiny Pennine textile village, no fewer than 700 attended a Women's Christian Peace Crusade meeting.[42]

But big cities remained stiff with tension. Manchester's Women's Peace Crusade committee planned a meeting in Stevenson Square, with Ashton, Barton and Snowden speaking. But they arrived only to find a large number of police – and the meeting banned. The women protested. The atmosphere was nasty; one newspaper reported:

> The crowd, which was seething with excitement, then surged round, and, amid threats of violence, the women were hustled out of the square, several of them seeking refuge in the Newton-street Police Station. . . . The crest-fallen women eventually made their escape. Later three attempted to start a peace meeting at the corner of Spear-street, which was abruptly terminated by a hostile crowd. One man who endeavoured to have the women removed was mistaken for a pacifist, and the police had to rescue him.

Florence Lockwood, travelling over specially, had to come home by the next train; she pasted the above press cutting into her diary as a record.[43]

Women began distributing leaflets outside churches on Sundays. In Burnley, Annot Robinson addressed 4–500 at a women-only meeting in the Co-op Hall: over a hundred signed up as local Crusade members. In nearby Nelson over 1,200 crowded into a Methodist Sunday School. 'I think', Selina Cooper said:

> that those who took part in the procession did something wonderful. It is one thing to come to a meeting like this; it is another thing to march through the street to be jeered at and booed at. . . . When the settlement comes, every woman who joined the crusade will be glad to be able to say, 'I joined the peace crusade'.[44]

Three thousand attended a meeting in Leeds. Over 4,000 listened to Despard in Leith. To mark this success, Bondfield, Bruce Glasier and Snowden published a Women's Peace Crusade 'Directory', listing addresses of local secretaries. By November 1917 this had risen to about forty-five 'Crusades', mainly in Scotland and South Wales, the industrial Midlands, Lancashire, the North, the North-East and the West Riding – significantly, a similar pattern to ILP strongholds.[45]

In October, WIL held a meeting in Central Hall to receive branch reports on the Crusade. Crawfurd went from Glasgow, Ingham from Nelson. Despite rumours 'that "a band of stalwarts, 100 strong" was being organized to break it up', it went well. The Huddersfield WIL delegate returned, according to Lockwood's diary, with a 'thrilling' report:

> The Women's Peace Crusade activities – very encouraging
> not reported
> Heaps of women awaking from the opium of false propaganda.

Lockwood finally resigned in despair from the local Women's Liberal Association: its members wanted whist drives, not politics. In November she went to the first public meeting of the Women's Peace Crusade in Huddersfield; she pasted into her diary the Crusade Leaflet *A People's Peace*, supporting open diplomacy and President Wilson's plans to 'make the world safe for democracy'.[46]

This was the fourth winter of the war. Shops were empty:

no butter, tea or sugar. Increasingly draconian DORA censorship angered WIL members: they attacked this 'Assassination of Opinion', issuing an *Is this Fair Play?* leaflet. The WIL office was raided. Police seized accounts, literature and all copies of a *Democracy and Peace* leaflet. WIL withdrew a few pamphlets, tied up remaining stock 'in a sealed parcel marked "withdrawn from circulation" and deposited it in the basement, where it will be useful to sit upon in case of air-raids'.[47]

Then news came from Russia that the Bolsheviks had seized power in the October Revolution. Encouraged, Women's Peace Crusade activity continued. Women like Despard and Snowden continually criss-crossed Britain. 'I am stomping the country again quite a lot for the UDC ILP WIL WPC', Swanwick joked to Marshall. ('Do you know your alphabet?')[48] In Glasgow the Women's Peace Crusade held anti-war meetings outside shipyard gates. A censorship order was placed on their leaflets; when the city corporation refused to receive their delegation, Dollan and Crawfurd forced their way into the council chamber; after scuffles they appeared in court, pleading their innocence. The stipendiary magistrate found them guilty – but imposed no penalty.[49]

But it was in London that the battle between the authorities and the Women's Peace Crusade was fought out most ferociously. 1918 was a ghastly summer: Germany had launched a new offensive, and by May was within forty miles of Paris. WIL had long believed that the London police, under Home Office control, determined that for WIL *'to tell London what the provinces are doing . . . is dangerous. London must not know.'* Yet plans went ahead for a major peace negotiations demonstration in Hyde Park on 14 July, supported by Guild, labour, suffrage and church groups. Patriots agitated for its prohibition, and the Home Secretary was questioned in the Commons. On 11 July the rally was finally prohibited – as 'likely to give rise to grave disorder and to cause undue demands to be made on the police'.[50]

Women's Peace Crusade activity continued right up to Armistice, but what did it achieve? Its exact *effectiveness* is difficult to disentangle from that of the other anti-war groups with which the Crusade and WIL were linked. But its *significance* is easier to measure, for the Crusade developed unique characteristics that crucially distinguished it from other peace groups – even from WIL.

Like WIL, the Crusade was born of the political and social 'separate spheres' of Edwardian Britain. It could appeal to working women as *women*; for their daily lives, particularly as mothers, were so different from men's. Also like WIL, the Crusade captured a *moment*, harnessing women's weariness with the war and its attendant authoritarianism, and transforming that into action. But unlike WIL it stressed not women generally, but *working-class* women – especially their own experience of war in terms of both gender *and* class. It had little time for theory linking anti-militarism with feminism – its language was an urgent, pragmatic mix of maternalist and socialist arguments. Also unlike WIL, it flourished mainly outside London, particularly in industrial ILP strongholds. It reached previously isolated working women, extending the women's peace movement into fresh territory well beyond its Liberal-suffrage roots. As a result, tens of thousands of women took to the streets demanding peace. In this way the Crusade, like the pre-war labour–suffrage pact, was part of a broader leftward shift of feminism from Liberalism to Labour and beyond.

But the Crusade was transitory; it flourished across Britain for less than two years and never won the support of more than a small minority of women. Yet it was the first truly popular campaign linking feminism and anti-militarism, and it is therefore extraordinary that it has been ignored for so long by historians of both the women's movement and the peace movement.[51]

7

Wars will cease when . . .
(1919–33)

The Armistice left women peace activists in Britain with a mixture of emotions: remorse at the number of young men's lives lost or maimed, yet hope that it might *never* happen again; empowerment – now that those over thirty were enfranchised their voices could be heard both at Westminster and in international counsel; yet anger at what had been done without consulting women. Few had greater reason to *live* the tragedy than Vera Brittain, who had lost not only her fiancé and two close friends, but now also her brother; she discovered that life would never, ever be the same again:

> Once an ecstatic idealist who had tripped down the steep Buxton hill in a golden glow of self-dedication . . . , I had now passed – like the rest of my contemporaries who had survived thus far – into a permanent state of numb disillusion. . . . Now there were no more disasters to dread and no friends left to wait for.[1]

Those women who had challenged such naive 'idealism', courageously opposing war from the very beginning, were totally exhausted. Gwen Chambers, veteran of Peace by Negotiation (and later of Morel's UDC), recalled years later her feelings of ennui:

> . . . when war was declared over I was very weary. . . . We were living in Leeds, Mother and I, and things were pretty bad, we couldn't get any firewood or anything. I went for a walk on the moor, gathering firewood. I came to a wall, I stood by this wall and just the other side a lark went up singing. I put my head down on that wall and I sobbed and

sobbed. It was just something that this lark had, you know, that we'd done without for so long. Working for peace during the war wasn't easy. . . . I mean you were a traitor to your country, you should have been shot at dawn.[2]

Women were not shot at dawn, nor did they suffer lengthy imprisonment like COs, but they did pay a high personal price for their peace protests. Alice Wheeldon returned home from Aylesbury Jail, weakened by her ordeal – only to find herself ostracized by her neighbours, and her second-hand clothes business ruined. For her, the post-war flu epidemic proved fatal: she died in 1919.[3] Other women's experiences, though less dramatic, were also bruising. Radical suffragists, who had campaigned all their adult lives for the vote, now found themselves, in Annot Robinson's words, branded 'a Bolshevik, a German spy, a traitor'.[4]

Other more fortunate peace activists felt empowered to use their new political rights. On Clydeside, Agnes Dollan immersed herself in municipal politics. She was appointed to Glasgow Education Authority, campaigning for better child and health care; eventually, in 1921, she was elected a councillor. Helen Crawfurd, always the more militant, followed a different trajectory. Increasingly critical of ILP 'reformism', she travelled to Moscow in 1920 to attend the Second Congress of the Third International. She was granted an interview with Lenin and, deeply convinced, returned to Britain and joined the newly formed Communist Party, working to recruit women members.[5]

But this was unusual: working women active in the Peace Crusade were more likely to join the Labour Party's new and extremely popular Women's Sections. Although Sections had little direct power, they did offer an accessible route into local political activity: attracted by the concern for welfare issues, tens of thousands of working women joined.[6] Minute books of one north London Section, for example, record attendances of about a hundred; it not only ran whist drives and organized visiting 'for sick and absent comrades', but also campaigned on peace. During 1924–25, for instance, it ordered a hundred copies of 'No More War' literature; listened to a speaker warn how the *next* war would wipe out of existence not only soldiers but also civilians; and sent four delegates to a conference on 'The suffering of women and children caused through war'.[7] For such war-weary working women, socialism now meant peace.

But for others, their despair at the devastation left by the war, and their hope that it had really been a 'war to end all wars', meant that peace remained *the* key single issue. 'People have no idea what a shock war was to us then', Kathleen Courtney reminisced later. 'We had no idea of the causes of war. I felt we must try to learn.' Now that most women had the vote, they felt that *separate* women's campaigning had become rather an anachronism and joined the new general internationalist and peace groups that sprang from the war. By far the largest and most respectable was the League of Nations Union, formed in October 1918; it tried to press through local branches and through the League structure then emerging at Geneva, for both arbitration of international disputes and multilateral disarmament to ensure that no conflict ever escalated into war again. By 1925, when it received its royal charter, the League boasted no fewer than 255,469 subscribers in Britain; by 1931 this had mushroomed to a phenomenal 406,868.[8] Some were undoubtedly just paper members; but many genuinely believed that League was *the* organization which could prevent future war. Vera Brittain was among the feminists so inspired. On leaving Oxford she contacted headquarters in London, offering herself as a League speaker, and eventually took her first tremulous public meeting – reading out an overly academic lecture to 'fifteen elderly females huddled in tweed coats' in a Baptist vestry in Watford. But the Union seemed to approve of her, continuing 'to urge me forth upon long hot journeys in trains, or long cold journeys in trams, until the halls and chapels at which I spoke . . . gradually merged into a vague

kaleidoscopic dream of swaying lights and upturned faces.'
Brittain's personal commitment remained strong. In 1923
she was in Geneva, reporting on a League Assembly for
Time and Tide, a new feminist magazine; here she witnessed
an exciting example of open diplomacy as Greece appealed
against Mussolini's attack on Corfu. 'The world really
seemed to care', Brittain recalled, that the League 'should
emerge with credit from the Greek–Italian crisis'.[9]

A few women joined the much smaller No More War
Movement, formed in 1921 and linked to other countries
through the War Resisters' International. It was predominantly socialist and pacifist, attracting COs and ILP members, and often criticized the 'imperialist' League. But for
feminists moving leftwards from Liberalism to socialism,
signing the No More Movement's pledge offered hope in
the post-war gloom. For a while it organized annual demonstrations on the anniversary of the outbreak of war;
Florence Lockwood made a banner for the (rainy) 1922
demonstration in Huddersfield and in 1923 joined the
Manchester procession, where 'a few tired enthusiasts
assembled under umbrellas'.[10]

But it was not Women's Sections, the League of Nations
or pacifist groups that gave sharpest focus in the 1920s to
feminism and anti-militarism. That specific perspective
lay, of course, with WIL – renamed the Women's International League for Peace and Freedom in 1919. (For
convenience, the British section is referred to here as
'WILPF'.) Although WILPF could not sustain its high levels of
wartime membership and activism, it remained a key
group within both anti-war and feminist campaigns right
up to 1933 and the rise of Fascism. Yet WILPF has been
badly served by posterity. Peace historians, building a
Procrustean bed around 'pacifism', find that WILPF does
not fit. So one author claims derisively that it had 'no clear
policy' and was 'evasive',[11] while another completely ex-
cludes it from his account.[12] Similarly, major histories of
the women's movement have been remarkably silent about
WILPF: Ray Strachey's classic account, *The Cause*, omits it

because she hated the women who seceded from NUWSS. With WILPF, therefore, we enter uncharted territory. Until recently, its history was recorded only in small-circulation pamphlets[13], and out-of-print biographies such as Swanwick's *I Have Been Young*. Eventually, Bussey and Tims's WILPF history was published in 1965 (and reissued as *Pioneers for Peace* in 1980). Since then, Greenham has provoked enough curiosity about the past to ensure that WILPF's early history has been given the attention it deserves.[14] Certainly, WILPF is crucial to any understanding of feminist and peace politics, particularly before 1933.

WILPF emerged from the war and the peremptory banning of its Hyde Park demonstration with an impressive membership of about 4,200, grouped into fifty-one local branches.[15] Although the move away from industrial areas like South Wales was already apparent, it could well take pride in its activity during its first post-war year. As well as large public meetings and smaller 'At Homes', it formed an Election Sub-committee to support the Labour candidacies of two leading members, Emmeline Pethick Lawrence and Charlotte Despard (though of course neither was elected); produced *Bibliography for Teachers of History*; protested against DORA Regulation 27C restricting freedom of opinion and against the notorious Regulation 40D on venereal disease as 'a degradation of womanhood'; and condemned the British government's repression in Ireland.[16] But of course the most significant event was the congress in Zurich in May, reaffirming WILPF's vital international links. The congress also highlighted the *cost* of war still being paid by non-combatants. For in Central Europe women and children were starving to death as a result of the food blockade imposed by the relentlessly 'victorious' Allies.

Once WILPF members read reports early in 1919 of the effects of this blockade, the harrowing images of starving children and wizened mothers haunted them. 'The account of the awful suffering in Vienna is appalling', Despard wrote after reading one such report. 'I threw it down choked – and we continue the blockade – it is almost unbearable.' But her Women's Freedom League would not share her outrage about the Viennese children. She lost her patience. 'Their usefulness I think is over', she declared – and resigned from the executive. Only WILPF offered hope: 'This League is more alive than the WFL, and has, I believe, work before it.'[17]

In fact, because the crisis provoked by the blockade was so appalling, and because WILPF had not been set up as a *relief* agency, it was necessary to create new food aid networks. Dorothy Buxton (who was married to Charles Roden), along with her sister Eglantyne Jebb and other sympathizers, formed a Fight the Famine Council. It held its first meeting on New Year's Day 1919, aiming to alert both public opinion and Lloyd George's government. 'The War', as Jebb's biographer put it, 'had killed ten million men; economic war was as deadly to women and children.'[18] The women's peace movement 'brunt of war' claim, battered by the realities of the Somme, now began to make better sense. Mary Sheepshanks, feeling that post-war hunger was more urgent now that so many women had the vote, had resigned from editing *Jus Suffragii* and became the Council's Secretary. She had already helped to organize a German Babies' Teats Fund. German mothers were too undernourished to breastfeed their babies and everything was in short supply; so over a million much-needed rubber teats were sent out to baby clinics there.[19]

Buxton and Jebb felt that still *more* needed to be done; and in May 1919, at a packed Albert Hall meeting, the new Save the Children Fund made its first appeal. Jebb became secretary. Emily Hobhouse was also active, as chair of a small Russian Babies' Fund. She travelled for Save the Children to Vienna and Leipzig and began a school feeding system; but, a maverick to the end, she soon parted company with the Fund over a squabble about whether German children were receiving less than others.[20]

WILPF itself organized a women's demonstration against

the hated food blockade. On 6 April 1919 about 10,000 people packed into Trafalgar Square to listen to Emmeline Pethick Lawrence, Theodora Wilson Wilson, Jessie Stephen, Guild and shop steward speakers. Afterwards, they marched down Whitehall to deliver an anti-blockade resolution. For the government, Bonar Law expressed cautious sympathy but 'maintained that the Blockade could not be raised until Peace was signed'. (However, useful publicity was inadvertently gained when Eglantyne Jebb, the WILPF secretary, and the National Labour Press appeared in court in May, charged under Regulation 27C with not submitting their leaflet – with its photograph of a starving Austrian baby – to the censor.)[21]

By now, of course, the WILPF Congress in Zurich had opened. The twenty-five-strong British delegation included Isabella Ford, Ellen Wilkinson, Ethel Snowden and Mrs Despard. This time everyone reached the congress. Chaired again by the ever-conciliatory Jane Addams, it was an extremely moving occasion. The Americans were particularly shocked by the effects of the blockade. 'The marks of war were visible for all to see in the faces of the delegates from the defeated countries,' recorded *Pioneers for Peace*. 'Some had been present four years earlier at The Hague, and the change in them was pitiful. Scarred and shrivelled by hunger and privation, they were scarcely recognizable.'[22]

Helena Swanwick, delayed by visa difficulties, arrived late, but in time to witness the most dramatic episode. Addams quietly announced that a French delegate had managed to get through from the Ardennes, devastated by German occupation. The Frenchwoman walked to the front of the platform and:

> spoke of what she had witnessed, appealing to 'les forces de demain', and Lida Gustava Heymann sprang to her feet, clasping the Frenchwoman's hands and pledging her German colleagues to work for reconciliation. The whole Congress was led in response by Emily Balch [from the United

States] lifting her hand to declare 'I dedicate my life to the cause of peace!'[23]

'Up shot all our hands and a great cry went up in many languages', '"We dedicate our lives to Peace!"' Swanwick added. 'I have never witnessed or imagined so remarkable an affirmation.' Zurich was indeed an extraordinary occasion. There were no recriminations. WIL's wartime organization was put on a permanent footing as a genuinely international body, its name amended at Catherine Marshall's suggestion to the Women's International League of Peace and Freedom (WILPF), with its headquarters sensibly moved to Geneva. But as the congress drew to an end, delegates were ominously reminded of the absence of real 'peace' in Germany and Central Europe. The pathetic Austrian and Hungarian women particularly haunted Swanwick:

> One woman was tortured by daily news of her daughter dying of tuberculosis in a sanitorium, who died before the close of the congress. The sanitoria and hospitals had no linen, and babies were born into newspapers, and dressings had to be washed again and again. One thin, eager, gentle woman died from exhaustion almost immediately after the Congress. . . .[24]

Worse still, the Congress coincided with the publication of the Treaty of Versailles; news came daily from Paris of the deliberations of Lloyd George, President Wilson and Clemenceau. The Peace Conference was grinding on. The news, Swanwick recorded, 'was worse than anything we had anticipated'. A strongly worded indictment of the Treaty and the savage terms imposed on Germany and Austria was telegraphed from Zurich to Versailles. WILPF determined that as the only international women's peace organization, its immediate priority *must* be revision of the Treaty terms now – before it was too late. So, as at The Hague four years earlier, the Congress sent personal envoys speeding to the statesmen conferring at Versailles, including Addams, Macmillan, Despard and Gabrielle Duchêne from France.

None of their proposals was accepted, and only Wilson acknowledged them. However, back in Britain, WILPF squeezed the maximum propaganda value from the occasion. There was a public meeting to welcome Addams and condemn the peace terms; a deputation to Labour MPs at the Commons; and a protest demonstration in Trafalgar Square. But it had little effect. 'The seeds of future war – poverty, disease, and despair – have passed the stage of sowing: their growth is visible everywhere', WILPF lamented.[25]

Post-Versailles Europe lay in ruins. WILPF soberly deliberated where it could take most effective action. Near home, fighting dragged on in Ireland: the notorious 'Black and Tans' were retaliating against the Irish who had rebelled against British rule. The 750-strong Manchester branch suggested a delegation to investigate. Irish WILPF welcomed this; so, in October 1920, ten WILPF members – including Swanwick, Wilkinson, Robinson, and Dollan from Glasgow – set out to see for themselves. Their conclusions were uncompromising: the recent electoral success of Sinn Fein meant that the British were governing only 'by force and fraud'; the armed forces should be withdrawn, all political prisoners immediately released, and authority placed in the hands of Irish local elected bodies – a real move towards Irish self-determination. The women returned and told crowded meetings in Manchester and elsewhere of the devastation they had seen; Robinson and Wilkinson then sailed to America to give evidence there. WILPF kept up the pressure during 1921 and in December rejoiced at the signing of the treaty to set up the Irish Free State.[26]

WILPF also sent twenty-one British delegates to its 1921 congress in Vienna – this time including twenty-five-year-old Mabel Phythian. The problems of Central and Eastern Europe dominated. WILPF, which had originally welcomed the Russian Revolution, passed a resolution – by just one vote – condemning *violent* revolution, even as an agent of social change. Anti-Semitic pogroms, especially in the Ukraine, were condemned. And Phythian could not forget, more than sixty years later, the harrowing impression post-war Vienna made on her. She had been advised to bring her own tea and sugar; but when she arrived it became tragically clear that such valuable commodities must be shared. She gave hers to two university students who were so poor they shared one pair of trousers, taking it in turns to attend lectures. People were so starved, they just fell down dead in the streets.[27]

More congresses followed: at the Hague again, and in Washington,[28] and other pressing issues were pursued: in 1923 WILPF despatched commissioners from the Swedish, American and British sections to investigate France's invasion of the Ruhr; it was impressively well-informed in such crises, which needlessly fuelled Germany's resentments. So, in the mid 1920s the Geneva office could claim a membership of 50,000 women across forty countries.[29]

But in Britain, at least, it was difficult to sustain the early momentum. WILPF's activists were being pulled in too many directions; Swanwick, Chair from 1915 to 1923, became heavily involved in League of Nations Assemblies, so Kathleen Courtney took over. Some of the golden generation of founder-members were growing elderly: Isabella Ford died in 1924. Younger women like Mabel Phythian might occasionally call in at the Manchester office; but now earning her living, she had scant patience for old-fashioned 'feminism' or taking 'refuge in a little bevy of women'.[30]

Membership fell – from about 4,200 in 1918 to about 3,000 in the early 1920s. But many of these seem to have become paper members only. The number of local branches halved between 1918 and 1922.[31] In 1921 WILPF opened an adventurous International House in central London, with a reading room, an 'American-style' café, and a small garden; it offered concerts and weekly discussion meetings but never became self-supporting, and closed in 1924.[32]

A women's peace movement is always highly cyclical, and a downturn in popular support cannot but be melancholy. With its workers creaking under the strain, WILPF had to acknowledge that it now had to revert to a small-scale peace pressure group. But it still valued its distinct identity, combining internationalism with feminism.[33] How could it use its unique influence most effectively? So that it did not become just one more 'head-without-bodies' peace organization, WILPF made an imaginative decision: in 1923 its constitution was amended to make local groups eligible to affiliate. Soon, affiliations included twenty-three Women's Co-operative Guild branches and eleven local Labour Parties and Women's Sections, mainly in London; there were also local affiliations to the bigger WILPF branches like Glasgow, Liverpool and Manchester.[34] Speakers were invited to address meetings of working women; and, despite shrinkage of its *own* branches, WILPF developed a new and broad peace network.

So what did a women's peace movement look like in the mid 1920s, ten years after the Hague Congress? How much popular support for peace issues *could* WILPF still count on, and what strands of feminist anti-militarist thinking predominated? For answers, it is easiest to glance back briefly to the debates about women's representation in the League of Nations.

Equal-rights feminism enjoyed a high profile immediately after the war. It was argued that now most women were enfranchised, women's voices must be heard at Geneva, on grounds both of rights to full citizenship and that women would bring different qualities to bear on international politics. Significantly, lobbying ranged right across the political spectrum, from the most nationalist patriots to the most idealistic internationalists. Mrs Fawcett led an

Inter-Allied (i.e. from the victorious nations only) Suffrage delegation to Paris in 1919; and, along with Margery Corbett Ashby, had some success in demanding that the League Covenant should include provision for all positions to be 'open equally to men and women'. In Britain the conservative National Council of Women initiated a Council for the Representation of Women in the League of Nations; and in 1925 a Joint Standing Committee of Women's International Organizations appeared, also at the invitation of the International Council of Women (ICW), and including the International Woman Suffrage Alliance (IWSA) and WILPF; it aimed to work 'unitedly for the appointment of suitable women on Commissions or other bodies in the League of Nations where women's opinion should be represented'.[35]

But two problems remained. First, women's voices were still virtually inaudible at Geneva. In 1924 Ramsay MacDonald's short-lived Labour government appointed Swanwick substitute delegate to the Fifth Assembly. But as late as 1929 only fifteen women attended the Tenth Assembly, mainly just as substitute delegates and technical advisers. Not until 1929 were women appointed to commissions other than the fifth (dealing with women's and children's welfare). Within the League's secretariat only one woman, Dame Rachel Crowdy, social section chief, reached high office. Second, the lobbying revealed the limitation of equal-rights feminism to a women's peace movement. Was there much point in encouraging representation from each and every woman, irrespective of whether she had been a staunch patriot in the Great War or joined the Women's Peace Crusade, and whether she was a genuine internationalist, conservative imperialist or, as was becoming conceivable, Fascist? Not so, thought Catherine Marshall. 'I think we should not content ourselves with asking that *a* woman should be appointed to these bodies,' she wrote. 'I don't want to urge the appointment of "*a* woman" for the sake of having a woman on.'[36] Certainly WILPF wanted *more* than just equal-rights feminism (even when that feminism also stressed women's difference from men).

The second strand, Gilmanite feminism linking maleness and violence, was scarcely visible in the 1920s. The reasons are easy to appreciate. The Somme was still an immediate memory. Every community had its share of wounded and shell-shocked soldiers. Too many mothers' sons had died: too many women had lost young men. Also, there was an optimism that women's new-found citizenship *would* give them the power to shape a peaceful future. So WILPF attacked, not any violence inherent in men, but the way men were conditioned. It protested at the growth of military drill in schools, Officers' Training Corps and war films. It readily co-operated with mixed peace organizations, voicing no criticism of maleness as such. This tended to spring from ex-suffragettes active in equal-rights feminism rather than in peace politics.

One was Elizabeth Robbins, an American who had moved to London in the 1880s, became an actress and playwright, joined WSPU, and after the war the equal-rights Six Point Group, contributing to *Time and Tide*.[37] In 1924 Robbins's *Ancilla's Share: An Indictment of Sex Antagonism* (Ancilla means handmaiden) was published – anonymously. Although the book is not lucidly written, its language has fascinating echoes for contemporary readers familiar with recent radical feminist critiques of patriarchy.[38] Robbins argues that:

> Wars will cease when woman's-will-to-peace is given equal hearing and equal authority in council with man's-will-to-war. . . . No war could be fought, it is doubtful if a war could be declared, in the face of the proclaimed non-consent of women.[39]

Robbins is critical of the way the League used women as little 'more than superior sort of charwomen'. 'It is not truly a League of Nations . . .', she wrote. 'It is a League of men served by women in the subordinate offices.' But she is less clear than Gilman before her, or Virginia Woolf some years later, about men's responsibility for condoning warfare. She expresses a hope for the future rather than any plan of action for the present, showing more sympathy for the conservative ICW than for WILPF, with its socialist links.[40]

Robbins's 'man's-will-to-war' polemic did little to shape the language of the women's peace movement in the late 1920s. It remained predominantly maternalistic, stressing first the effect of the food blockade on women and children; later education and the influence of mothers on the next generation of soldier-sons. These concerns were increasingly expressed by Guildswomen. The Women's Co-operative Guild, though smaller than the Labour Party Women's Sections, was growing fast: after the war its membership was 44,500; by 1930 it had risen to 66,566. Like the Sections, it could speak for working women, almost all of them mothers.

From the outbreak of war, the Guild had played a largely supportive role rather than initiating peace campaigns of its own. But an International Co-operative Women's Guild was formed in 1921, and Guildswomen became increasingly involved. 'There is no class to whom the cause of Peace can make a stronger appeal than to International Co-operative Guildswomen,' wrote Llewlyn Davies, 'for war casts its dread shadow in a special way on the lives of wives and mothers.'[41] The Guild condemned militarist material in textbooks, and campaigned for an annual peace day in schools. From 1927 it could report that hundreds of branches held special Peace Celebrations during Armistice Week, 'to secure a peace of mind in opposition to the militarist mentality aroused by the official glorification of war'.[42] Uncompromisingly, it also demanded the abolition of war films, with working-class mothers on the board of film censors, and for peace to be the main plank of Labour's programme at the next general election.

Maternalist feminists were concerned, as before, not only with the *cause* of a 'next war' but also with how 'the brunt' might fall on non-combatants. WILPF members remembered what they had seen in Zurich and in Vienna. 'This modern massacre of the innocents haunted us for years', Swanwick wrote.[43] For such women, opposition to war grew into an absolute pacifism. Any use of violence to achieve social change, or any 'blockade' of one nation to force the hand of another, was condemned as violent – a condemnation fuelled by the growing fear that in any future conflict aerial bombardments would annihilate civilian women and children. This absolute pacifism grew stronger – and more contentious – in the 1930s; but in the 1920s campaigns for disarmament and international arbitration to end war were popular, uniting an impressively broad and optimistic women's peace movement.

In November 1924 MacDonald's Labour government fell; with it went hopes for strengthening the League of Nations by the adoption of a Geneva Protocol offering proper provision for the international arbitration of disputes. The new Foreign Secretary, Austen Chamberlain, was no imaginative internationalist. His Conservative government rejected the Protocol, and so killed its chances of acceptance by other nations. When WILPF heard of this ominous snub it quickly organized an Arbitration Petition in conjunction with other peace groups. Members swung into activity, setting up Petition Shops, running stalls in marketplaces, and organizing house-to-house canvassing. In August 1925 there were over 500,000 signatures on the Petition, which was lodged at the Foreign Office.[44]

That winter the Locarno Pact (much weaker than the Geneva Protocol) was signed. Amid this optimism a WILPF member suggested an Arbitration Pilgrimage, along the lines of the dramatic 1913 suffrage pilgrimage. The idea caught on. Representatives from twenty-eight women's organizations, including the National Council of Women, met in January 1926; they greeted the suggestion enthusiastically and a Peacemakers' Pilgrimage Council took shape. Soon it became clear that the Pilgrimage would be about arbitration *and* disarmament; for in December the League had appointed its Preparatory Commission for a proposed Disarmament Conference.

Plans for staging the Pilgrimage unfolded. There would be about eight main routes, converging on Hyde Park from all over the country, each headed by a great two-pole blue banner bearing the route name, with women carrying staffs with a dove of peace on top. Groups of 'Pilgrims' would walk along each route, talking to bystanders and handing out literature. And it worked. The Pilgrimage followed hard on the heels of the General Strike;[45] but women found that wherever they went, passers-by came out to greet them and join in the meetings. Newspapers reported how far the nearest group of pilgrims had reached each day. 'Tanned and Tired but Triumphant', ran the *Western Daily Mail* headline about the South Wales Women. 'From our first meeting at Pen-y-gwes in the hills of South Carnarvonshire,' a north Wales pilgrim recorded, 'to which came pilgrims of seventeen quarry villages and seaside towns, until Chester, the same enthusiasm followed and sustained us.'[46]

Women who could not leave their homes for more than a few hours were especially encouraged. In Halifax, the Women's Liberal Association ran charabancs to take women to join pilgrims in a service in York Minster. 'Fare 7s. 6d. return', ran the advertisement. 'This is not a Party Political Campaign.' Across the Pennines in Nelson, Selina Cooper and sixteen other women, with blue and yellow rosettes pinned to their coats, unfurled their 'Peace our Hope' banner, and clambered aboard their charabanc for Manchester. The service in the Cathedral was crowded, and afterwards women marched through the city to Platt Fields, where 2,500 people joined the demonstration. 'Law can be substituted for war,' Courtney told the crowd, 'as law has been substituted for duelling.'[47]

This demonstration was billed to coincide with the first contingent of marchers reaching London: those from

Brighton, Hastings and the Sussex villages. They carried long staffs bearing the names of the three dozen communities which had passed arbitration resolutions. They marched to an open-air meeting at Crystal Palace; another was held at Fulham Palace for the pilgrims from Wales and Land's End. Thousands of women were now pouring into London. The following day, 19 June, 10,000 marched to Hyde Park through brilliant sunshine. Many more joined them in front of twenty-two platforms to listen to Pethick Lawrence and Corbett Ashby, Fawcett and Bondfield, Ellen Wilkinson and others. At the end a bugle was sounded, and from every platform the resolution was put, urging the government to support disarmament and arbitration. With hardly a murmur of dissent, it was carried.[48]

This was the women's peace movement at its imaginative best: unified, coherent and effective. The Pilgrimage had been very cleverly stage-managed, and politicians found it difficult to ignore. Austen Chamberlain agreed to receive a deputation. He listened sympathetically to Swanwick, Royden, and Barton of the Guild; and pointed out that preparations were already under way for the Disarmament Conference. But he was, of course, wary about arbitration – for he was conscious that Britain remained a major *imperial* power and his government wanted its traditional free hand to settle disputes in her colonies.[49]

Chamberlain's sympathy was disingenuous. Soon after the Preparatory Commission for the Disarmament Conference began its work, differences – caused in part by British obstinate self-interest and security paranoia – slowed progress down to the speed of a cautious centipede.

However, this could not be foreseen in the summer sun of 1926, and WILPF felt delighted with the outcome of the Pilgrimage. In 1927, some branches staged mini-pilgrimages. Particularly impressive was the Carnarvonshire and Anglesey Women's Peace Council, which held two dozen meetings.[50] WILPF could take stock optimistically. The Disarmament Preparatory Commission might be tiresomely slow. But in 1928 the Kellogg–Briand Pact – aiming, at least in theory, at a renunciation of war – was signed in Paris. And in Britain an election was imminent. All pointed towards a campaign to educate voters on the key issues: disarmament and arbitration. The Pilgrimage Committee, which somehow kept going after 1926, was in touch with organizations which were already working to similar ends in the States. (It changed its name to the Anglo-American Crusade Committee, and later – recalling the heady days of 1917 – to the Women's Peace Crusade.)[51]

The Women's Peace Crusade campaigned hard in the run-up to the 1929 general election. All-party deputations from twenty-seven women's organizations lobbied candidates in 300 constituencies, questioning them on the Kellogg Pact, arbitration and disarmament. This energetic pressure for a 'Parliament of Peacemakers' even provoked a sympathetic cartoon in the *Evening Standard*: a new woman 'flapper voter' was depicted saying *no more war in our name*.[52] Afterwards, with MacDonald's Labour government returned promising active support for the League of Nations, the international outlook was extremely hopeful. The women's peace movement felt strong and could still command broad support: not all would go as far as WILPF's radical demand for *complete* disarmament, but under the Women's Peace Crusade umbrella it could orchestrate effective campaigns.

Despite the Kellogg Pact and MacDonald's new Labour government, this earlier optimistic consensus on peace through arbitration and disarmament soon began to crumble. The Depression followed the Wall Street Crash. In Germany, unemployment reached three million; five million by the end of 1930. In the Reichstag, the National Socialists grew in strength. In Britain, MacDonald's government was struggling as unemployment rose from 1,500,000 to over 2,600,000 by 1931.

WILPF still clung to hopes focused on the long-awaited World Disarmament Conference. Its petition headed 'War is Renounced – Let us Renounce Armaments' began in May 1930 to circulate in Britain, America, France, Germany and elsewhere. Soon, petitions were circulating in no fewer than eighteen languages across ten national WILPF sections, and signatures leapt to 240,000. In January 1931 the League of Nations announced that the conference would open in February 1932. Margery Corbett Ashby, still an idealistic old-style Liberal, was included in the British delegation (though only as substitute). All this gave an added fillip to the petition. In the States, WILPF organized a Peace Caravan: in June 1931 it left Hollywood, travelled nearly 9,000 miles, and reached Washington – and President Hoover – in October.

Petition enthusiasm now spread far beyond WILPF to the older and more conservative organizations. ICW and Corbett Ashby's smaller International Alliance of Women (as IWSA was now called) were working closely together; a new Liaison Committee of Women's International Organizations emerged (including the Young Women's Christian Association – YWCA). It claimed to speak for a staggering forty million women in fifty-six countries, and in September 1931 it set up a special co-ordinating group to focus on the coming Disarmament Conference, with Mary Dingman of the YWCA as president, Kathleen Courtney as a vice-president, and headquarters in Geneva. By the end of 1931 over half a million signatures had been collected worldwide; remarkably, half came from Britain alone.[53] This, surely, was the worldwide women's peace movement, if not at its most feminist, then certainly at its most effective.

But autumn 1931 cast a shadow over all this. In the face of mounting economic depression, the Labour government had resigned in August. MacDonald moved treacherously sideways to lead a new right-of-centre 'National' government. Then in September Japan invaded Manchuria, using bombers to maintain 'control'. This was an act of obvious military aggression; but despite all the Kellogg Pact rhetoric, the League was too weak and too slow to be able to impose effective sanctions. Japan got away with murder.

The clear-cut 'never again' certainties of the 1920s looked increasingly shaky. *Pioneers for Peace* vividly captures all the tensions and expectations as the first World Disarmament Conference opened in Geneva on 2 February 1932:

> War raged in the Far East, unemployment blanketed the USA, Europe shivered on the threshold of new chaos – and as the 'peacemakers' assembled the world held its breath and waited for the words and deeds of hope. What hope was there for success? The hopes of the 'ordinary people' of the world . . . lay piled in despatch boxes in the library of the conference hall – those millions of petitions, collected . . . by peace societies and ex-servicemen; by religious and labour organizations; above all by the women, mothers of one slaughtered generation and now another threatened.[54]

No fewer than eight million signatures from women's organizations alone were presented at the receiving ceremony. An eye-witness recorded how:

> The women entered the Hall in a long procession, two abreast, each wearing a scarf bearing a nation's name; the end of the procession was lost to sight beyond the doorway, so that one could imagine it stretching round the world. . . .
> [Mary Dingman] then addressed the Conference, on behalf of the greatest collective effort that women have ever undertaken. . . . 'Behind each of these eight million names stands a living personality, a human being oppressed by great fear – the fear of the destruction of our civilization – but also moved by a great will for peace. . . . It is not for

ourselves alone that we plead, but for the generations to come. To us women, as mothers . . .

. . . The women in procession filed up to a table below the President's dais to deposit their petitions. . . . The pile on the table mounted higher and higher, till it began to topple over. Again and again the bundles were carried away in baskets, to make room for more. The President leaned over from his seat to watch. Everyone was stirred. At last the pile was complete.

Outside, WILPF members demonstrated, proclaiming: 'The Disarmament Conference is meeting in Geneva. Japanese bombs are falling on Chinese cities. What will you choose: War or Disarmament?' The answer soon became tragically clear. The politicians were prepared to concede little, and soon adjourned. The verb 'to disarm', one French states-man joked cynically, is 'conjugated only in the future tense, and it has only the form of the second person'.[55]

Events, especially in Germany, also cast an increasingly black shadow over Geneva. Japan withdrew from the League of Nations. And the day before the Disarmament Conference reopened in January 1933, Hitler became Chancellor. Discussion seemed to shift from *dis*armament to *re*armament. Britain held out for retaining bombers. Further elections in Germany strengthened the Nazis: they soon dissolved all other political parties, and herded Jews, pacifists and Communists into concentration camps. In May, the National Council of Women in Germany was ordered to submit unconditionally to the Fuehrer, and to recognize the 'special tasks' assigned to women by the Nazi state. It decided to disband. The German section of WILPF could no longer function openly either: Anita Augspurg and Lida Gustava Heymann fled to Switzerland; others were arrested.

Then, on 14 October, Germany announced her with-drawal from the Disarmament Conference and, worse still, from the League of Nations. Hitler demanded the return of the Saar from France. 'Not only the draft Disarmament

Convention died on that day,' summed up *Pioneers for Peace*; 'with it were buried all the hopes of a peaceful political settlement in Europe.'[56]

Even the ever-patient Corbett Ashby eventually resigned in complete despair in 1935, the time of yet another adjournment. Britain had just committed itself to increased armaments spending. It was, she later recalled, 'the most unhappy period of my life', when 'the last opportunity of securing international action for safe guarding [*sic*] peace was frittered away'.[57]

8

Pacifism – or Anti-Fascism?
(1934–39)

The rise of Nazism, the collapse of the Disarmament Conference and the subsequent spread of Fascism in Europe stimulated flourishing peace movement activity. Peace historian Martin Caedel recently noted how around 1936 these events 'generated grass-roots activity of a type not matched until the 1980s'. Local 'peace councils' sprang up, and there was an outbreak of 'Peace Tableaux, Peace Pageants, Peace Exhibitions, Peace demonstrations, Peace Flags, Peace Bands, Peace Pennies' (though, as we shall see, often with very contradictory political programmes).[1] Yet such peace movement historians have remained gender blind, uninterested in the 'separate spheres' which still so significantly shaped the lives of the great majority of women, and so much of their peace activity.[2]

Caedel's earlier *Pacifism in Britain 1914–1945*, so dismissive of WILPF, looked at the pacifist Peace Pledge Union (PPU), commenting on the middle-class nature of its support and the 'disappointing' response from women. But it neglected even a glance at the other major pacifist organization, composed predominantly of working-class women: the Co-operative Guild.[3] Yet gender remained a crucial key to understanding how individuals and organizations responded, against the background of the Depression and memories of the Great War, to the deteriorating world situation.

Equal-rights feminism had its back against the wall in the 1930s. High unemployment and pressure on women to take up domestic service and leave work on marriage meant that access to higher education, training and equal pay remained highly contested.[4] These social, political and economic shifts and tensions also significantly shaped women's peace activities; for women seemed to be on the receiving end of a considerable amount of eloquent but contradictory advice – about *both* feminism *and* peace.

Some argued that traditional equal-rights feminism had grown old-fashioned now that there were other, more urgent political issues. Meanwhile maternalist feminism, stressing gender difference, was less on the defensive; its form of welfare feminism, with demands around family health, was more acceptable – though Nazi Germany's highly pronounced separate spheres ideology cast a dark cloud.

Similarly, among peace activists in the late 1930s there was growing confusion and tension between pacifists who clung to their absolute anti-war faith; those who still hoped a League of Nations policy of sanctions against bullies would stop the world being dragged into war again; and those who had already lost faith in the so-respectable League's ability to combat Fascism, and looked instead to build an anti-Fascist alliance of the Soviet Union and the West against Nazi Germany.

A combination of these contradictions within peace ideas and feminism meant that a women's peace movement lost its earlier coherence. This is reflected by the writers of the day. Virginia Woolf protested eloquently against male militarism and male power, proclaiming women's internationalist and pacifist instincts – but was a very isolated voice. Helena Swanwick, still closely involved in peace politics, now despaired of women's ability to rouse themselves against war.

So many contradictory ideas were pressed upon women – pacifism or anti-Fascism, general campaigns or separate women's actions – that it is impossible to encompass the full range of contemporary organizational or individual experiences. Rather, here are the stories of the two key women's peace organizations: WILPF and the Guild. An account of WILPF's decline is complemented by the experiences of the large (and still growing) Guild – and in particular of one north London branch where the friction between pacifism and anti-Fascism is clearly revealed. Into these two accounts are woven the life stories of two young women, both born in 1913 – too young to have known the great pre-war suffrage campaigns – and growing up in the Depression. One, Emma Chatterton, lived in Yorkshire; the other, Vera Leff, in north London: both joined their local Guild branch (though for very different reasons) in about 1937; and both cared deeply about peace but, due to differences in their personal experiences and their politics, moved in opposite directions. Together these narratives help to illuminate how women, confronted by the increasingly desperate choices between pacifism and anti-Fascism, broad campaigns or women-only organizations, sped along different trajectories.

The rise of Hitler, which had so enfeebled the League, also prompted real disagreements about peace and freedom. Was the prospect of another war so horrific that every peace lover should refuse to participate or condone it, or was Nazism so terrible that every democrat should resist Fascist aggression by every means possible – including, if necessary, military? Confronted with this dilemma, the earlier consensus fractured and the conservative-dominated National government could more easily fudge, evade and procrastinate. As the peace movement lost its earlier coherence, the women's peace movement factionalized and entered a very long hiatus.

WILPF remained the doyenne of women's organizations, the only one in Britain devoted solely to international peace. The British section, while not brutally persecuted like the German section, weakened visibly as the policies of the government at home and of Fascists abroad unfolded. It became difficult to keep members: WILPF shrank to a scattering of brave loyalists (often Quakers) and a handful of active branches. One key resignation in around 1933 was that of Kathleen Courtney from the chair; she increasingly transferred her energies to the larger and far more respect-able League of Nations Union.[5]

Divisions among peace activists became dramatic only in the late thirties. During winter 1934–35, for instance, an impressively wide range of organizations took part in a Peace Ballot, initiated by the League of Nations Union to muster support for its policy of imposing sanctions on aggressor nations. A staggering 11,640,066 people were canvassed by a volunteer army of no fewer than 500,000. Many of these determined door-knockers (never an envi-able task during a British winter) were women. 'The work involved, viz., a nation-wide house to house canvass, is greater than that of a general election,' WILPF noted soberly, 'involving very often repeated calls at one house in order to collect the voting papers.' In some areas WILPF branches did much of this work; in others it was Guilds-women and Labour Party Women's Section members, while elsewhere National Council of Women branches were active. The Ballot revealed that a massive 87 per cent of those questioned supported *economic* sanctions; however, only just over half (59 per cent) were prepared to support *military* measures.[6]

This broad agreement, however, was vague, and easily manipulated by the centre-right government. Crises over the ensuing fifteen months – the Italian invasion of Abyssinia, a general election confirming the National government in power, German troops marching into the Rhineland and, in July 1936, the landing of Franco's Fascist troops in Spain, leading to the outbreak of the bitter Civil War – tumbled one after another. Peace activists seized on various conflicting strategies, and the women's peace movement consensus finally dissolved.

Many of these conflicts were painfully played out within WILPF. Should there still be a separate women's peace organization, or should everyone now join together – and if so, in what? How should WILPF advocate resistance to

Fascism: nonviolently – or by force if necessary? (This debate about violence stretched back to WILPF's 1921 resolution condemning violent revolution, even to bring about social change.)[7] WILPF's policy was nonviolence, though not all the national sections were happy with this. In the 1920s the influential German and French sections grew more militantly socialist. Yet the sizeable British, Scandinavian and American sections remained rooted in a more Liberal tradition, veering towards nonviolence and absolute pacifism. This crucial division between leftist anti-Fascism and Anglo-Scandinavian pacifism led to tremendous tension, which gripped WILPF in the 1930s. Mary Sheepshanks became international secretary in 1927 but within three years she resigned, infuriated by what she saw as pro-Communist tactics by the French and German members of the executive.[8]

A particularly dramatic example of the growing belief in Britain in the power of nonviolence (in this case, Christian pacifist) was Maude Royden's proposal, in a sermon in early 1932, for a 'Peace Army' to go out to Manchuria. 'Men and women who believe it to be their duty should volunteer to place themselves unarmed between the combatants', she suggested. 'We make our appeal to men and women alike. . . . Let us, therefore, ask the League to send us, unarmed, to the scene of the conflict.' This proposal caught the public imagination, and no fewer than 800 people volunteered; but the story that any of them actually set out for Tilbury seems unfounded.[9]

The continental sections of WILPF did, of course, face mounting oppression in the 1930s. Camille Drevet, who replaced Sheepshanks as international secretary, fell victim to anti-Soviet smear tactics and was threatened with expulsion from Geneva for being pro-Communist. As Fascism spread, the British section therefore found itself increasingly out of step with WILPF in Europe. It made the right gestures about opposing Fascism; but in 1934 it still criticized the international executive for 'passing political resolutions' and demanded a change in WILPF's constitution to give national sections more autonomy – and so to weaken the executive.[10]

These divisions deepened. Edith Pye, a Quaker and the only British member of the international executive, had grave doubts about the French section; and these were shared by the Swedes and Emily Balch (who was now running the Geneva office). This Anglo-Scandinavian group took particularly strong exception to Gabrielle Duchêne's role in organizing a large women's conference in Paris 'against war and Fascism'. British WILPF, wary of anything linked to Communist initiatives, merely sent an observer. At its Annual Council in 1935 a motion to withdraw completely from international WILPF was only just defeated. Britain, rather grumpily, remained a member.[11] (It seemed that WILPF in Britain could not win: what drove Kathleen Courtney away was both 'the extreme lines' of the international executive, and her feeling that the British section 'was becoming too pacifist'.[12])

To mount the Paris conference, a Women's World Committee Against War and Fascism was set up in summer 1934; its British sponsors included not only women inside the Communist Party but also an impressive sprinkling of those outside: Charlotte Despard and Sylvia Pankhurst, Ellen Wilkinson, and writers Vera Brittain and Storm Jameson. The British Section of Women Against War and Fascism, aiming for a broad appeal, produced a 'Women's Charter' including the right of married women to work, birth control at local clinics – and only in the final section a demand for the disbandment of all Fascist organizations and support for the Soviet call for total disarmament.[13]

Pacifist WILPF held such organizations at arm's length, but became increasingly isolated. With lingering memories of a food blockade, it even hesitated over the use of *economic* sanctions against aggressor nations. For instance, in spring 1936 Nazi troops occupied the Rhineland, and international WILPF recommended economic sanctions against Germany; but Edith Pye and a Dutch member rejected such 'punitive measures', and relations between the British

Section and the others chilled yet further. Even when the Civil War broke out in Spain, timid WILPF would go no further than urging non-intervention, with mediation and relief from the League of Nations.[14]

Like so many pacifists in the 1930s, WILPF tragically underestimated the full horrors of Nazism and Fascism, alienating many of its socialist supporters. Yet when it came to imaginative *peace* campaigning, WILPF had its clothes stolen by two large pacifist groups: the new Peace Pledge Union and the Women's Co-operative Guild.

Hitler's rise to power brought with it real fear of war; but this fear did not strengthen support for the League of Nations Union.[15] Rather, Nazism stimulated two very different anti-war movements, both popular and both sharing a cynicism about the effectiveness of the League's policies: the anti-Fascist movement, and a new pacifism – a personal refusal to support or condone war. Vera Brittain's *Testament of Youth* mirrored this new pacifist mood. 'The story became a memorial', Brittain wrote later, 'to the generation of young men who were swept from the threshold of life by the First World War.'[16]

Brittain grew increasingly disillusioned that 'the League had become an instrument of French policy': party politicians and their evasive compromises could no longer be trusted. To such people a highly charismatic Anglican clergyman, the Reverend Dick Sheppard, now offered an *un*compromising, almost religious pacifism – and so a new hope. With his very simple 'I renounce war and never again, directly or indirectly, will I support or sanction another' promise, Sheppard soon received 80,000 postcard pledges. In May 1936, this surge of personal renunciation grew into the Peace Pledge Union (PPU), which began its own newspaper, *Peace News*. Then in July Sheppard opened the pledge to women: Brittain, who had become weary of speaking in support of collective security, was among those suddenly magnetized by his evangelical message:

In that moment I saw that my study of peace had been too superficial. . . . For fifteen years after the First World War, th[e] wide moral division between the supporters of collective security and the exponents of revolutionary pacifism had always existed but had not been emphasized. But with the threat of a Second World War, the gulf became clear. Individuals who believed war was wrong in all circumstances could no longer join with those who were prepared to fight in the last resort.[17]

With other writers like Rose Macaulay, Brittain joined the PPU's galaxy of glittering 'sponsors'; by the time of Sheppard's death in October 1937, the total number of pledges had risen to an impressive 120,000. Around the country, women became extremely active – driving the PPU van, addressing crowded marketplaces.

But over two-thirds of PPU support still came from men.[18] Rather than joining such a general organization, pacifist women – particularly working-class women – were much more likely to be found in the Women's Co-operative Guild. The number of Guildswomen continued to rise: to an impressive 87,246 members in 1,819 branches by 1939.[19] And it was increasingly pacifist. Among older Guildswomen there was

the tremendous surge of these women 'never again, never again'. . . . And determination that – 'OK no grandson of mine has got to go through this. No daughter of mine has got to see her children taken off into khaki.'[20]

Many younger Guildswomen felt that the devastation of the Great War had tragically scarred their childhoods and adolescence. One was Emma Chatterton, born in Clayton, a hillside textile village near Bradford. She was just a year old when war broke out; her brother was born in 1915. Emma's father, a miner, was killed by mustard gas in 1918.

He was twenty-four. She remembers seeing him only twice, on both occasions in uniform when he was home on leave. But Emma retained sharp memories of what his death meant:

> It was a very difficult, hard time, when you look back on those days, for mother to have to bring up two young children, because we were both very young. . . . Mother had to go out to work. In fact, when we were very little, she was working on night turns. . . . I always said we were latch key kids.[21]

Emma's mother could not allow her to go to grammar school. Instead, when she was fourteen,

> my mother was waiting for me to leave school, to go to work with her. And she worked in the mills in Clayton, and I worked with her. She was what they call a gill-box minder . . . and I was a spinner and a rover,

– with wages of 13*s*.7½*d*. [about 68p]. Emma married in 1930 and worked until her daughter was born; in 1937 she had a son. This second birth – at home, with a midwife – proved a turning point:

> Now my mother's sister, who was Aunty Becca to us, always went out with the midwife and helped produce the babies. And she did this for Winnie [my friend], and for me. . . . Anyhow, when we'd got over the birth, and starting an ordinary life again, she says, 'Now I've gone and done what I could to help *you*', she says. 'And now it's your turn to do something for me. I've been made a member of the committee of the Clayton Co-operative Guild; and my job is to get new members. Now, you, and Winnie and Mary' – that was the lady next door – 'and Emily and Doris' – two more friends – she says, 'You can all come to the Guild'. So I says, 'I'm not going to the Guild.' I says, 'They're all old women like you.' . . . And she says, 'Never mind whether we're old

women or not', she says. 'You come. And then, if you don't like, fair enough. But if you *do* like, then that's it'. And so we went. . . .

Chatterton did like: the Guild fitted her needs precisely:

'I fell for it, hook, line and sinker. It must have been something I was waiting for. . . . And for the first time from being married, I was able to think about something outside my home. And I *really* went for it. It *fascinated* me, the way that the women came from the District Committee of the Guild and gave 'Subjects', and stood up and discussed things.

The Guild changed Chatterton's life; soon she was going as the Clayton delegate to the national congress, and was made her branch's secretary. Among other things, it introduced her to a pacifism that helped to make sense of her father's wartime death. She remembers a joint Guild meeting with the Peace Pledge Union, and how a local WILPF activist, Florence White, leant on the Guild and came to speak to the Clayton branch about peace.[22]

How did the Guild's pacifism arise? Its open anti-war campaigning had shifted to a narrower, personal-witness style of pacifism. Its current general secretary, Eleanor Barton, a Sheffield City councillor and ILP supporter, was a strong pacifist. As early as 1933, even before Sheppard launched his pledge campaign, Barton introduced a Guild Peace Pledge Card committing signatories – a few thousand Guildswomen and their friends – to take no part in war or preparations for war.

More startlingly memorable were the Guild's symbolic white poppies. In 1933 some branches asked the central committee for an emblem that was distinct yet unassociated with the evils of war. The committee agreed to the wearing of a white poppy on Armistice Day. Before long, white poppies as a symbol of personal pacifism caught on. Certainly Chatterton wore hers each November. Although there was no special local Armistice Day ceremony, there were in places like London. Sometimes there was harassment, because 'it was absolutely unthinkable not to wear a red poppy on 11th November'. But Guildswomen were determined. 'I've never bought a Flanders poppy in my life,' recalled one. 'Not that I'm disrespectful to the boys that lost their lives. But we believed in peace poppies. . . . That's my training in the Guild.'[23]

But local Guildswomen were still subject to contradictory messages about peace: both Barton's sectarian pacifism and a more robust anti-Fascism. To take one particular example, the cosmopolitan Hampstead Garden Suburb branch in north London, whose minute books survive from at least January 1933, had a flourishing weekly afternoon attendance of two to three dozen. Partly social, it also received invitations for support from competing peace organizations. In spring 1933, hard on the heels of a WILPF appeal, came an invitation from a local Anti-War Council, part of an international Communist peace initiative. The branch was evenly divided about this Council, but seemed to prefer a more liberal approach, inviting a very well-informed UDC speaker to talk on Nazi Germany; and in November five members ordered Peace Pledge cards.[24]

The Hampstead Garden Suburb branch grew increasingly wary of 'united front' and anti-fascist appeals. Significantly, though, in summer 1934, when the branch was asked to help to fund a delegate to Paris for the Women's World Congress against War and Fascism, members enthusiastically arranged a whist drive, perhaps because of the practical welfare proposals – maternity hospitals and birth control – of the 'Women's Charter'.[25]

But the Guild's central office grew suspicious of such enthusiasm. In 1935 it issued a warning against receiving visits from 'strangers' asking for help, and provided a bracing talk on 'Unity' from a Guild official. So what was happening? A considerable internal struggle. Barton's right-wing hostility to Guildswomen who were members of the Communist Party was combined with her sectarian pacifism. Despite strong and diverse opposition, Barton and her supporters managed to silence her critics; she imposed both pacifism and, in January 1936, a 'Black Rule' which effectively prohibited Communist members from holding office, however lowly.[26] The Hampstead Garden Suburb branch seemed to absorb both Bartonisms: it ordered a hundred copies of the new rules, and a dozen white poppies. This rather authoritarian tightening up continued through 1936, with officials coming to speak on the new 'Black Circular'.[27] Peace also remained a contested area. The branch still seemed to opt for pacifism rather than anti-Fascism: as soon as Sheppard opened the PPU to women, the branch ordered no fewer than a hundred pledge cards.

But the Spanish Civil War forced some Guildswomen to reconsider their pacifism. By spring 1938, when Hitler's troops crossed into Austria and entered Vienna, feelings ran high between Barton's absolute pacifism and an anti-Fascist 'United Peace Alliance'. At the June congress, the debate was bitter. 'Absolute pacifism is not wrong but is impracticable at the present moment . . .' proclaimed a Watford Guildswoman. Delegates voted to retain the Guild's pacifist policy – but only by 897 votes to 623. The bitter argument rumbled on into the pages of *Co-operative News*.[28]

For Chatterton in the semi-rural Clayton Guild, the 1938 congress decision was not a problem: she wore her white poppy with pride, and Vienna still seemed far more remote than her father's death in the war. However, in more cosmopolitan Hampstead Garden Suburb there was now greater resentment against the official Guild pacifist policy and the Barton regime: members resigned and attendances slumped. There were nasty wranglings over the 'Black Circular': the branch even planned its own protest deputation to the central committee.[29] Its minute books suggest that a women's peace movement scarcely existed any more.

Vera Leff was one member for whom the Guild's new pacifism was increasingly unrealistic. Her origins were Jewish and Central European: one grandfather had fled to Edinburgh from anti-Semitism in Lithuania. The family shop did not do well; and in the early 1920s Vera and her family moved to London. Their business did indeed eventually go bankrupt, and when Vera left school she was sent to a commercial 'college' to learn typing and shorthand. She began working in drab office jobs. In about 1934, influenced by a particularly charismatic socialist cousin, Vera stumbled upon the local Communist Party – and a new life:

> The evening of our first cell meeting came. . . . There were about nine or ten of us. We were all young, and mostly Jewish. The idea that there could be Communists who were middle-aged or elderly never entered my head. I began to feel exhilarated. At last I was among people to whom I felt akin. I loved them all. When [my cousin] said, 'Comrades, we will now begin the meeting', I suppose I felt a thrill of a new initiate to a ritual ceremony.[30]

Vera was made secretary. When someone mentioned Mosley's Fascists, 'the temperature in the room immediately rose'. Anti-Semitism was rife. For the young Jewish people present, 'the ideas of Marx and Lenin were intriguing and aroused much curiosity, but it was the threatening Fascism which prodded us into action.' During the Spanish Civil War, for Vera and her comrades, *Fascism meant war*. 'Bombs on Madrid today. Bombs on London tomorrow', they declaimed.[31]

In 1937 Vera married Sam Leff, an energetic doctor and fellow cell member. Back in north London after their honeymoon in Stalin's Soviet Union, the Leffs found themselves a target for blackshirt abuse, with swastikas daubed on their front gate. By now, Vera was in the thick of anti-Fascist agitation. 'Events seemed to be telescoped and speeded up like one of the early films. We were living so intensely. . . . We felt only that time was not on our side.'[32] In these last frenetic years of peace, Leff wondered what in particular she could do. She had been told to join a trade union, but there was no housewives' union. Then someone, presumably another cell member, told her:

> 'You must join the Women's Co-operative Guild.'
> I felt my heart sink at that instruction. I was used to the exciting give and take of male-dominated political talk and action. . . .

Leff, unlike Chatterton, saw little point in women-only organizations, but:

> . . . on the next Wednesday afternoon . . . I walked through the doorway of the large Co-operative Hall in Seven Sisters Road, to join the Holloway Branch of the WCG. . . . I prudently took a seat at the back of the Hall. I saw in front of me rows and rows of be-hatted women, many of them middle-aged and even older. . . .
> A pianist struck a chord on a tinny piano and seventy female voices joined together on a shrill, high-pitched note. To my dismay, I was overcome with uncontrollable giggles. . . .
> Someone pushed a small, paper-covered book into my hand. A finger pointed to Hymn Twenty-Seven. I read the words I had not been listening to:
>
>> 'When wilt thou save the people,
>> . . . Not thrones and crowns, but men!'

The people, yes, the people. And that was why I was here. Tears came into my eyes. . . . We communists were not the only ones who cared. . . . These women, even with their hats, were my sisters. I opened my mouth. It was the first hymn I had ever sung in my life.[33]

Leff became one of the Guild's many new members; although Barton's 'Black Circular' officially circumscribed her actions, she recalls arguments about Spain and about peace. A child at the time of the Great War, she found it virtually impossible to understand the pacifism of older Guildswomen, so fearful that 'If we get drawn into the war in Spain, we will soon be at war with Germany and Italy.' Leff happily wore her white peace poppy on Remembrance Day, but in fact most of her time was filled with increasingly frenzied 'Popular Front' activity.[34] For Leff, first and foremost a socialist and internationalist, seeing so many Jewish refugees desperately trying to flee Nazism made the Guild's pacifism no longer tenable.

The choices, and the speed at which they had to be made, had become impossibly bewildering. Like the Guild and other pacifist groups, WILPF, which *over*estimated the danger to civilians from bombing, still *under*estimated the evils of Fascism. In summer 1937, Japanese troops invaded north China and bombed undefended Chinese cities. The League of Nations weakly offered China 'moral' support. WILPF also responded inadequately: it was undecided about a boycott of Japanese goods, leaving it to 'individual conscience'. And it still could not come to terms with Spain, wanting 'genuine non-intervention' but 'recognizing that non-intervention has lamentably failed in practice'.

Its pioneer generation was passing away: a new 'In Memoriam' section of its annual reports recorded the deaths of Margaret Ashton, Chrystal Macmillan, Esther Roper and Florence Lockwood.[35] By 1938 a weakened women's peace movement had long been split and demoralized. Connections between feminism and antimilitarism were no longer obvious. For Nazism and Fascism offered an unparalleled threat to equal-rights feminism – and even to general women's organizations: shortly after Hitler occupied Austria, its National Council of Women was banned. So, if feminism meant anti-

Fascism, did it now perhaps also mean war? The peace movement had lost all coherence. Particularly despairing of the destruction of all her earlier hopes was elderly Helena Swanwick. Still opposed to the use of sanctions, she increasingly feared the aerial bombing of non-combatant women and children. 'Yet how little women do repudiate war!' she lamented. 'Women . . . still have remains of the primitive instinct to idealize the hero in battle.'[36] Yet into such unpropitious times sprang a great feminist anti-militarist classic, still undimmed in its appeal, unrivalled except perhaps by Schreiner's *Woman and Labour*: Virginia Woolf's *Three Guineas*, published in June 1938.

Woolf, born in 1882, had long been a feminist. While her brother went to Cambridge, a protective Victorian girlhood had denied her access to higher education. Later, friendship with Llewelyn Davies brought her into close contact with the Guild. Woolf knew that however much she admired their courage, she had little in common with the hard-pressed Guildswomen, 'because one's body had never stood at the wash-tub; one's hands had never wrung and scrubbed and chopped'.[37] Yet even as an established writer, Woolf still felt that she – denied access to education, salary and professions – remained, like the Guildswomen, an outsider. Her resentment was rekindled when, in 1935, she learnt that she could not sit on the London Library Committee because she was a woman.

Woolf's feminism might seem out of step with the late 1930s. So did her pacifism. ('We were all co's in the Great war', she wrote.[38]) For the younger generation of intellectuals – like her nephew Julian Bell – adopted a more urgent anti-Fascism. He went to fight against Franco and was killed in July 1937. Woolf was already writing *Three Guineas*, but increasingly the book became an argument with her nephew.

Her feminism and her anti-militarism came together in *Three Guineas*. It presents an eloquent and impish attack on patriarchal structures and on the reluctance of middle-class men to share their privileges with their sisters.

The book takes the form of a letter to a man who has written to Woolf asking how 'are we to prevent war?' Woolf, identifying with other middle-class women, protests that 'we' are without power. Education, property, professional salaries, patronage – all these distinguished such daughters from their brothers. Look, says Woolf, at the absurd ceremonial clothes men put on when conferring power and status on each other – curly wigs, jewelled crucifixes, cocked hats, glittering medals. And, significantly, 'your finest clothes are those you wear as soldiers'.

For men's power under patriarchy is dovetailed with militarism. How are these structures to be challenged? 'The most effective way', Woolf suggests, 'in which we can help you through education to prevent war is to subscribe as generously as possible to the colleges for the daughters of educated men.' Otherwise marriage is the only profession open, and women would still welcome war as a thrilling escape from such suffocation. So Woolf subscribes a guinea to rebuild a college – to help prevent war. And she subscribes her second guinea to help women find employment in the professions.

The third section of *Three Guineas* focuses on the letter-writer's request for Woolf to help prevent war by supporting a society 'to protect culture and intellectual liberty'. But why *should* women want to contribute anything, Woolf protests, when they remain outsiders? Reality ('so kind to you, so harsh to us') is not like that. Women cannot join the *same* society as men.[39] They must form their own Outsiders' Society. And in her much-quoted passage, Woolf explains:

Their first duty . . . would be not to fight with arms. . . . They would refuse in the event of war to make munitions or nurse the wounded. . . . The next duty . . . is, briefly, not to incite their brothers to fight, or to dissuade them, but to maintain an attitude of complete indifference. . . . The outsider will make it her duty to base her indifference . . . upon reason. When he says, . . . 'I am fighting to protect our country' and thus seeks to rouse her patriotic emotion, she will ask herself, 'What does "our country" mean to me, an outsider?' . . . The outsider will find . . . that she has no good reason to ask her brother to fight on her behalf to protect 'our' country. '"Our country"', she will say, '. . . has treated me as a slave; it has denied me education or any share in its possessions. . . . Therefore, if you insist upon fighting to protect me, or "our" country, let it be understood, soberly and rationally between us, that you are fighting to gratify a sex instinct which I cannot share; to procure benefits which I have not shared and probably will not share; but not to gratify my instincts, or to protect either myself or my country. For,' the outsider will say, 'in fact, as a woman, I have no country. As a woman I want no country. As a woman my country is the whole world.'[40]

From cataloguing women's lack of equal rights, Woolf finally stresses – even exaggerates – gender difference, and so argues for a form of separatism. But was she *really* saying, as late as 1938, that whatever tyrannies Fascism imposed upon Jews (including her own husband), the outsider should resist war?

It seemed so. According to one biographer, Quentin Bell, 'a great many women' were enthusiastic about *Three Guineas*, but 'the book was pretty severely attacked' because the connections between women's rights and anti-fascism were 'tenuous'.[41] Certainly it was an oddly timed book, less connected with late-1930s crises than with echoes back to J. S. Mill and the suffrage era. Its attacks on male militarism are more akin to the pre-war writings of Gilman or Schreiner than to the Hitler years. Yet it also has a contemporary 1980s ring to it. Anachronistic? Yes. But *Three Guineas* offers an important bridge between the earlier feminist flowering and the later 1980s wave of a women's peace movement.

Woolf seemed unaware of either women's peace movement history or current struggles. A couple of months after *Three Guineas* was published, Hitler moved again. Under the infamous Munich pact, Czechoslovakia was virtually dismembered. The final twelve months of peace were frantic, a desperate clutching at short-term solutions. Pacifism appeared a morally comforting option. On Armistice Day 1938, the sale of white poppies reached a record 85,000. The Guild remained so strongly pacifist that it even decided not to be officially represented in Air Raid Precaution (ARP) discussions.[42] The following year conscription was announced. The Guild still ferociously opposed it – but, unlike Woolf, with a maternalist logic. One Guildswoman wrote to Chamberlain:

> Please be notified that I have not nurtured a son for twenty years ... for you, or any other Government, to claim him. ... Since I am responsible for his being, I mean to see to it that he shall have the life which I thrust upon him and not the living death which you seek to offer him, nay to demand of him. So if you choose to collect him, you will first have to collect me. ...[43]

WILPF similarly opposed conscription and left ARP work to 'individual conscience'. It despaired at news from its beleaguered continental sections. Like many other organizations it threw itself into relief work, helping members of the Czech section and their children flee to Britain.[44] Then, on 2 September 1939, Chamberlain declared war on Germany.

The war was now recognized as just by all but a tiny minority of pacifists. Maude Royden, for instance, who had recently joined the PPU, now resigned, confessing: 'I ought not to have joined'.[45] The war was certainly a devastating blow to those who had believed *nothing* was worse than war. Helena Swanwick, aged seventy-five, died in November from heart disease, apparently accelerated by a deliberate overdose of sleeping tablets. Woolf rationally discussed suicide with her husband as the Germans neared Paris; in March 1941 she drowned herself in the River Ouse.

Guildswomen were also stunned by the outbreak of war: Chatterton remembers the deep distress of the Clayton members. But their sons would now be called up, so they agreed to help with knitting and providing comforts for the soldiers. WILPF, still promoting peace by negotiation, lost yet more members and branches.[46]

However, some of their fears about the aerial bombing of civilians were shown to be correct. Although Britain did not suffer badly, the bombing of German towns like Dresden killed in all over 500,000 German civilians. In the Far East, America dropped atomic bombs on Hiroshima and Nagasaki in August 1945. Earlier predictions about blurring the distinction between non-combatants and the armed services – and where 'the brunt of war' fell most heavily – were now becoming increasingly appropriate to the post-war atomic age.

9

Hiroshima to Aldermaston
(1954–64)

The 1950s are just one generation away. Post-war peace debates continue, for passions still run high – and I have written this chapter conscious of those controversies. The major conflict stemmed from the Cold War. From mid 1941 the Soviet Union had fought alongside Britain and the Allies: it numbered twenty million dead in *its* fight against Hitler. But those staggering sacrifices seemed to count for nothing in the post-war chill. Hopes for a new peaceful democratic Europe shared by those fighting Hitler – in the army, in the Resistance, as partisans – crumbled. Western governments grew paranoid lest the Soviet Union, their wartime ally, might acquire the new secret knowledge which had exploded so fatefully at Hiroshima and Nagasaki. In 1947 a British Labour government secretly decided to develop its own atomic bombs. The Soviet Union had not yet test-exploded *its* first atomic bomb, and the West continued to guard its murderous secrets fiercely.

A particularly tragic victim of these Cold War divisions was any attempt in the West to form a peace movement opposed to atomic weapons and their testing. Such attempts were instantly branded as a Communist front – as they often were. In 1950 a newly formed World Peace Council, instigated by the Soviet government, tried to hold its Peace Congress in Sheffield; but Attlee's Labour government refused to grant visas to the East Europeans, and so at the last minute the congress had to move to Warsaw. Dora Russell was among those who despaired at such virulent anti-Communism; the peace movement, she lamented, 'was driven towards the East. The efforts of its peacemakers were smeared and derided. . . . Peace became . . . a dirty word.'[1] Local Peace Councils found their meetings shunned and their 'Ban the Atom Bomb' leaflets derided.[2] Russell and others like her refused to be deterred; perhaps naively, she became involved with the Women's International Democratic Federation (WIDF), centred in East Berlin and associated with the World Peace Council.[3]

The second debate concerned feminism – and current reappraisals of whether there was a 'women's movement' in the 1950s. Around 1970, a new generation of young feminists, understandably impatient for women's liberation to happen *fast*, wanted urgently to forge a revolutionary break with the past. Growing up in the 1950s, recalled Sheila Rowbotham in 1973, meant we 'inherited a political feminist hiatus. . . . My recognition of women as a group was as creatures sunk into the very deadening circumstances from which I was determined to escape. Most older women seemed like this to me.'[4]

Since then there has been time to reassess whether feminism in the 1950s *had* degenerated so completely: the title of a book of feminist conversations published in 1983, even claimed: *There's Always Been A Women's Movement This Century*. The editor, Dale Spender, marvelled on 'the sheer absurdity of the fact that we of the post-sixties women's movement had *ignored*' older women's experience: 'we had contributed to their invisibility . . .'[5]

But it is misleading to suggest a timeless, unchanging constancy to feminism. The 1950s and 1960s were more complex, with tensions between equal-rights feminism and a maternalist feminism that asserted women's needs, yet within the separate domestic sphere. For much of the post-war debate about women concerned their work as housewives and mothers. After wartime disruptions, a focus on the family was part of a longing for peace and stability. Nurseries closed; the notion of 'the housewife's home is her factory' encouraged women to think of 'home-making as a career'. But women were still faced with a rigid alternative: *either* a wife and mother, *or* a single career woman. 'Experts' like Bowlby encouraged child-centred childcare – and that meant full-time mothers. Mothers who worked were prey to terrible guilt feelings. While there were campaigns around equal pay, these could, with a rather narrow maternalist feminism commanding the progressive high ground, contemptuously be dubbed 'old-fashioned'. Elizabeth Wilson summarized how women:

> were not passive. They *organized*. . . . They were everywhere – and yet they were nowhere. . . . Feminism did not die in the years after the war. There continued to be women's organizations that made feminist demands, even if there was no movement to combat the general oppression of women. . . . What made their struggles difficult and lonely was that this oppression was invisible and was silenced. Feminism led an underground . . . existence.[6]

Certainly, this complex, half-buried image of feminism best illuminates a women's peace movement in the 1950s. The emphasis on gender difference and on women's special nurturing attributes stressed their peace-loving qualities. Yet the older internationalist women's groups found it hard to recover after the war's devastating blow to their pacifism: Guild membership was now on a downward spiral.[7] It was also difficult for WILPF to recapture its earlier certainties, before Nazism crushed its spirit. The first generation of pioneers was dying – Rosika Schwimmer in 1948, Maude Royden in 1956, Catherine Marshall in 1961. Yet new times demanded new campaigns. WILPF, in the face of the chilling hatreds of the Cold War, tried to remain even-handed and scrupulously honest. It opposed the setting up of the North Atlantic Treaty Organization (NATO) in 1949, protesting to the Foreign Secretary, Ernest Bevin; it also remained wary of pro-Soviet organizations like WIDF. But the Cold War left little room for openness and fairness.[8]

Dora Russell was among the few who refused to give up. While she believed in equal rights, 'for me the struggle of the women's movement for peace was first on the agenda'.

She included issues raised by Hiroshima in the Six Point Group manifesto; but the more conventional equal-rights feminists were unhappy: 'members began to resign' – and so peace had to be dropped.[9] Generally, women's peace groups – small, struggling, and usually overmodest – regained little of their pre-1933 vitality and broad support. But it would be wrong to think that *nothing* happened. Links between the first and second waves of the women's peace movement – shaped by the Olive Leaf women and by WILPF – and the third wave – dominated by Greenham – were weak – but never completely fragmented.

So this chapter describes three phases of women's peace activity: 1954–57, when the Guild roused public alarm to the horrors of atomic (and later, hydrogen) bomb testing; the great days of CND from 1958, and CND Women's Group; finally, the new women's peace groups sparked off around 1961 by very real fears about weapon testing.

None of these was a 'mass movement'; the problem of being half-buried remained. One of the unique features of the first great burst of CND energy (1958–64) is that the popular impact of feminism and the peace–gender debate was extremely limited, in contrast to the new youth and student culture. Yet, ironically, the women's peace groups, particularly those predating CND, played an important historical role in successfully offering a *legitimate* space for campaigning, despite the Cold War. Hiroshima and Nagasaki had dramatically dissolved the traditional dividing line between civilians and combatants. Women and children now became arguably *more* vulnerable: atomic radiation affected children's milk and even possibly damaged unborn babies. The atomic warfare threat seeping into the home brought fear of radiation directly to the mother-as-homemaker. This understandably fuelled women's anxious peace activity. That this occurred only slowly, falteringly and on a small scale was partly due to Cold War suspicions; partly to the lack of unity and confidence of women's groups; but also to the secrecy still cloaking Hiroshima. Radiation and atomic warfare's genocidal effects must at all costs be kept from mothers.

For many, anxiety about the distant bombings in Japan in 1945 was pushed aside by the enormous sense of relief that the World War was at last over. John Hersey's *Hiroshima*, published in 1946, offered a coolly factual account of the bombing which had killed at least 100,000 people.[10] But such investigative journalism was no match for the official secrecy machine. Labour politicians pushing for Britain's *own* weapons programme cocked a snook at democratic processes. The 1947 decision to develop atomic bombs had been shared neither with Parliament nor even with the Cabinet, but taken furtively by a caucus of six ministers. If MPs and the Cabinet felt uninvolved in decision-making, it is small wonder that there was scant debate beyond Westminster.[11] Indeed, for the first ten years after the war, peace protest focused on specific issues – the rearmament of West Germany and the Korean War – rather than on the bomb.

Despite all this secrecy, the unsalubrious atmosphere of spy scandals and President Eisenhower's bland 'Atoms for Peace' propaganda, there was small-scale protest against atomic weapons. In Britain it arose from three very distinct peace traditions, each unfortunately still speaking a different language. The first, and oldest, was Quaker-led pacifism, still centred on the Peace Pledge Union (PPU) and *Peace News*. But post-war revelations of Nazi extermination camps had put pacifism on the moral defensive: in the early 1950s it had shrunk to a small sect. However, in the wake of Indian Independence, pacifism was re-energized by Gandhian ideas. In 1952 a tiny 'Operation Gandhi' group sat down outside the War Office in Whitehall; thirteen were arrested. Later there was a small demonstration at Aldermaston in Berkshire. Here an Atomic Energy Research Establishment factory, linked to the manufacture of bombs, was being built. The group soon changed its name to the Non-violent Resistance Group; but its fundamentalist pacifism isolated it from popular support, and by 1956 it had almost fizzled out.[12]

The second peace tradition lay with left dissidents within the Labour Party. Since Attlee's government was the original arch-demon of atomic plotting, it demanded considerable courage from Party members to challenge Labour's guilt. But there were always a few fiery rebels – like Aneurin Bevan. In 1951 Churchill's Conservatives won the election, and the brave 'Bevanites' grew into a left opposition *within* the Opposition. In 1952, when Labour agreed to support Churchill's defence plans, the fifty-seven MPs who voted against were threatened with expulsion. Then, in spring 1954, after America had tested a hydrogen bomb at Bikini in the Pacific, a hundred MPs urged a halt to H-bomb tests; delegates from churches, labour and peace organizations met six Labour MPs to form a Hydrogen Bomb National Campaign. But by the end of the year, it too had fizzled out.[13]

The third peace tradition lay, of course, with the World Peace Council and its British Peace Committee, highly critical of Labour's foreign policy. Vicious Cold War suspicions meant that Labour Party members risked expulsion if they became involved in such proscribed organizations; yet some brave socialists felt so strongly about peace that they willingly took this risk.[14]

Alongside these three distinct traditions, particular specialist groups – scientists, doctors, intellectuals – also tried to raise the alarm. Quaker atomic scientist Professor Dame Kathleen Lonsdale wrote on 'The Hydrogen Bomb and International Control' for WILPF. Dr Sheila Jones, who took over from her as secretary of the Atomic Scientists' Association, spread information about the genetic effects of radiation. But it was hard going.[15] On 23 December 1954 Bertrand Russell warned against the H-bomb in his influential 'Man's Peril' radio broadcast; and he worked to bring together eminent scientists to oppose the bomb. But there were still no real signs of how a popular broad-based disarmament movement could spring up.

This, then, was the political log-jam early in 1955. The beginnings of moves to unjam it came from a seemingly unlikely quarter: north London Guildswomen. By now the Guild, with its decaying membership, was not short of critics from both right and left. Certainly, CND's first historian was among those who readily wrote it off. In *The Disarmers*, published in 1964, Christopher Driver wrote his much-quoted passage on CND's origins:

> In March 1955 a Socialist doctor's wife in Golders Green, Mrs Vera Leff, mentioned to her local Women's Co-operative Guild the problem of the radiation risk from H-bomb tests. Women's Co-operative Guilds being what they are, it is probable little would have happened but for another of the Guild's members, a retired civil servant called Gertrude Fishwick. . . . If any single person can be said to have triggered off the chain reaction which ended in CND it is Miss Fishwick. . . .[16]

This version was, until recently, the account that prevailed. However, recent research suggests the crucial role played by the Guild.[17]

Of course, many currents – pacifist and Labour, Communist and intellectual – fed in to create CND. Here it is suggested that in the vital years 1955–56, the Guild offered something rare: a legitimate political space in which the very first post-war stirrings of a mass peace movement could begin to be heard. Crucially, its language was not only against atomic militarism, but also audibly maternalist. In a history of feminism and anti-militarism it is therefore important to listen to these pre-CND developments. Readers can then judge for themselves whether – perhaps cynically – Guildswomen were being manipulated by outside groupings; or – more straightforwardly – they initiated and ran their *own* campaign, which took off so dramatically in 1958 with the birth of CND.

The small-scale world of the Golders Green Guildswomen in the mid 1950s can be reconstructed from a variety of sources: newspaper reports, oral testimony, Vera Leff's unpublished autobiography and – invaluably – the branch minute books, which survive.[18]

Richenda Barbour retains memories of the weekly meetings – held on Wednesday afternoons, for all members were outside the world of paid work. Many, like Barbour, were at home looking after children. Some were middle-class, yet were denied their husbands' access to higher education and an independent income. Other members were working-class, steeped in trade-union and labour politics; retired teachers made up a third, smaller group. Barbour came to the Guild through a Workers' Education Association (WEA) evening class, a welcome break from childcare. There, someone asked: 'Now, who's going to be class secretary?' There was a hush, and Barbour found that she had volunteered: 'And then I found that if you were the class secretary, you had to report the class to the committee of the WEA branch.' The branch secretary was Marion Clayton, also secretary of the local Guild branch; it seems to have been through her that Barbour was invited to the Guild – though with young children in tow, she could not attend regularly. But the branch chair, a working-class woman called Agnes Simpson, 'was so good at bringing me *Woman's Outlook*', the Co-operative magazine, that Barbour, touched by their warmth and friendliness, kept in touch.[19]

The Golders Green Guildswomen *were* friends: summer outings were arranged, sick members were visited. Discussion at meetings covered literature and politics; and, despite differences stirred up by the Cold War, there was no obvious political bickering. Yet this particular branch, with its many 'friendship' links with Eastern Europe and to the new National Assembly of Women, was as pro-Soviet as possible within the Guild rules. Some members, like Barbour, belonged to no political party; others to the Labour Party; and a few – including Leff and Clayton – to the Communist Party.

Branch meetings during winter 1954–55 focused on opposition to German rearmament and proposals for revising the Guild's restrictive rules.[20] Then, on 26 January 1955, members learnt of a London Co-operative Education Department conference on 'The Hydrogen Bomb and You', to be held in Central Hall on 26 February. (This was probably sparked off by America's H-bomb test at Bikini, which had already killed a Japanese fisherman; the Hydrogen Bomb National Campaign; protest by some Labour authorities against civil defence; and, of course, Russell's Christmas broadcast.) The branch duly ordered a dozen tickets.[21]

Then in mid February, the government's Defence White Paper (craftily shielded behind news about nuclear power) announced that Britain would manufacture her own H-bomb; and the Labour Party began to grapple with this.[22] On 22 February the Golders Green Guild committee – Leff, Clayton, Simpson, and three others – met to discuss the branch's spring programme. They planned a joint meeting on 28 March on German Rearmament and the H-Bomb; and on 6 April a visit of 'Japanese Women'.[23]

The H-bomb issue was debated in the Commons on 2 March: Bevan and sixty-three other MPs abstained from supporting Labour's official pro-bomb amendment. On 3 March Leff reported back to the Guild branch about the Central Hall H-bomb conference, attended by about a thousand 'delegates'; the minute book records that she was particularly active on this issue.[24]

However, in her autobiography (1978), Leff gives a slightly different version: her husband Sam, now a local Medical Officer of Health, brought home some papers 'about the genetic effects of radiation. "Even unborn children can be affected," he said.' So next Wednesday afternoon:

> I told my friends about the technical paper on the genetic effects of radiation. It sounded coldly scientific and distant, but in our little meeting room, the effect was explosive.

'We should _do_ something,' said ... [one of the retired teachers].

'Doing something' for Guildswomen meant getting together, co-operating with others. We decided to call a local meeting on the subject, approaching all ... organizations in the area.[25]

This is what happened. On 25 March the first sign of a public campaign appeared in the local paper, the *Hampstead and Highgate Express* (known as the 'Ham and High'; its proprietor – Arthur Goss, a local Quaker – was active on peace but unsympathetic to what he saw as pro-Soviet initiatives.) Under the headline 'H U-Bomb Must Be Banned', Simpson was quoted: 'First it was the A-bomb, then the H-bomb, and now this hydrogen-uranium bomb.'[26] Three days later, the joint meeting brought together a few local groups; afterwards two Quaker women stated how 'surprised and pleased' the trade unionists present had been to learn that the local Council of Churches was concerned – and vice versa.[27]

However, local opposition remained strong: one Labour MP derided pacifists and 'fellow-travellers'; and seventy-seven-year-old Dame Kathleen Courtney declared at a local United Nations meeting: 'I would rather die at the hands of the H-bomb than see my children brought up in a totalitarian state.'[28] Yet the small circle of concern *was* beginning to widen; for on 5 April no fewer than fifty-seven Guildswomen and friends assembled to listen to Kikue Ihara. Ten years earlier, she had been teaching in her primary school in Nagasaki – when the bomb dropped. Simpson chaired the meeting as Ihara spoke through her Japanese interpreter. The headlines in the local paper capture the moment:

'TERRIBLE BOMBS' MUST NOT BE DROPPED
NAGASAKI VICTIM WARNS BRITAIN

Holding up photographs of charred bodies of atom-bomb victims, a pretty Japanese schoolteacher from Nagasaki, Miss Kikue Ihara, made this appeal. ...

'Look at these wretched victims, good mothers of Britain, and then do all you can to help put an end to the making of atom and hydrogen bombs.'

. . . Miss Ihara said . . . 'I would never again like to see charred bodies lying in the streets or innocent children crying for their dead parents.'

Mothers all over the world should make sure there would never be another nuclear war.[29]

Richenda Barbour was in the audience. Even though she had already read Hersey's *Hiroshima* she could still recall, thirty years later, the impression Ihara made on her:

She talked about skin hanging off. . . . And then this hand, this shadow of a hand on the tile, which they actually brought. . . . We held – passed [it] round; and we held it. And you saw this . . . [print of a hand of somebody] who'd perished. . . . Well, you couldn't really believe it. But it was so strong. . . .[30]

Ihara's visit had tremendous impact: the Golders Green Guildswomen could talk about little else. Their meetings increasingly resembled a nuclear disarmament group; and a wider popular campaign began to take shape. The Quakers produced leaflets and on 17 May the local Council of Churches organized an H-bomb meeting, addressed by Methodist minister Donald Soper; although it was just before the 1955 general election, well over 120 attended.[31]

The following day Leff reported back to the Guild committee on the success of the Soper meeting. Up to now, the initiative had been shared among a small group – particularly Simpson, Clayton and Leff. Now, as the campaign expanded, Leff played a leading role. On 25 May she reported back again; and an open meeting was agreed for 13 June, with an autumn showing of the powerful film *The Children of Hiroshima*. On 6 June a special committee meeting 'was called at short notice to deal with an emergency situation in relation to further activity re H B[omb]'; at

Leff's house were Simpson in the chair, Clayton, Leff and a
fourth Guildswoman; the main item was planning, with
Quaker help, the 13 June meeting, with Leff giving a
'statement on past activity'. Other local Guilds, trade
unions, churches, Labour and Communist Parties would
be invited.[32] This plan worked. The local paper, under the
headline 'These Foul Things Must be Banned: Women's
plea to the PM', reported that at least eight groups had been
represented; Clayton stated that the aim was 'to stir up this
neighbourhood. . . . I think it is about time women did
something'; and a scientist warned that 'if bombs are
dropped many people will become sterile'.

This seems to be when Gertrude Fishwick first appeared:
she probably attended the 13 June meeting, for two days
later she came to the Guild, where Leff and Clayton
reported on its success. The Guild was obviously extremely
excited by the growing support, and this must have rubbed
off on Fishwick.[33] Leff's autobiography records:

> A tall, thin, rather melancholy looking woman stood up. I
> had not seen her at the Guild before. 'I'd be glad to help,'
> she said. 'I don't often come to the Guild but I'm very glad I
> came today.' So that was how I and Miss Fishwick ('G. F.
> Fishwick, you can call me Jeff!' she said shyly) got together
> in my kitchen and worked out a plan to persuade local
> people.[34]

As Driver suggested, Fishwick was a retired civil servant.
She was also a member of Finchley Labour Party and,
apparently, of the Anglican Pacifist Fellowship – and a
one-time suffragette. Leff remembers her as 'very frugal in
her life style, and deeply devoted to the cause of peace. . . . I
had confidence in her dedication':

> We turned out to be an unlikely but good team. I could find
> contacts in the local trade union groups and other organiz-
> ations, and she would go on her bicycle and visit the local
> churchmen and political groups. I would draw up the letters

or circulars and she would 'vet them' with Civil Service precision. She was often on the telephone to me before I was out of bed in the morning. 'I think that should be a semi-colon, not a full stop,' she would say. Sam would pull on his trousers, grumbling. 'Doesn't that woman ever give you peace?'[35]

So on 20 June, at a meeting called by the Guild and chaired by an Engineering trade unionist, the name 'Local Committee for the Abolition of the H-Bomb' won support. Leff reported this to the Guild, and on 24 June Simpson, as chair, sent out multiple copies of a historic circular letter. It summarized the H-bomb protest since New Year, noting that scientists warned that 'H-bomb experiments taking place *now* will cause the suffering and death . . . of children *not yet born*.'[36] Leff continued to report back to the Guild; but from now on the 'H-Bomb Committee' became autonomous of the small world of socialist Guildswomen. Certainly, by mid July 1955 the group was established with its own headed notepaper ('Joint Local Committee for the Abolition of H-Bomb and other Nuclear Weapons'), with Fishwick as 'Hon. Sec.', and plans to commemorate the tenth anniversary of Hiroshima.

'Jeff went off on her bicycle, a tired ageing woman with an unbeatable spirit,' Leff wrote later. 'We really were poor – in support, publicity, influence, funds of course. We had no idea how rich we were in potential success.' The two women approached Arthur Goss, who later recalled what hard workers they were. He was impressed by Leff's very genuine commitment (only long afterwards did he discover that she was a member of the Communist Party). Through his Quaker links, Goss became actively involved. By early August Fishwick was able to appeal through his 'Ham and High' on behalf of her committee, quoting the Russell broadcast and urging readers to help put pressure on the government.[37]

By autumn 1955, therefore, the Joint Local Committee for the Abolition of Nuclear Weapons was well established,

with Goss as chair. The Guild ran a poster parade on
1 October on Golders Green Road. And on the 3rd, 200
people crammed into the local Methodist Church Hall for
what the 'Ham and High' described as 'The Largest Ever
Public Meeting in The District To Discuss The Hydrogen
Bomb'. The walls were covered with slogans – 'Ban the
H-bomb' and 'Mothers, would you let your sons drop this
bomb?' – and a geneticist warned: 'If two people with
damaged cells marry, their children will probably be deformed physically and mentally. There will be numerous
miscarriages and still births.'[38]

So, if anyone 'triggered off the chain reaction which ended
in CND', it was three Golders Green Guildswomen: Agnes
Simpson, Marion Clayton and, particularly, Vera Leff.
The support of Fishwick and later of Goss was, of
course, vital – but came only after six months' determined
campaigning.

This small group grew into the National Council for the
Abolition of Nuclear Weapon Tests, and so into CND; but
that story is told in detail elsewhere.[39] Briefly, anti-bomb
campaigns now rippled outwards from Golders Green,
often triggered by a showing of *The Children of Hiroshima*.
First Hampstead: Dr Sheila Jones recalls that her local
Labour Party branch was invited to affiliate; already familiar with the genetic effects of weapon testing, she found
her imagination gripped and agreed to go. Before long,
she too was being constantly badgered by Fishwick. A
'Hampstead Joint Committee' was formed about Christmas
1955 as anxiety about Britain's own testing plans grew.[40]

During 1956, enthusiasm spread across north and west
London – to Willesden and Hornsey, Finchley and Crickle-
wood, Paddington and Muswell Hill.[41] Later that year,
Khrushchev's revelations about Stalin were followed by the
Soviet Union's crushing of the Hungarian uprising, and
Britain's own crisis over the Suez Canal. These events
jolted many people out of their Cold War mind-set, and

into reappraising Britain's ambitions to remain a nuclear superpower. Fishwick used the crisis to send out another sobering circular:

> We have been, and may still be, very near a war, in which the use of nuclear weapons has been forecast. . . . Even without a war, we are in increasing danger from the Tests. It seems that our Government is determined to conduct its own H-Bomb Tests in the New Year. . . .
>
> Apart from the noticeable increase of Strontium-90 in sheep feeding on high pastures (Wales, the Black Forest, etc.), already the bones of YOUNG CHILDREN IN BRITAIN show an increase in this cancer producing element.[42]

It certainly seems to have been the imminence of Britain's own H-bomb test plans that increased the movement's support. In November a conference on the tests was held and an *ad hoc* committee – including Fishwick, Goss and Jones – was formed. From this, the National Council for the Abolition of Nuclear Weapon Tests (NCANWT) was inaugurated in February 1957, with Goss as chair and Jones as secretary.[43]

NCANWT grew impressively during 1957, and began to look for prominent personalities to act as figureheads. The movement's modest origins in the Guild were increasingly forgotten; women and women's groups were increasingly marginalized as popular and respectable support grew.[44] Fishwick fell ill and ceased to play a key role; Leff also seemed to be edged out. Yet, as could be expected when tangible fears about weapon testing and Strontium 90 were growing, at least two-thirds of NCANWT's support still came from women. By mid 1957 it could boast seventy-five local groups. NCANWT remained strongest just north of the Thames, but had now spread to other cities and towns – Glasgow and Edinburgh, Cardiff and Swansea, Leeds and Sheffield, Birmingham and Nottingham. In the average local group, women activists apparently outnumbered men by two to one.[45]

There were immediate fears about the tests. A Quaker called Harold Steele had volunteered to travel out to Christmas Island in the Pacific, the site for the British H-bomb test explosion; and an Emergency Committee for Direct Action against Nuclear War was set up. Macmillan's government even began muttering about 'the more extreme elements of public opinion' being mobilized against 'the next nuclear weapons test'.[46]

At this highly appropriate moment, NCANWT launched its women's demonstration. Sheila Jones recalls that just a short, sharp campaign was thought necessary to persuade Britain to abandon the tests, as a means to stop proliferation; and that a women's march, rarely seen since suffragette days, would win publicity. 'In view of the especial danger to children likely to result from the continuation of H-Bomb tests . . .', the publicity leaflet called upon all women supporters to join. 'Even if you have never before taken part in such a demonstration. . . . Ask Your Friends to Come With You.' Inspired by South African women who had demonstrated in black sashes, they bought yards of black crepe and began sewing neatly. But Jones remembers increasingly anxious phone calls from mothers fearful about radioactivity and whether they should bring their babies. In the end, the sash-sewing became more like factory production, with women hastily cutting out strips and just pinning them together.[47]

The demonstration on 12 May 1957 – amid publicity about Steele's departure, and debate whether radiation from tests caused sterility in women[48] – was a great success. About 2,000 women braved drenching rain to march in silence through London, many wearing the black sashes, some in complete mourning, others carrying homemade banners: 'Stop The Tests' and 'Save Your Child'. The crowd in Trafalgar Square swelled to about 3,000. Speakers included Diana Collins, wife of the St Paul's Cathedral canon; Vera Brittain; Sheila Steele, whose husband was then nearing the explosion area; and Dr Edith Summerskill MP, who warned that the kind of downpour they were then enduring could carry radiation that could render women sterile. Three days later, the explosion in the Pacific was announced.[49]

On the high note of this women's march, NCANWT took on as secretary Peggy Duff, veteran Labour activist and chair of the newly formed St Pancras and Holborn Committee against Nuclear Weapons Tests. (The movement still operated from a room in Sheila Jones's house. Later it moved to a small office in central London, lent by the veteran National Peace Council.) Meanwhile, Bevan startled the Labour Party Conference with his 'naked into the conference chamber' speech, swinging delegates against Britain's giving up her H-bombs; J. B. Priestley wrote an influential disarmament article in the *New Statesman* in November; and the new Direct Action Committee welcomed back Harold Steele on his return, and began to plan a march to Aldermaston.[50]

As the need for an extraparliamentary campaign grew, the number of NCANWT groups rose to 112.[51] It planned an expanded campaign, but eventually agreed (though not without some understandable resentment at behind-the-scenes manipulations) to merge its organization into a new and bigger campaign initiated by Kingsley Martin, editor of the *Statesman*.[52] So, on 16 January 1958, the Campaign for Nuclear Disarmament (CND) was born.

Just as the birth of NCANWT had nudged the original Guildswomen aside, so, in the speed of events, CND now moved very far from its modest NCANWT origins. Indeed, Priestley was scathing about 'well-meaning nonentities'.[53] Russell became president, Canon Collins chair, and Peggy Duff secretary. The public launch in February attracted well over 6,000 people. At Easter the first Aldermaston march, organized by the Direct Action Committee, took place; and the following spring over 20,000 people packed into Trafalgar Square. By 1960 the crowd had swelled to over 60,000, and CND could boast no fewer than 459 local groups. (However, tensions over tactics soon grew between 'official' CND and the newly formed Committee of 100, which now became *the* direct-action group.)

Nobody was more involved in this Aldermaston era, or wrote about the new generation of marchers more affectionately afterwards, than Peggy Duff:

> They carried their banners – 'Twickenham CND', 'Harrow Society of Friends', 'Gorbals Young Socialists', or 'North London AEU'. . . . They did not require names. They were just the sort of people who marched, most of them young, wearing anoraks and sandals, a few with bare feet, a few with funny hats. . . . Yet it was . . . these people who marched, and planned the marches, who booked the halls for the meetings, flyposted the posters, gave out the leaflets, sold the pamphlets, wrote letters to the local press and every year organized the contingent to the Aldermaston Marches – these were the people who created a fever of opinion which for a time the orthodox political leaders could not stay. They were the ban-the-bombers.[54]

Were there any visible remaining links between this new generation of popular protest and the modest socialist maternalism of the Guild? Not many. Nor did equal-rights feminism seem to have much impact on the new peace politics of CND: one Aldermaston coach, Duff reported, 'was nicknamed "the brothel"', and certainly Duff herself had little sympathy with feminism.[55] So the inherited image of CND is predominantly one of angry young men. It was almost as if Woolf had never written *Three Guineas*. But if gender politics scarcely surfaced during the Aldermaston Marches, this first wave of CND *did* offer a valuable non-sectarian political space. Certainly women still made up a very high proportion – probably a majority – of activists.[56]

What is very unusual about this popular peace movement between 1958 and 1964, distinguishing it from campaigns described in previous chapters, is how marginal women-centred peace activities had become. The best-known example was Dora Russell's Women's Peace Caravan, in which about fifteen women travelled to Moscow in summer 1958. Russell did manage to win support from the national Guild, but this success was short-lived. When she returned, what she saw as the old, bitter suspicions remained: 'CND and the Left remained blindly parochial. . . . No one wanted to hear us.'[57]

Less well-known was the women's group *within* CND. While Russell's Caravan was travelling in Europe a 'Women Against the Bomb' conference was held in London, chaired by Jacquetta Hawkes, a co-opted member of the CND executive and wife of J. B. Priestley. She planned to stress 'the genetic dangers which are of such special concern to women, and to work up to a deliberate and controlled evocation of emotion' with readings, including letters written by a man dying of radiation sickness to his wife. But perhaps because of a feeling of control from the top down rather than something springing up spontaneously, such ideas never won broad support. The CND Women's Group characteristically compèred 'events', rather than responding to grass-roots demands; and in 1960 it apparently ceased to operate as a separate group.[58]

But in autumn 1961 this changed, and a third women's peace grouping was sparked off by fears about renewed weapon testing and increased international tension over Berlin. The Committee of 100 was then very active: mass sit-downs led to mass arrests, on several occasions outside the Embassy of the Soviet Union, which had resumed tests. Then on 5 November 'Pram-pushing mothers led four hundred ban the bomb marchers' to the Embassy to deliver a protest letter. This action, combined with the language of the letter to Khrushchev, suggests something more urgent and assertive than the CND Women's Group – something reminiscent of the earlier 'sisterhood is international' spirit:

Up to now women have not had much say in politics; but . . . we can't just go on cooking food for our families when we know it is being contaminated with radioactive poisons. We know that women all over the world, especially those who have or hope to have children, feel as we do. . . . Your censors and frontier guards may have been able so far to prevent women in your country from knowing what is going on. . . . We shall find a way to communicate with them and they will join with us in taking action to end the present intolerable situation.[59]

Particularly affected by the Berlin crisis was Judith Cook from rural Cornwall – thirty-four years old, a Quaker attender and mother of three young children. Later, she recalled how one night:

. . . we watched a programme that showed the Russian and American tanks facing each other in Berlin, and the commentator interviewed an American colonel who reckoned they'd be using nuclear weapons by next Tuesday. I was horrified. I sat down and wrote a letter to the *Guardian* – from the viewpoint of an anxious mother . . . express my fears and feeling of powerlessness.

She got a tremendous response – 120 people wrote asking what was to be done:

I'd just been reading about American women's strike for peace [WISP] so I wrote another letter and suggested we formed a women's peace movement to see if there wasn't something, however small, we could do to prevent a nuclear war. The second day the postman staggered up on horseback with 89 letters, then there were a hundred, and so on.[60]

Cook received a thousand letters in four days. 'Voice of Women' (named after a similar group in Canada) was born. Most members were mothers with young children, though many were older: even one or two in their nineties of the suffrage generation.[61] Cook threw herself into organizing, and on 7 March 1962 Voice of Women held meetings in

London, Manchester and Liverpool to 'observe a national day of peace'. The background to this was Committee of 100 activity at a base at Wethersfield, prompting a major Official Secrets trial at the Old Bailey. Cook explicitly distanced herself from such tactics, from any suggestion of being anti-men, and asserted Voice of Women's respectable, maternalist 'ordinariness': 'You don't have to believe in CND to be one of us, but I think we're all against any more tests. . . .'[62] The daring of 'Greenham women' was still a million miles away.

One outcome was the revival of the CND Women's Group at New Year and activity around the Day for Peace: a mime on the steps of St Paul's Cathedral, and later a deputation to see the Prime Minister.[63] As a result of this bubbling up of activity, another new umbrella group was formed: a Liaison Committee for Women's Peace Groups. It aimed to co-ordinate both the old-established organizations – WILPF, the Guild, the National Assembly of Women – and the newer groups: CND women, Voice of Women groups, an East Anglian Federation of Women for Peace, 'Women for Peace' in Birmingham, 'Women against War' in London and Manchester.[64] This small-scale Liaison Committee began a monthly newsletter, *Call to Women*, which did have some echoes of *Three Guineas*:

Education, the Law, the Health Services, Defence and Foreign Policy are all firmly controlled by men. . . . It is inconceivable that women could spend as much on two Polaris submarines as is spent in one year on all our universities, as is now the case. . . .

Does it matter if women drift on in the same old way? Yes, if they want their children to live. Men are brought up from early childhood to admire those who fight to destroy enemies. Once, this may have. been necessary, but in the nuclear age it is primitive madness to solve problems by violence – even before Hiroshima one air raid on Dresden killed 130,000 people.[65]

By now, however, the Committee of 100 was in decline.[66] The 1962 Cuban crisis revealed that the nuclear superpowers could, on this occasion anyway, control their own lethal weaponry; and the 1963 Partial Test Ban Treaty outlawed the atmospheric testing that had prompted so many fears. By 1964–65 activists felt exhausted and Aldermaston Marches seemed almost passé. Britain's cringing support for American bombing and napalming in Vietnam felt far more urgent than the timeless question of 'the bomb'. From then on, CND's decline was unstoppable.

As CND shrank away, the few dedicated peace women in and around the Liaison Committee refused to give up: Richenda Barbour, now an active Guildswoman, was its Guild representative:

> By being in the Liaison Committee, I was able to think that perhaps the immediate Strontium 90 in the atmosphere was over, and that now we had to see about getting rid of war, the idea of war. . . . I think they had a feeling, 'Well, *that*'s looked after, and now we'll get on with . . . Vietnam.'[67]

But this small-scale women's peace movement, while more unified and energized than ten years before, grew increasingly out of step with anti-Vietnam militancy and the alternative culture of the 1968 student generation.

Guildswomen had been crucial to providing the space that allowed the political log-jam to be broken in the mid 1950s; subsequently women provided an extremely substantial proportion (at times, apparently, a two-thirds majority) of NCANWT and CND support; yet their active role seems subsequently to have become marginalized. Frank Parkin's study of CND supporters, *Middle Class Radicalism* (1968), looks in detail at class, jobs and education – but omits gender. Women emerge in a comically shadowy way, their paid work invisible. ('Because so many of the female respondents classified themselves as housewives or part-time workers it was decided not to include them.') Their lack of access to higher education, training and an independent income goes unrecorded. Indeed, the only place women crop up in as mothers of young activists – where, of course, they emerge as considerably more sympathetic to CND than fathers. This, Parkin suggests, 'is perhaps somewhat surprising'.[68] Not surprising – and no 'perhaps' about it – is that such gender-blind studies should help to fuel a new, vigorous women's liberation movement in the 1970s.

Part III

LIBERATION AND PEACE CAMPS
(1970–88)

10

Feminism, Eco-feminism,
Nuclear Power and Cruise
(1975–80)

Peggy Duff, who finally left CND in 1967, published her
autobiography *Left, Left, Left* four years later, and dedicated it to '. . . the Aldermaston Marchers, whom I loved –
I wonder where they've gone?' It was clear that they too
had abandoned CND (whose membership slumped almost
as low as 2,000 in the early 1970s). Those still on the move
were marching to a less peaceful tune. A survey conducted in
1978 of over four hundred people who had been CND and
Committee of 100 activists nearly twenty years earlier
showed that many had become caught up in anti-Vietnam
protests, in Trotskyist socialism, or in single-issue campaigns around the environment, Ireland, squatting and
community politics. And significantly, a sizeable number
had become active in the Women's Liberation Movement.[1]

Diana Shelley, born in 1943, was one. She joined the
second Aldermaston March in 1959, then became caught
up in the Committee of 100 mass sit-downs; in October
1961 she was arrested near the Russian Embassy and fined.
By 1962 Shelley had discovered anarchism, and eventually
she was admitted to the London Committee of 100. Then in
1967 she became involved in the occupation of the Greek
Embassy following the military coup in Greece. On trial at
the Old Bailey, Shelley was found guilty – this cost her her
secretarial job. Understandably, she retired from politics
for a while.[2] 1968 passed her by; but a year or two later an
old Committee of 100 comrade, back from the States, said:

'Oh, you know, there are a lot of women getting together in
groups in America and talking about what it's like to be a
woman.' . . . And he said, 'And how come you always did
the cooking when you lived with [Chris]?' I just thought,

'Good heavens, yes. How come did I always do the cooking when I lived with [Chris]?' That was – that was a turning point.[3]

The powerful re-emergence of a women's movement in Britain in the early 1970s changed everything. Feminism would never be the same again. It affected not only women in their late twenties like Diana Shelley, who had already cut their political teeth in CND, but also a new generation of slightly younger women born in the post-war baby boom and able at last to take advantage of easier access to higher education and jobs.

For these feminists, whose lives soon assumed a very different shape from their mothers', there were suddenly new methods of working: small women-only consciousness-raising groups, in stark contrast to the formal structures of the political parties, now fiercely criticized for relegating women to the bottom of every political agenda. And there were new demands which, while we now know they were not completely new, were suddenly being expressed with a highly effective urgency. There was an energetic resurgence of equal-rights feminism, particularly among women in waged work. The Women's Liberation Movement also formulated demands for equal educational and job opportunities, and for equal pay. And why *should* women have to make a choice between rewarding paid work and motherhood? So women demanded practical changes – access to free contraception, abortion, and adequate childcare provision. And they took to the streets in support of their demands: for instance, in 1979 about 80,000 marched on a trade-union demonstration against Corrie's restrictive anti-abortion Bill.[4]

Yet one of the effects of the eruptions of 1968 and of the Women's Liberation Movement (WLM) was that much of what had gone immediately before seemed to get forgotten. CND was now seen as irrelevant. Peace and nonviolence became old-fashioned words. The Committee of 100 sit-down tactics were derided as 'a near-obsessional form of self-restraint'.[5] No one predicted the peace campaign's rebirth in 1980, and few wanted to remember their links to a movement that had so completely fallen from vogue.

The dramatic events of the early 1970s seem particularly to have fractured continuity for those of us caught up in the WLM. So much happened, politically and personally, in the 1970s that Aldermaston was relegated to a daring moment of teenage rebellion, a chance to escape the discipline of school and family – to be laughed about later. For younger women, it was just an outing with parents, a childhood memory easily overlaid by later events.

This process of forgetting was codified by historians of the first wave of CND, Driver and Parkin, whose accounts, written before the eruption of women's liberation, leave out gender.[6] Then, when the WLM came to reflect upon its origins, women tended to record not CND and the Committee of 100, but feminism as a reaction to the chauvinism of the Marxist left or underground press. As a result, links between women's experiences of CND and the revival of feminism only six years later have been largely neglected.[7] Feminism sprang up again with scarcely any knowledge of its anti-militarist past. For instance, *Sweet Freedom*, an excellent guide to the WLM, referred neither to CND nor to peace.[8]

The 1970s were also a period of détente, when East and West seemed to have reached an accommodation, through agreements like SALT (Strategic Arms Limitation Talks). Women's liberation flourished – but the disarmament movement remained moribund. *Peace News*, which once could sell thousands of extra copies during an Aldermaston March, slipped back to a small-circulation paper, even at one time self-deprecatingly calling itself *P Snooze*. It did, however, broaden its remit to include community and sexual politics, becoming *the* paper to read for the minority who demanded radical but nonviolent change; and in 1971 'for non-violent revolution' was added to the masthead.[9]

Also small-scale was the Liaison Committee of Women's Peace Groups and its constituent organizations – like WILPF and Voice of Women. They struggled on, but found the new WLM generation extremely critical of their traditional maternalist peace campaigning. In the early 1970s, the Liaison Committee's *Call to Women* newsletter voiced its members' hurt about how, 'to add to the mother's growing sense of inadequacy, she is being made to feel by the more "liberated" of her own kind that she ought to be out in the streets fighting for her rights.'[10]

A few younger women did join such peace groups. One was Margot Miller, born in 1939, who left school to work as a secretary but grew frustrated with office jobs and became a mature student. Miller, with her mother and sister, joined Voice of Women, which happened to have a local branch in their village, Claygate: just a dozen women, all friends and local Labour Party members. Such peace groups were now limited to modest actions – local vigils, a Voice of Women annual meeting. This low-key activity sucked Miller into its close-knit world; she was invited to join a visit to the Soviet Women's Committee in 1968–69, and when she returned someone suggested she should join WILPF, and she did.[11]

WILPF's membership was dwindling, but its antennae remained alert. Miller was impressed by members' grasp of nuclear power and radiation dangers. She became as involved as her two young children allowed, and began co-editing *Call to Women*, reporting, among other things, on 'women's lib'. As a new recruit, Miller developed enormous respect for the older rebels who kept going. 'To *survive* like that, very often alone in your own community, you've got to be strong. . . . These women . . . are the women who kept the flame alive.'[12]

It was not easy. Their lobbying seldom hit the headlines. One rare occasion was during 1975, International Women's Year, and a 'Letters-to-Downing-Street Campaign'. Liaison Committee women delivered letters to Number Ten asking for practical steps towards nuclear disarmament. 'If the Liaison Committee', the *Guardian* commented sympathetically:

> could get a million people to demonstrate then publicity would be guaranteed. But how do you rouse a million people. . . ? That is their dilemma. Abortion, homosexuality . . . are now openly discussed. . . . Campaigning for peace remains unmentionable and a cause of embarrassment.[13]

The following year an international disarmament forum, sponsored by the United Nations, WILPF and other peace organizations, drew attention to the stark fact that the nuclear madness had *not* disappeared – even though the Aldermaston Marchers had. Jill Tweedie, again in the *Guardian*, wrote a prophetic jokey-but-serious ('Oops, I've dropped a stitch – oops, they've dropped a bomb') article, 'Exploding Myths':

> Take the Campaign for Nuclear Disarmament. . . . I must admit now, about the Bomb at least, that as things became more complex I rather lost track . . . so I stopped reading. . . . [Women's] work is raising babies, their eventual megadeaths we leave to the boys. . . .
>
> But recently . . . I read the papers with a new eye. Good heavens, those men aren't rattling rifles any more, they're rattling plutonium. . . . I felt it was high time I put my knitting down and went and saw someone. What the hell, I said to the room, ever happened to CND?
>
> . . . Down at the CND HQ in Bethnal Green . . . three men sit in a room. There used to be 18 of us in the old days, they say, like aged retainers. . . .

Tweedie took a sober look at the Non-Proliferation Treaty, widely ratified but weakly worded; and at how the export of nuclear power technology had *not* stopped:

> If the Big Boys think nuclear power gives them strength and prestige, why on earth should they expect the little boys to

think differently? . . . The appalling thing about the whole nuclear threat . . . is the awful similarity to quarrels in a nursery. . . . And the funny thing is, women are in nurseries all over the world but not in this one. Our voices aren't heard in the nuclear nursery. . . . Women have a lot to do, but none of it is much use if it is wiped out because their children and their grandchildren are wiped out.[14]

She urged women to sign a Women's Declaration, proposed by actress Peggy Ashcroft and signed by sixteen eminent women. The *Call to Women* groups were delighted. But even such publicity had little effect. CND recruited under 500 new members that year,[15] and the minuscule women's peace movement remained outside popular consciousness. Women's liberation had other priorities – and different definitions of key ideas.

Ideas about violence and nonviolence had changed radically. Not only had there been a reaction against the nonviolent techniques of the Committee of 100; but in addition women's liberation undertook a wholesale redefinition of 'violence'. Declaring 'the personal is the political', women shifted the focus away from global nuclear violence and state militarism, to personal experience of men's domestic and sexual violence. As feminism developed in the late 1970s, anger against this grew stronger, with campaigns around rape and pornography. Identifying violence as based within gender difference was a key contribution of 1970s feminism, as any woman who has needed to seek out a Women's Aid refuge would testify. But it also provoked argument among feminists about the prevalence of male violence; and, in Britain anyway, left little space for discussion of *military* violence – or about *non*violence as an empowering feminist strategy for confronting militarism.[16]

There was a similarly revolutionary shift around ideas about motherhood. Much of WLM equal-rights anger in the early 1970s was a reaction against narrow maternalist values. Practical campaigns for childcare ran alongside a critique of the family and its oppressive structures. In many ways this echoed back to Gilman's attack sixty years earlier on 'the man-made family'. A pamphlet, *The Myth of Motherhood*, voiced the anger:

> From Bowlby to *Woman's Own*, it is everyone's prerogative to state with absolute certainty that a child needs its mother, and, deprived of her constant and exclusive care and attention, the child will ... probably turn out to be a delinquent. ... [But] mothers are no more essential to their children than are fathers, grandmothers, or indeed anyone who loves them with the right kind of care and understanding.[17]

Much of this new feminist anger reacted against any stereotyping of women as naturally *more* caring, *more* peaceful, *less* violent than men. Impatient with earlier 'mothers-for-peace' images, it was at odds with Gilman's, and particularly Schreiner's, anti-militarism. Despite the vigilance of CND and Liaison Committee groups, détente lulled people into forgetting Hiroshima and the inconvenient nuclear bomb. So the 1970s were the nadir of a popular women's *peace* movement in Britain. Feminism and anti-militarism seemed a million miles apart. An article in the new feminist magazine *Spare Rib* called 'Nuclear War' turned out to depict – conflict within the family.[18]

To understand why, seemingly from nowhere, a popular women's peace movement sprang up in 1980–81 around the Greenham Common peace camp, it is necessary to glance at the *un*popular peace politics of 1975–80. In retrospect it becomes clear that Greenham was presaged by tiny women's peace groupings, by imaginative actions against nuclear power, and by debates about feminism and nonviolence in Britain, America and Northern Europe. So the rest of this chapter examines how these small-scale debates and actions prefigured the 1980s.

Oral testimony from grass-roots activists committed to both feminism and nonviolence in the 1970s suggests how difficult it was to find a language for making these links. Diana Shelley was involved with *Peace News* and the British Withdrawal from Northern Ireland Campaign (BWINIC). Making links between nonviolence and Ireland in the 1970s was scarcely easy, but at least the BWINIC campaign was possible.[19] Even discussing links between nonviolence and feminism was problematic. Shelley recalls going with another woman to an Anarchist-Feminist Conference in 1977, and organizing a workshop on feminism and nonviolence,

> and getting incredibly frustrated because we wanted to talk about political struggle in terms of nonviolence and how it related to feminism. And the *entire* workshop talked about domestic violence. . . . Even talking about *that* felt quite new. But it wasn't the only thing we wanted to talk about . . . because I was very committed to trying to find ways of making revolutionary changes in a nonviolent way; and that seemed to link up for me with the ways of working in the women's movement.[20]

In fact, women very far removed from any popular peace movement began to make these connections. They were pacifists, connected not only to *Peace News*'s 'nonviolent revolution' but also to older anti-conscriptionist networks, such as the Fellowship of Reconciliation and the War Resisters' International (WRI).

Gay Jones's experience provides a narrative thread to this particular story. She grew up a Christian pacifist; Vera Brittain 'was one of my mother's heroines and a household name'; her father had been a Conscientious Objector, and her parents sold *Peace News* on the streets during the war. Jones, born in 1949, was taken along as a child on the last days of Aldermaston Marches. By the time she left school in 1966 opportunities had opened up for girls' higher education. At university she became involved with Christian groups, *Peace News* activities – and nonviolence training, led by an American Quaker. Later, she worked as a secretary in Manchester. Then in 1974 she went to Copenhagen, where the International Fellowship of Reconciliation (IFOR) collective was based, 'and that was where it all fell into place'.[21]

At the collective Gay Jones came across four women: one Danish, one French, and two Americans, who:

> had just begun to discover feminism, so *MS* [magazine] arrived every month; and we just sat and talked. . . . And we sat over our typewriters, and we typed and we duplicated and we talked and we talked and we talked. . . .

Jones had fallen for the women's movement in a big way. Back in Manchester, she and a few friends set up a consciousness-raising group; at Christmas 1974 she went back to IFOR (which had moved to Brussels) and talked to one of the American women again:

> and she said she had this vision of getting women in the peace movement together, as internationally as possible, and talking about feminism and the peace movement. . . . And this seemed like a *really* exciting idea.[22]

Plans took shape for a women's workshop in summer 1975 at the WRI triennial in Holland. About thirty British, American and European women attended, including Jones (who came out as a lesbian at about this point). There was resistance from some European men, she recalls: 'because the peace movement in Europe was about conscription, resisting conscription, women didn't have very much say in it at all'. But there was a strong feeling, especially in America, that feminism *was* relevant to peace issues. 'It was agreed generally that we needed a women-only event for women around the peace movement – and particularly where the WRI and IFOR had branches.'[23]

A planning committee of women from five countries met

during winter 1975–76; over 300 letters were sent out. 'It must have touched a chord somewhere, because', Gay Jones recalls, 'women just wrote back with suggestions, feelings, reactions, ideas.'[24] Eventually a venue was agreed: Les Circauds, a large French farmhouse near Lyons. For five memorable days, ninety women and ten children attended this historic gathering. Jones remembers the excitement: the dry July heat, a rain dance in the nude (which worked), massage and self-examination workshops, and discussion of the specific lesbian contribution to nonviolence. And, as *Women in the Nonviolent Movement*, the document that resulted from Les Circauds, makes clear, part of the excitement also sprang from clarifying ideas – such as the limits of equal-rights feminism:

> If violence can be defined as the struggling for power over other people, we would like to ask whether the struggle for equal rights is striving for power and therefore violent? . . . (We would say that struggling for equal rights within the armed forces is bolstering up the patriarchal capitalist system and not revolutionary at all.) . . . We would like to talk about these issues fully in the women's movement. . . .[25]

Significantly, there was very little interest in nuclear weapons or radiation hazards, but a nonviolent feminism based on gender difference was beginning to be emphasized. Maternalist values, traditionally focused on the family, were being imaginatively reshaped in the light of discussions about crimes against women, about lesbianism, matriarchy and 'the way in which institutionalized religion has done violence to our female spirituality'. For Les Circauds wanted 'to extend the positive value recognized by feminists of female nurturing to a world view, of nurturing the world'.[26]

For 'practically anybody that went there, it was one of the most important events of our lives so far', enthused Gay Jones. 'Sisterhood reigned.'[27] Les Circauds also introduced a new hedonistic note into the women's peace movement. Impulsive women-centred pleasure and magic ritual predominated over WILPF's tradition of reasoned argument. Les Circauds was tiny, isolated from popular feminism and from disarmament groups, but its spirit lived on afterwards. The British women organized a conference in Birmingham in autumn 1976 to explore links between feminism and nonviolence. 'It was more of a *feeling* that there were a lot of connections, but very hard to actually articulate at that stage,' Jones explained. The older women's peace groups were not identified with women's liberation; nor as yet was nonviolence on any mainstream feminist agenda. So it was agreed to form a 'long-distance' Feminism and Nonviolence Study Group, linking the few women 'who had been in the peace movement and discovered feminism' with those equally few who had 'been in the women's movement and discovered *Peace News*'.[28]

But the group still searched for a sharper definition of its central concerns. At a women's liberation conference in 1977, they convened a workshop on nonviolence and women. 'A lot of women there did feel similarly, that instinctively they did react against the idea of violent revolution or behaving in ways they felt were very tied up with masculinity,' Jones said, 'but we all found it very difficult . . . to get beyond that.' Indeed, the Study Group 'very quickly realized, apart from bits of American input in particular, there was so little written. "So, OK, we are going to have to write it".' They began working on a special issue of *Shrew* – and reading what was coming over from America and elsewhere.[29]

Barbara Deming was a particularly influential American feminist writer. Born in 1917, she went to a Quaker school and later read Gandhi; in 1960 she joined the Committee of Nonviolent Action's anti-Polaris symbolic 'civic disobedience' and anti-racism 'Walk for Peace'. Deming became involved in WISP (Women's International Strike for

Peace) and was frequently jailed. Her thinking offers a bridge between traditional Gandhian pacifism and the 1980s' dramatically symbolic peace actions:

> To resort to power one need not be violent, and to speak to conscience one need not be meek. . . . How, then, does one distinguish nonviolent from violent action? . . . The distinction to make is simply that those committed to a nonviolent discipline refuse to injure the antagonist. . . . It is precisely solicitude for his person *in combination with* a stubborn interference with his actions that can give us a very special degree of control. . . . The more the real issues are dramatized, and the struggle raised above the personal, the more control those in nonviolent rebellion begin to gain over their adversary.[30]

During the 1970s Deming had to think hard about feminists whose hatred of male oppression meant that they *were* prepared to take violent action. 'It was very painful for me to look at this new anger; and it is only gradually I am learning to transmute it – into determination,' she admitted. In 1973, aged fifty-six, Deming came out as a lesbian; she now became more immersed in feminism, agreeing with writer Andrea Dworkin that 'patriarchy is a system of ownership wherein women and children are owned'; with Mary Daly that 'If God is male, then male is God'; and was influenced by Adrienne Rich, whose *Of Woman Born* (1977) stressed the centrality of woman's power to give birth.

Deming's feminism increasingly stressed gender difference, especially around motherhood. Despite her fierce critique of patriarchy, she still remained committed to nonviolence – including nonviolence towards men. '"There is a lot of anger against men amongst us,"' she told one young man, '"but you don't have to be afraid that we want to eliminate men. Don't forget that women gave birth to men".' But, she added, because of all the ancient wrongs done to women, a 'temporary separatism' is necessary:

I think we have to *begin* by trying to form again a kinship circle that is simply a circle of women and children. I don't think we can form that necessary larger circle, which includes men, until we have found our courage to assert with great clarity . . . that we do not *belong* to men. . . .

Perhaps as we sat together in these new circles of women, remembering together who we were, we began even to remember the long-ago – to remember, with that part of the brain that is nonverbal, not only our individual earliest experience . . . but also the earliest experience of the race – an experience, too, of knowing well women's strength.[31]

This American focus on men's original wrongs against women did not always translate smoothly to Britain: indeed, writers like Mary Daly have recently been criticized by feminists.[32] But Deming's own past commanded respect; and her writings, now recognizably prefigurative of Greenham, were acknowledged in the late 1970s by feminists around *Peace News*. Diana Shelley remembers the paper's role in 'explaining feminism to the male-dominated peace movement' – albeit by lifting Dworkin and Deming articles from *WIN*, an American war-resistance magazine. Gay Jones also recalls how Deming's writings were 'filtering through; she was like a bit of a guru in that sense'.[33] Certainly Deming's ideas about patriarchy and motherhood increasingly complemented a broader shift in the late 1970s: away from socialist feminism, with its stress on equal opportunities at work and welfare rights, towards an emphasis on female-centred culture and a hatred of male violence. (Amid controversy, a new women's liberation demand was added in 1978: 'freedom from intimidation by threat or use of violence or sexual coercion' and an end to the perpetuation of 'male dominance and men's aggression towards women'.)

The Feminism and Nonviolence Study Group's issue of *Shrew*, published in summer 1978, demonstrates its sharpened thinking since Les Circauds two years earlier. Its opening quotation from Dworkin on feminist assertiveness – 'As women, nonviolence must begin for us in the refusal to be violated, in the refusal to be victimized' – was followed by a statement of why the group had decided:

> We did not want simply to inherit and pass on 'male notions of nonviolence'; secondly we had all experienced at some time a dismissal by other women . . . of the ideas of nonviolence . . . ; thirdly we felt that the Women's Liberation Movement was, and is, in danger of perpetuating some of the patterns which are an integral part of the male value system in respect to violence. . . . Too often violent revolution has involved the substitution of one group of rulers for another. . . . To us, nonviolent revolution means . . . a growing and evolving process . . . until the concept of power itself is destroyed. As feminists we believe there are no good hierarchies.[34]

Next came an attack on American feminists' campaign for equality in the army; but particularly galvanizing was news about nuclear power and radiation hazards. CND might still be small and reduced to sharing small offices with WILPF. But a new and imaginative anti-nuclear campaign was gathering momentum.

The dangers of nuclear accidents had long been shrouded in secrecy. Knowledge of the 1957 Kyshtym disaster beyond the Ural Mountains had been suppressed by the Soviet authorities. More than thirty years passed before they admitted the nuclear explosion at an atomic weapons plant.[35] That same year, there was a reactor fire at the Windscale nuclear power plant on the Cumberland coast; a 'high airborne contamination of strontium and iodine' meant a six-week ban on milk distribution over 200 square miles. But the thirty-year rule on the release of official papers means that such truths are only now emerging.[36]

Instead, the British public was lulled into believing that nuclear power was safe and unconnected with the production of bombs to kill people.

The campaign began elsewhere. In Denmark in 1974 the impressive Organization for Information on Atomic Power (OOA) was formed. Its smiling-sun logo, 'Atomkraft? Nej Tak' ['Nuclear Power? No Thanks'] became widely translated and instantly recognizable. New forms of protest sprang up: nonviolent but assertive, imaginative, sometimes influenced by feminism – and usually fun. In 1975 at Whyle in West Germany, where a gigantic camp was set up at a proposed nuclear site:

> Faced by armed and helmeted police, women called out: 'Look here, we cannot talk to you while you are wearing those helmets. Take them off and we'll talk.' . . . Two companies of police, defying orders from their headquarters, then refused to take action against the demonstrators.[37]

At Seabrook, on the east coast of America, resentment against a proposed nuclear power plant grew, and in 1976 a 'Clamshell Alliance' was formed. An occupation to stop construction led to hundreds of arrests. Then, in 1977, 2,000 pitched a 'tent city' there, and over 1,000 were jailed. Jo Somerset of the Feminism and Nonviolence Study Group was present and reported enthusiastically to *Shrew*: the nonviolence training and small affinity groups profoundly impressed her, though she criticized the absence of a feminist consciousness.[38]

Protest spread – against nuclear power, and also against the newly announced 'neutron bomb'.[39] In Holland, the influential Interchurch Peace Council (IKV) launched its campaign: 'Help rid the world of nuclear weapons. Let it begin with the Netherlands'. In Britain, however, antinuclear protest remained small-scale until April 1978, when there was a large protest march through London against expansion plans for Windscale. And in Scotland, a new Alliance held a mass occupation of a proposed nuclear reactor site at Torness near Edinburgh, introducing many to 'affinity groups' as a way of organizing large nonviolent actions.

Among the women who went to Torness, one remembers a notice pinned to a tent: 'Free bed for free birds' – suggesting that in Britain the debate about feminism and peace had got stuck.[40] However, American news now crossed the Atlantic fast. *Spare Rib* began to mention 'Feminists Against Nuclear Power'; and a London conference was planned for April 1979 to bring feminists together before the next Torness event.[41] But even before this, nuclear power hit the world headlines. Hard on the heels of the prophetic film *China Syndrome* came the real Three Mile Island reactor panic. On 28 March, at a nuclear generating station in Pennsylvania, a serious radioactive accident was only narrowly averted: the state governor had advised the evacuation of pregnant women and pre-school children from within a five-mile radius. In Denmark, OOA mounted two enormous demonstrations; and a big Torness Gathering in May was attended by over 7,000 supporters.[42] Also, news came through that the family of the late Karen Silkwood, an American believed to have suffered internal plutonium contamination, had been awarded substantial damages for radiation negligence by her employers.

Only at this point did concern about the nuclear threat as a gender issue begin to broaden. In February 1980 *Spare Rib* ran a 'Nuclear Power – it'll cost the earth' feature which argued: '. . . women are twice as likely as men to get cancer from radiation . . . foetuses and young children are even more affected.' Its emphasis was part maternalist, part a *Three Guineas* argument with a new anti-urban, anti-authoritarian twist – in other words, the greening of feminism:

> Feminism is about individual and local decisions. The will to have control over our own lives – and nobody else's – is fundamental to Women's Liberation. . . . As feminists we're

attacking the stability of the system by challenging the power of a few men to hold all the money and power. . . . The technology of our male culture is based upon the imposition of the technologist's skill. . . . Nuclear power is the extreme manifestation of a technology that relies on subjugation and exploitation. . . . It is our energy against their power.[43]

The link between plutonium production in nuclear reactors and the manufacture of weapons was building an effective argument. For 1980 saw the dramatic resurgence of a new, popular campaign against the missiles, catching the anxieties and imaginations of hundreds of thousands of British people. And with it, the feminist critique of the nuclear threat grew from a prophetic minority, still looking outside Britain for inspiration, to something broader and more sturdily home-grown.

The 1979 general election produced Britain's first woman Prime Minister; but not much else seemed immediately to change. 'This year I'll remember Hiroshima in the same way as I have the last few years,' wrote a *Peace News* reader, 'as one of a pitifully small group of a vigil in a main street.'[44] For most of us had forgotten 'the bomb'. Why should we remember? However, among the tens of thousands of other lapsed CND activists, historian Edward Thompson was watching television:

> Early in October, 1979, . . . an 'expert' sort of a young man came upon the BBC news, and informed us that we are to have 140 Cruise missiles with nuclear warheads stationed on our soil. . . . They are to be 'our' contribution to NATO.
> . . . As is the manner with the 'news' these days, this young man offered us all this in a comforting, normative kind of way. . . .
>   [But] Civil liberties and 250 Cruise missiles cannot co-exist in this island together. East Anglia is not Arizona nor the Nevada desert. . . . Informers will be put in. . . . The most awful trials will become habitual.[45]

Thompson's predictions were grim. So was reality. On 12 December, the NATO decision to site Cruise and Pershing II missiles in Europe within the next few years was officially 'taken' – that is, with no discussion in Parliament. (There was a protest rally in Brussels; but only about twenty British people – from WILPF, CND and Labour Action for Peace – went.[46])

To combat this new threat to peace, Thompson helped to form European Nuclear Disarmament (END) and hastily wrote a pamphlet, *Protest and Survive*, whose mockery of official 'protect and survive' civil defence did more than anything else to rouse people from their nuclear sleep. Local organizations sprang up from early 1980 onwards: some were CND groups which had refused to die or were now re-formed; but many completely new ones, wary of CND's fusty image, opted to become anti-nuke or anti-missile groups.[47] Research student Meg Beresford, just back from New York and exhilarated by a mammoth Three Mile Island demonstration there, recalls an attempt very early in 1980 to revitalize the small Oxford University CND group. It decided to organize a demonstration and invite Thompson and CND's general secretary, Bruce Kent – but to call itself ' "Campaign Atom", because we were *quite* sure that CND was a defunct organization'. They marched to Upper Heyford, then predicted to be a probable Cruise missile site. *Peace News* people with experience from Torness helped Campaign Atom with nonviolent direct action.[48]

'The demonstration was *immensely* exciting', Beresford recalls. But their prediction was wrong. In June Francis Pym, first of Thatcher's many Defence Ministers, announced that ninety-six Cruise missiles were to go to Greenham Common in Berkshire. Near by, Joan Ruddock, a Citizens' Advice Bureau worker and chair of Newbury Labour Party, helped to launch a local 'Campaign Against Cruise', which eventually became a CND group. Up in York, Lynne Jones, a qualified doctor completing her surgery training, recalls the local CND group starting up, and a nonviolence group, mainly of *Peace News* people with experience of Torness and affinity-group structures. And in Halifax, our local Nuclear Disarmament Group started in summer 1980 as an END group, and only much later affiliated to CND.[49] But national CND, guided by the wise counsels of Bruce Kent, generously helped these energetic upstarts, each with its own origins. As a result, its national membership rose to over 9,000 by late 1980.

Amidst all this bustling activity, there was still very little linking of peace and gender at a popular level. For the great majority of feminists – myself included – such connections were scarcely raised in local anti-missile or CND group discussions.[50] But in North America and Northern Europe, they were beginning to be made.

American feminist writers like Susan Griffin were developing an increasingly Manichaean view of life based on gender difference. 'Bad' was male, science, high technology, centralization, power, violence, oppression. 'Good' was female, nature, low technology, nurturing, spirituality, ancient mythologies, the oppressed. The rise of Western science and 'the death of nature' meant that 'the earth was no longer regarded as a nurturing mother to be cherished'.[51] This eco-feminism saw maleness as so destructive that women should want no share in its power. Equal-rights feminism was rejected; instead, this particular philosophy offered an anti-patriarchal maternalist separatism.

After Three Mile Island, New England feminists, inspired by such thinking, began to organize. The 'Vermont Spinsters' wove shut the gates of a nuclear power plant with wool. In March 1980, over 600 attended a 'Conference on Women and Life on Earth: Eco-feminism in the Eighties'. Significantly, 'the Pentagon emerged as a symbol of all the male violence we opposed'; and meetings to plan an action continued all summer.[52]

In Britain, plans were – as yet – less dramatic. However, anti-nuclear discussions among small women's groups did develop a strong anti-missile emphasis once plans for Cruise became known. Leeds feminists were particularly active. Among them was Bridget Robson, a libertarian already involved in an anti-nuclear action group. She very clearly remembers the winter of 1979–80, and the fateful NATO decision:

> It was an incredibly powerful time. . . . I just went through that whole winter . . . absolutely terrified. And was very, very sure that every day was going to be the last. . . . A lot of women I knew had nightmares about the bomb and nuclear war. . . . So, yes, that was several months of private terror – but starting to talk to other women about it. And that was when Erika [with whom she worked at Corner Books] and I held a workshop within the Women's Liberation conference in Leeds. . . .
>
> We said we'd like one on the nuclear threat. Which we had; and quite a lot of women came. . . . And I think that was a *new* idea; to think that we wanted to talk about it with women, and that it was an issue we could bring into a feminist conference, and *expect* to get support, and *expect* that other women would want to talk about it as well. . . .
>
> Quite a lot of us [were] women with children, small children. . . . We saw it as an exchange of *feelings* . . . just to say how we all felt. Which was mainly that we all felt scared stiff.

The group began to meet regularly: 'We were very uncertain how we saw ourselves. A lot of women felt they couldn't really say they were pacifists. A whole discussion about pacifism and militarism came up.'[53] Tiny tentacles like these began to spread across the country during 1980. In March there was a conference in Nottingham on 'Women and the Military', attended by women from Leeds and from the Feminism and Nonviolence Study Group; it concluded: 'we must act together against nuclear destruction.' In June, a women's anti-nuclear power conference decided: 'since nuclear reactors produce plutonium, the main ingredient in atomic bombs, nuclear electricity and nuclear weapons are like siamese twins. We need to campaign against them both.'[54] Also that summer, the Study Group organized another international conference, on 'Women and Militarism', in Scotland. Gay Jones remembers how some of the American women who attended then 'went back to the States much more conscious of what was happening in Europe'. (And vice versa, Diana Shelley noted, remembering that a 'Vermont Spinster' came.)[55]

By then, the Leeds women had formed WONT. Its original name was 'Women Versus War'. 'I can remember us actually originating [the name]', Robson recalled:

> We were very angry and indignant that all this was being done to us. . . . We just wanted to refuse to allow it to happen. The title was 'Women Oppose the Nuclear Threat'. We were very aware of language. We didn't want to say 'Women Fighting the Nuclear Threat' or even 'Women Against the Nuclear Threat'. It was definitely 'Oppose'. Strong but non-aggressive.

Anti-missile groups were springing up. WONT soon found itself between two camps. 'There was a straight peace movement,' Robson explained, 'and there was the feminist movement. And they were both saying, "*Why* are you in this feminist anti-nuclear group?"' There were also differences within WONT:

> We don't all call ourselves very strongly feminist. There was a feeling about women and motherhood; and women creating and nurturing life. That still seems quite important to me, really. . . . On the other hand, other women were saying, 'Well, it's just as important to stop nuclear war for *me*. I want to survive. I've got a right to demand a peaceful world for *myself*. Not just for somebody else. Women have always been trying to do things for other people . . .'. So there was a very strong feminist debate going on.[56]

Was 'opposing the nuclear threat' a *feminist* issue? And were women-only groups within the peace movement divisive?

The debate continued. Meanwhile, the WONT group organized a telephone tree, sewed a banner, and drew up a petition to Mrs Thatcher: 'We refuse to prepare for or suffer a war which we have not made and which can never be in our interests'. It demanded 'An end to the manufacture and stockpiling of all weapons of mass destruction'. During autumn 1980, copies were circulated to women's groups and peace groups around the country. Other WONT groups sprang up; and *Spare Rib* ran a 'Take the Toys from the Boys' feature, explaining Cruise missiles and CND's strategy.[57] At the same time, news of 'Women and Life on Earth' travelled across the Atlantic, firing a few women in Britain to form a similar group.

That autumn in New England, plans for the first 'Women's Pentagon Action' took shape. Lynne Jones, visiting the States, remembers: 'I was very stroppy, because I'd come from an *intensely* anti-nuclear group to an America that was not the *slightest* bit interested in the peace movement.' She trooped around, met up with older women's peace groups like WISP, and:

> They thrust a leaflet into my hand, and said 'You're a woman. You'll be interested in this.' And it was this poster for this demonstration ... called Women's Pentagon Action. And there's a beautiful poster, and on the back of it this extraordinarily beautiful statement called 'The Unity Statement'. . . . And I thought, 'Well, this is really lovely. Must go'.[58]

Writer Grace Paley had helped to draft this brilliantly clear, strong statement:

> We are gathering at the Pentagon on November 16 because we fear for our lives. We fear for the life of this planet, our Earth, and the life of the children, who are our human future. . . . We have come here to mourn and rage and defy

the Pentagon because it is the workplace of the imperial power which threatens us all. . . .

We want the uranium left in the earth and the earth given back to the people who tilled it. . . . We want the sham of Atoms for Peace ended, all nuclear plants decommissioned and the construction of new plants stopped. . . .

We want an end to the arms race. No more bombs. No more amazing inventions for death.

We understand that all is connectedness. The earth nourishes us as we with our bodies will eventually feed it. Through us, our mothers connected the human past to the human future.[59]

Two thousand women assembled in Washington. To the sound of a slow drumbeat, they began with ritual *Mourning* for the victims of the war machine – including Karen Silkwood. The second stage was *Rage*: women chanting 'Take the toys from the boys' railed at the Pentagon. Third was *Empowerment*: women encircled the Pentagon, holding hands and scarves, singing feminist and civil rights songs. Finally came *Defiance*: women sat down and blocked the entrances; at one, the Vermont Spinsters 'wove the door shut' again. 'I've never seen such a *beautiful* demonstration', Lynne Jones stated. 'The whole thing was like an *enormous* piece of theatre. . . . No speeches, no rostrum. . . . Women just sitting down and being dragged away and sitting down, dragged away.'[60] It had a profound effect on her.

Also during 1980, the small women's peace groups in Britain began to hear of actions in Northern Europe. WILPF's newsletter, now edited by Margot Miller, reported how Scandinavian 'Women for Peace' were collecting a million signatures, demanding 'Disarmament for an ever-lasting peace on earth'; this Scandinavian appeal was adapted in West Germany, and German Women for Peace started. By early 1981 it was clear that not only was there a very large trans-European peace movement – linked through groups like END and IKV – but that women in

Holland, Germany and Scandinavia were also taking imaginative feminist action. Scandinavian women were even organizing a march from Copenhagen to Paris.

In Britain, by March 1981 CND had 16,500 national members and many, many more in local groups: total membership was now around 200,000. A Nuclear-Free Zone movement was also spreading fast, with over fifty local councils refusing to take part in preparations for nuclear war.[61] Meanwhile, Meg Beresford, now on CND's ruling National Council, produced a 'Women and Nuclear Disarmament' supplement in *Sanity*, drawing together news from Europe, America and Britain. Yet it was still not apparent in Britain that *feminist* opposition to nuclear-militarism was spreading very far beyond WONT, WILPF and the small Women and Life on Earth networks.[62] That summer, a modest Women's Peace Alliance was also being planned to bring together both newer and older groups. Margot Miller was asked to represent WILPF at a preliminary meeting in Oxford in early September, and remembers:

> I went down there, and when I got there they said, 'Oh, the women have arrived at Greenham, and they're chaining themselves to the fence. And we can't have our meeting *here*. We must go down *there*.' So off we went ... down to Greenham. ...
>
> And we got down there, and it was all quite peaceful and quiet. Because there were the women chained to the fence; and the other ones had gone back to Wales with their children. ... And I sat there with a woman from VOW – Voice of Women – who I'd known from Claygate, who'd come to the meeting. And we'd worked together for *years*, and we just sat there talking about old times. And Voice of Women and all that. And little did we know that this was the beginning of the next era.[63]

11

The Pebble that Started the Avalanche
(1981–82)

In every community across the land there are women who became caught up by the Greenham Common women's peace camp in the tumultuous years 1982 to 1984. Perhaps it is still too early to record the complete story of the 1980s women's peace movement. In the celebrated phrase attributed to Mao when asked about the effects of the French Revolution: it is too soon to say. And for Greenham, of course, not all source material is as yet available. For the peace camp was nothing other than a direct confrontation – and struggle for credibility – between the Greenham women and the nuclear state; and whereas the peace movement has been open-handed with its own memoirs and documents, the state and its officials have not. The bland reassurance of successive Ministers of Defence may be readily accessible. But source material for the *real* 1980s peace history remains more elusive. The most sensitive documents may already have been weeded by civil servants. For many other categories of official papers, we will have to wait (under the thirty-year rule) until early next century; for other documents a hundred-year closure period is more likely. Peace historians may have to wait until 2082 before they can begin to assess what impact *we* had on *them*: the British state and its NATO allies.[1]

So these final chapters offer an interim report: a narrative, from 1981 onwards, of events at Greenham and elsewhere, drawn from the sources currently available. As far as possible I have referred to primary documentary evidence – newsletters and newspaper reports – supplemented where necessary by the half-dozen Greenham books published in 1983–84. I have also traced the individual trajectories of half a dozen women peace activists, based on interviews

recorded during 1985–86.[2] I have drawn extensively on
their eye-witness testimony to reflect the tremendous variety of personal 'Greenham' stories, both of women living
at the camp and of those rooted in their local communities.
Together, this evidence offers a reappraisal of the women's
peace movement in the 1980s.

The peace camp sprang from a 'walk for life' to Greenham
from Cardiff in summer 1981; this began as the brainchild
of Ann Pettitt, living at Llanpumsaint in Dyfed, west
Wales.[3] Pettitt, born in 1947, grew up in Surrey. Her father,
like so many other middle-class idealists in the late 1930s,
had been converted to the Communist Party; after the
wartime upheaval he returned home with his foreign bride,
a French factory worker. So, Pettitt recalls, her parents
never fitted in with the general norms of suburban society.
She herself was always stroppily iconoclastic. She lost
patience with the earnest socialism of her parents' circle,
and found the local CND group boring: 'I'd go with my dad
to the last days of the CND marches, but my parents never let
me go on the whole three-day march.' This was frustrating:
Aldermaston spelled freedom – and meeting boys.[4] By
1965, when Pettitt left to go to university, CND was in
unstoppable decline.

Later, Pettitt, living in east London, found herself in the
midst of a local squatting campaign, resisting eviction and
protecting her living space. She worked as a teacher and
became involved in the Women's Liberation Movement,
though she grew disillusioned with certain aspects of
feminism.[5] London seemed arid, a city to escape from. The
new ecology movement excited her. With her partner Barry
Wade, she planned to move out. Pregnant and involved
with a local maternity services campaign, she grew disturbed by what city pollution did to living beings.

So, in 1977, the couple and their baby left London for a
one-acre smallholding in Llanpumsaint, Dyfed. They
worked hard on the derelict homestead; a second baby

followed. These first three years in Wales rushed past 'in a whirlwind of pregnancies and mud and cabbages and nappies and cows and *mange-tout* peas and planting . . . and building and repairing'.[6] Then, in spring 1980, Pettitt emerged from the whirlwind, found she had time to read, and then:

> There was just one day when I got fed up with cutting up newspapers and putting them in folders labelled 'Nuclear Power, radiation, leaks, etc.', 'Pollution', 'Third World', 'Arms Race, weapons', and so on. That day, after the umpteenth 'Minister rejects enquiry findings' and 'radio-active leak denied' . . . I sort of literally blew a fuse, and I think I started shouting. And I went to the understairs cupboards and got out these rolls of old white wallpaper and unrolled them along that kitchen floor, got out a black felt tip [pen].
>
> . . . I wrote something like 'Nuclear power – poisoning our environment – nuclear weapons – more and more built every year', and something like 'This cannot go on. This must stop' – in great big letters, like a Chinese wall newspaper. And I made several rolls of this.[7]

Meanwhile, the owner of the local wholefood shop in nearby Carmarthen, a well-informed *Guardian* reader, readily displayed her posters and they agreed to call a meeting for the following Wednesday. Thirty people came, some from miles away, for there was fierce local opposition to nuclear waste dumping in mid-Wales. Carmarthen Anti-Nuclear Campaign (CANC) was formed, with Pettitt its informal chair. CANC's focus was nuclear *power*; Pettitt read up on how 'plutonium, daughter of the split uranium atom, goes on killing, turning cells cancerous and deforming genetic material . . . for a quarter of a million years.' Only some months later did CANC turn to nuclear *war*. It then booked the film *The War Game*, invited a CND speaker and campaigned along CND lines. By this time, Pettitt had read *Protest and Survive*; she was impressed by its message that

Cruise was a crucial turning point in the arms race and that, being ground-based, it 'was *get-at-able* in a way that no other system was. . . . Straight away I realized how vulnerable it was to . . . just people lying in the way'.[8]

By early 1981 CANC was busy lobbying Dyfed county councillors over the Nuclear-Free Zone issue.[9] Pettitt recalled that during this feverish local activity, she just happened to flick the pebble that started the avalanche. While the men were cooking and looking after the children, she and the other women were writing a nuclear-free zone leaflet, 'trying to make it sound clear, simple, direct'. Stuck for words, she reached for a copy of *Peace News* to divert herself and read about the march from Copenhagen to Paris led by women. She read it again – aloud:

> Immediately, we got off on the notion of a similar march happening in this country . . . marching to one of these damn military installations in the middle of nowhere . . . led and organized by women, with a women's 'core' group.
>
> . . . And then we tailed off. . . . I tried to find out if anyone was organizing a march in Britain like the Scandinavian one. Nobody was. . . . I tried to persuade other women I knew to take on responsibility for planning and organizing a march here. They were all too busy, they said. . . . I grew despondent, as I had by then collected fantasies about a march. . . .
>
> [But] as soon as I said those magic words, 'I'll do it', other people's attitudes changed.[10]

Among others who became involved was Lynne Whittemore, a student in Carmarthen. Her encouragement was crucial. 'We got the map out and said, "Where should it go?" . . . And we decided it should go to Greenham Common, rather than Aldermaston, because of Cruise.' A march would help to publicize this obscure Berkshire base. The date was chosen: two weeks in August, just three months away.

Pettitt lay awake at night worrying about what she had

taken on. The CND office in London was busy organizing the Glastonbury Festival. *Everyone* seemed busy. She hit upon the title 'Women for Life on Earth', and called a meeting in Bristol, halfway along the planned route. Only two women came; and although one, Angela Phillips from Newbury, was extremely helpful, the other scoffed at such a mad idea. Pettitt felt discouraged – until she heard about a woman called Carmen Kutler, who had started an anti-nuclear group nearby and had matter-of-factly said: '"That sounds a very good idea. Tell Ann I'll help her get that together."'[11] Kutler's organizing experience fleshed out Pettitt's obsessive fantasy. Another woman, Liney Seward, now joined. Kutler and Seward also had young children. That made four restless women, six kids – and an idea about Greenham.

The origins of the 'Women for Life on Earth' walk were humble and haphazard. Only around June did the plans begin to take shape. The walk would start from Cardiff and take ten days. Phillips contacted peace groups across south-west England. Kutler liaised with police stations along the route. They radiated a fearless optimism that *of course* it would work. A simple leaflet was produced; and the group began to gain publicity that took the march beyond the small women's peace movement of committed activists. The aim was to prise ordinary women away from their kitchen sinks and daily routines.

Letters appealing for support now rippled out from west Wales. The scribbled sheets of names and addresses which survived that frenetic summer suggest that extremely impressive networks were being activated. Contacts were made with the towns along the route – Newport and Chepstow, Bristol and Bath, Devizes and Marlborough, Hungerford and Welford; and with groups further afield – Friends of the Earth, Meg Beresford at END, Crèches Against Sexism, Quaker women, Campaign Atom at Oxford, the Feminism and Non-violence Study Group, Leeds WONT, Welsh anarchist-feminist artists and, perhaps a little more obscurely, the Radical Pagans of Swindon.[12]

By mid July, Pettitt was receiving daily letters from women interested in the walk. A WILPF member in Newport wrote excitedly; she had read of the walk in *Call to Women* and could hardly believe that the women's peace movement in Wales was at last reviving. In Reading, the women's group of Berkshire Anti-Nuclear Campaign (BANC) offered strategically placed help. CND promised a loan of £250. Cambridge WONT had a whip-round. Newport Women's Aid offered support.[13]

By early August plans were finalized. The title 'Women *for* Life on Earth Peace March '81' had been chosen, though without much direct contact with the 'Women *and* Life on Earth' group in Britain.[14] But although the west Wales women must have been at least *in*directly inspired by the American eco-feminists, and although both 'Life on Earth' initiatives shared the same anti-nuclear views, differences between the two were already clear. In America, the emphasis was on anti-patriarchal separatism and mysticism. By contrast, Women for Life on Earth was home-grown, rooted in the experience of running anti-nuclear groups in rural communities. It had little interest in feminist theory, and attempted to give voice to a wide range of women *without* excluding men. (Pettitt's own reservations about separatism were now strengthened by practical considerations: a march through sparsely populated areas meant they would have to rely for hospitality upon mixed CND groups.) The group's earthy pragmatism is clearly revealed in its press release:

> Women from all over Britain and their children will be marching across the border from Wales into England, bearing a message of peace. . . . Like the Copenhagen to Paris peace-walk this summer, this demonstration will be led by a 'core' group of mainly women and children who will go all the way. But everyone concerned at the deadly peril in which we are put by the escalating nuclear arms race is welcome to join in along any stretch of the march. . . .
>
> A unique feature of this march is that it is being organized

by unpaid individual campaigners in the CND movement who are fitting all the work into their spare time. Most are women with young children. . . .

The march is led by women to show everyone that women are active and prominent in the peace movement. Men are welcome as supporters, but most of the speakers at meetings and events along the route will be women. . . .

The other 'why women?' reasons stressed both maternalist arguments and equal rights. Much of women's work lies in the 'caring' professions and 'bearing and nourishing children', the press release stated; they 'feel a special responsibility to offer them a future – not a wasteland of a world and a lingering death'. Also, women bear the brunt of the cuts in public expenditure on schools and social services; yet 'most women have played no part in the decisions and delusions' whereby 'a few people hold the lives of us all in their control'.

By early August the march was becoming known. The *Sunday Times* mentioned it – prompting a flood of enquiries.[15] Kutler and Pettitt duplicated a leaflet for all the women who said they wanted to come. It gave information about the route; transport planned for luggage and children; what to bring (two pairs of walking shoes and plenty of socks); and it urged everyone to try local publicity and fund-raising. Leaflets were also printed to hand out on the route. They were impressively stark: 'Why are we walking 110 miles across Britain, from a nuclear weapons factory in Cardiff to a US base for "Cruise" missiles in Berkshire?' Overleaf was a picture of a badly deformed Hiroshima baby, born dead after its mother was exposed to radiation. The caption merely stated: 'This is why'.[16]

'We had no idea how many women would end up coming on the march,' Pettitt later wrote, '. . . so we made a guesstimate and plucked the figure of fifty out of the air.' Her original vision was now engulfed in last-minute rush and panic, as they hastily made the banner ('out of a sheet dyed pink; someone happened to have tins of dye that colour') with the CND symbol sprouting into a tree, and 'Women For Life On Earth, Peace-March '81' written across it. The four organizers travelled to Cardiff together. Pettitt's blood ran cold thinking of what she had started:

> And the amazing thing was, when we all talked afterwards about the feelings we brought to [Cardiff]. . . . Everybody had gone there feeling sure that what they would *find* would be female experts of some variety or other – women who were either all young and single and very politically astute, or who were all cleverer than them, or who all had done this kind of thing before. . . . Everybody thought that everybody else would be very intimidating.
>
> And it was such a revelation. We were such a revelation to each other. Because we looked around and my first thought was, 'Oh, my God, they really do all look so ordinary'. Quite a lot of them were quite old. And then I just got – got talking to them. . . . And all these young single politicoes that I'd expected to come on it . . . I don't think there was anyone in that category at all.[17]

So who were these women? A fifty-eight-year-old grand-mother and market gardener from Fishguard; a fifteen-year-old from Luton; a woman doctor from Abertillery; an Aldermaston March veteran from Cardiff; Eunice Stellard, another grandmother, from the Swansea valley; Helen John, a forth-right nurse, Labour Party supporter and mother of five from Llanwrtyd Wells; Denise Aaron, a mother of four young children from Chester, who felt she was very unpolitical.[18]

All the women congregated outside City Hall for a rally. Then the small cluster of walkers – thirty-six women, four men (a last-minute decision, despite the original 'core' marchers' intention) and three children set off on Thursday 27 August 1981. It was a historic moment – but hardly looked it.[19]

The pink banner, with its sprouting tree and CND symbol,

went ahead. A Methodist church hall in Llanrumney on the Glamorgan–Gwent border was the first stop; that evening the walkers rested in a church hall in Newport. Friday the 28th was a long, hot walk to Chepstow, with a detour to a US base at Caerwent; the marchers handed in a letter but were studiously ignored. Saturday the 29th was a tramp through the early-morning drizzle. Watching the bedraggled group approach was Denise Aaron, who was,

> I suddenly realized with horror, going somewhere ALONE for the first time since I'd been married thirteen years previously. It felt extraordinarily good. . . . Confidence and exhilaration evaporated instantly . . . when I saw marching towards me over the Severn Bridge a ragged, motley little – very little – band of women, dressed in all sorts of odd garments, carrying what was already a very faded banner proclaiming them to be Women for Life on Earth. . . . The oddness of their appearance was explicable after half a day's marching in the intense heat. Clothes had to be shed but heads and backs protected. Feet were blistered. We took it in turn to push pushchairs . . . and carry the banner. . . .[20]

As the forty walkers snaked their way eastwards towards Greenham, they began to meld together. 'We seemed', Pettitt wrote later:

> to have created a kind of force-field into which events fitted easily into our pattern, and setbacks became opportunities. . . . Coincidences abounded and even things dreamed beforehand came alive before our eyes. We just joked about the march magic. . . . We came to seem more and more special, at once more of a single forty-headed body and yet each more individual.

Each was an essential part of the group; the men looked after the children during meetings. Near Bath, as the walkers grew weary and footsore, the Fallout Marching Band suddenly arrived from London. 'We almost danced into Bath singing "Take those toys away from the boys" and "No More Hiroshimas",' recalled Denise Aaron. In the ancient villages and market towns of Avon and Wiltshire, hospitality abounded. They were crossing a forgotten, older England. Along the old A4 road, the landscape still conjured up a vision of a nobler time, uncluttered by nuclear death-missiles.[21]

The beeches of the Savernake Forest and US bases and Silbury Hill and Cruise missiles and women with pushchairs trundling slowly from village to village handing out Hiroshima leaflets – the mix was surreal. But not surreal enough to attract national media coverage. Fleet Street was uninterested in the march: each morning Pettitt rang their newsdesks, but they remained immune. Peace had been 'done' and was no longer an issue:

> And this was the biggest *shock*; because we thought . . . to walk 120 miles through a heatwave and in three cases pushing kiddies in pushchairs . . . seemed quite a thing. And we thought that this would be *bound* to produce a national impact . . . and it didn't *at all*. And this was why it became evident that we were going to have to do *more*.[22]

By this time they were halfway to Greenham. It was this realization that the media were ignoring them that prompted more confrontational tactics. One evening, at a stop-over in Wiltshire, someone mentioned the suffragettes. Why not chain themselves to the fence at Greenham? The whole group discussed this stunning proposal. It was a tense and frightening time: everyone was forced to reassess why they had come on the march.[23] Pettitt felt that the idea was right, but thought:

> Oh, no, God, I knew it! . . . This is not one of those finite things. No. . . . This is one of those trains that you don't bloody get off. This is one of those things that takes over your life and *forces* you to change.

She was very concerned that everyone should agree on the chaining action, but not everyone did. Then two women suggested that everyone should speak, without any comment. Pettitt said:

> And that was how we came to the consensus decision. . . . We realized that if we were going to do this . . . we *all* had to do it; but without bullying, without bad feeling. And so we did that for two *long, long* meetings. We just went round and everybody said what they felt.[24]

It was the first of many lengthy Greenham discussions.

By now it was early September. They wended their way through Marlborough; detoured to deliver a protest letter to the US nuclear weapons base at Welford; and then continued down the Berkshire lanes, 'past startled thatched villages where sleek streams flowed beneath houses, singing and inventing songs and ransacking the hedges for garlands of bindweed and bryony. We were building up this rumbustious spirit, which was *very* communicative,' Pettitt added. 'It all seemed very easy then.' 'It' was the chaining action. Four women would chain themselves to the Greenham fence: Eunice Stellard and Helen John, Linnie Baldwin and Lynne Whittemore, with Carmen Kutler as legal observer. (Already there were some doubts: Ann Pettitt was wary about the almost paramilitary secrecy needed; and Diana Shelley, contacted in London, was aghast that direct-actionists should so casually leave it to the evening before to enquire 'What's the law on chaining yourself to airbases?'[25]

A large contingent from Newbury Campaign Against Cruise was waiting to greet the walkers. The four women sprinted over to the base and duly chained themselves up at the main gate at about 7.30 a.m. Meanwhile, the rest of the walkers awoke at their Newbury church hall, and duly proceeded towards the base for the grand finale. Pettitt, busy liaising with the police, recalled the atmosphere as they approached the main gate: it was 'one of those "great emotional moments" when we – I think it was a very emotional moment for *them*, actually chained up there, getting rather bored by now – when they heard the singing coming down the road.'[26] Kutler then read out a prepared statement: an open letter to the Base Commandant, US Air Force, Greenham, explaining why 'Women for Life on Earth' had walked 120 miles from Cardiff to the proposed Cruise base, ending: 'We represent thousands of ordinary people who are opposed to these weapons and we will use all our resources to prevent the siting of these missiles here.' Another letter, demanding a televised debate between the women and a government representative, made its way to John Nott, Minister of Defence.[27]

It was the first of many such epic moments at Greenham, combining pandemonium with drama. The chained women stayed chained. Telegrams arrived congratulating the 'Protesters at Fence' – from Harrogate Women's Liberation Group, Berkshire Anti-Nuclear Campaign (BANC), Cardigan Peace Group and others. Adrenalin flowed. A rally was held, with CND speakers including Joan Ruddock and the Greenham walkers, some for the first time. Letters arrived – including one from Greenham's RAF Commander, offering to discuss 'domestic arrangements' (seemingly they were on common land) but not national defence policy.[28] A fire was lit. The vigil continued.

There was some rather prurient news coverage of the chained women, but as yet no response to their demand for a televised debate. So, Pettitt recalled:

> By day, we deliberated over our fire about how to spread our news. By night, we took it in turns to sleep chained to the fence [and] lay insomniac with fear and excitement under the early autumn stars. The American soldiers jeered and wondered at us.
>
> And then it became, well, we had to stay. . . . And people

in the Newbury group came along . . . and lent us camping equipment, because we didn't have any . . . and kept saying 'You really ought to stay here, you know'. And of course it was very difficult for those of us with children. . . . So what happened was that a group of older women and some of the younger women, the ones with less commitments, said to those of us who were rather chafing to get home – or those who had jobs to go back to – 'It's all right, because we can . . . stay on'.

Once it was clear that what had been started was now unstoppable, Pettitt returned home. She told an aghast family (both her children were still under school age) that she was going back in a week. Back at Greenham, there was a meeting in a tent and a vote: enough people were prepared to commit themselves to staying, and forming a peace camp. According to legend, this was the moment they emerged from the tent to discover a double rainbow arched over the common. It was a fortuitous start to the small, defiant Greenham peace camp.[29]

Back in Wales, Pettitt kept up a fearless barrage of pressure on the BBC and John Nott for a public debate.[30] In its first couple of months the peace camp remained remarkably low key. News about its existence criss-crossed southern England on the slender tendrils of CND, peace movement and feminist grapevines. Margot Miller, invited to the preliminary Women's Peace Alliance meeting, had stumbled only by accident upon the chained-up women. And other peace activists were busy elsewhere: Diana Shelley was involved with nonviolent direct-action training; Gay Jones, visiting the States, was at a second Women's Pentagon Action – she was joined by one or two Greenham women. For among those who *did* know about the camp, the effect was extremely energizing. Denise Aaron returned home and within a week organized Chester Women for Peace. And at the camp itself there was always a small but steady stream of visitors – including Bruce Kent and an old man who brought greens from his allotment. These comings and goings helped to spread the news. Fistfuls of letters from people inspired by the camp continued to arrive from Britain, Europe and further afield.[31] Yet there was still little popular news coverage, so the camp had to rely on word-of-mouth and articles in sympathetic small magazines (though *Spare Rib* included grumbles from a WONT member about its being a mixed camp still).[32]

Greenham was a fragile flame of defiance: a dozen people and a few tents. Work began on a high-security fence round the base. But already, in what would become a protracted war of attrition with the authorities, there were some victories. Greenham Parish Council wanted to be rid of it; but, significantly, the police refused to move people on, as no obstruction was being caused. And there were disputes whether they were camping on Ministry of Defence land or common land. The authorities already feared publicity if they attempted eviction.[33]

As winter approached, the camp dug itself in – and began to become better known. Ann Pettitt was invited to address CND's 250,000-strong Hyde Park rally on 24 October, part of the two million peace demonstrators across Europe that autumn.[34] In November, Joan Ruddock was elected CND chair, so helping to raise the profile of a new generation of women in Britain's flourishing peace movement. At Greenham money arrived from well-wishers, camp-dwellers became rate-payers, the Post Office delivered letters, and the local council even replaced their standpipe. But with this recognition came changes – and tensions. Some of the original Women for Life on Earth walkers became disillusioned with 'dossers' and the lack of a decision-making structure. The mud got deeper; the damp grew more penetrating; and there were already arguments about money.[35] At the same time the camp generated a uniquely infectious optimism: it *could* force the government to change its mind. 'Suppertime with Mrs Pettitt's pickets', announced a cheery *Standard* article, reporting over a hundred people at Greenham at weekends. 1981 ended on a revivalist note.[36]

At this point various shifts occurred which would, within twelve months, propel Greenham right to centre stage. First, confrontation between the peace camp and the authorities escalated. Relationships soured when updating the base's sewage system was given as a reason to dismantle the camp. News of this threat spread. In Halifax, for instance, our CND group was alerted and agreed to send volunteers down when bulldozers moved in.[37] The authorities had made their worst move.

Second, the isolated women's peace groups, so tiny compared to CND, began to link up. Partly this was because the new Women's Peace Alliance now offered an umbrella, with a newsletter encouraging contact between WONT, WILPF, and Women and Life on Earth; partly it was because Greenham increasingly now provided a central focus. Bridget Robson in Leeds WONT, among those receiving appeals from the camp, remembers her initial resistance:

> It felt as though these women were saying '*This* is where the women's peace movement is at, and you've all got to rush and support us.' [We felt] 'We're all very busy already. We've got lots to do.' . . . I remember definitely thinking peace camps *weren't* where it was at all.

But after a visit in March, Greenham became important to Leeds WONT too.[38]

Also, from February 1982 onwards, the camp became not just women-*led* but women-*only*. Amid controversy and some acrimony, the men were asked to leave. Like the original chaining decision it was a bruising moment, very hard on men genuinely committed to nonviolence. The immediate reason was that with eviction now threatened (and a nonviolent blockade planned in response), women-only actions offered a more complete guarantee of nonviolence in confrontations with the police or army squaddies. But perhaps, more generally, such a change was inevitable, in the face of criticism that something calling itself a 'women's peace camp' included men. It certainly sharpened Greenham's focus and imagery, so encouraging many more women to participate.[39]

Nearly as controversial as the women-only decision, the camp grew increasingly mystical and spiritual; the gates (i.e. entrances) round the base were named: New Age Gate, Forgotten Gate (and later called by rainbow colours). The pragmatism of the original Welsh women was overtaken by talk of witches and goddesses and being nice to trees. At first sight, such mumbo-jumbo might seem irrelevant to stopping Cruise missiles. But extraordinary times call for extraordinary responses; and ritual, symbols and incantations soon assumed a vital role in sustaining such an unlikely being as a women's peace camp outside a nuclear base. Certainly Dr Lynne Jones, who had seen how effective theatricality had been at the Women's Pentagon Action and who visited the camp that winter, took this shift in her stride:

> A woman walked up carrying a large puppet; an enormous woman's head with long red hair and brightly coloured hand-painted robes. 'This is the Goddess,' she said.
>
> 'Right,' said Helen [John], 'let's walk to Newbury.'
>
> We set off, the Goddess in the lead, bright against snow-laden branches and clear sky.[40]

All these four developments around spring 1982 helped strengthen Greenham's resolve to stay put and take on the government. A women-only action was planned, linking nonviolent confrontation and spirituality. On 22 March (following a Spring Equinox Festival) there would be a twenty-four-hour blockade of the base. Amid more eviction threats from Newbury Council, appeals for support went out, and the Greenham women began to organize in small groups for nonviolence training. On the day, 150 women chained themselves together across the gates; thirty-four later appeared in court, charged with obstructing the highway. Lynne Jones, one of those taking part, now resigned from her hospital job to work full-time for the peace movement.[41]

By this time, Greenham had inspired other peace camps: at Molesworth in Cambridgeshire, also due to receive Cruise missiles; at Upper Heyford in Oxfordshire; and there was a long vigil at Faslane on Clydeside, base for Polaris submarines. 'A new craze is sweeping Britain,' reported *Sanity*. 'Peace Camp mania.'[42]

But Greenham remained queen of the peace camps. Its pre-eminence was assured by the increasingly imminent arrival of Cruise missiles *there* rather than anywhere else, as well as by the shifts already described within the camp itself. Yet during summer and early autumn 1982 – dominated by the futile Falklands War in the South Atlantic, when ugly nationalism effectively throttled rational discussion on defence – Greenham remained marginal to most women involved in CND or the women's movement. Yet a series of events, crescendoing on 12 December 1982, transformed Greenham into a household name.

24 May was the first ever Women's International Day for Disarmament. Lynne Jones, now joined by Margot Miller with her long women's peace movement experience, worked hard to encourage local groups. In the event there were at least seventy actions, ranging from Birmingham WONT's vigil in the Bullring to an anti-Falklands petition in Bath, while in Holland a Dutch women's peace camp was set up.[43] But in a Britain mesmerized by 'bashing the Argies', the day received little national press coverage.

Meanwhile, court cases and eviction attempts at Greenham pushed their way into the newspapers. Women at the peace camp began to develop spontaneous spot blockades of the base. Then on 14 May a High Court judge, at the request of Newbury District Council, ordered eighteen named women to leave. However, forty other women added *their* names to the list during the hearing; so the judge adjourned the proceedings to move to a larger court. Outside, Greenham supporters were accompanied by jugglers, a band, and monks from the Milton Keynes Buddhist Centre beating loud and persistently on hand-held drums. 'The noise penetrated the neo-Gothic recesses of the courts,' one newspaper reported, 'and apparently several judges complained.' But its headline 'Judge Breaks Up Peace Camp' was premature. On 27 May the long-awaited eviction began; although caravans on council land were moved, those on Ministry of Transport land stayed; and when a bulldozer began shovelling up personal belongings, several Greenham women lay down in front of it; one even climbed into the cab and was dragged away by police. Four women were arrested. A sympathetic Berkshire county councillor complained of Newbury's 'Argentinian' methods. The peace camp stayed.[44]

The due processes of law work only if sufficient people respect them. Yet *can* a legal system which permits violent nuclear missiles to be sited deep in the English countryside, but forbids nonviolent women to camp on the common beside them, command that respect? The Greenham women exposed this juridical humbug in a series of surreal court hearings, using imagination and a sense of fun to mock the judiciary's support of the unsupportable. When the 'bulldozer' women appeared in court they hummed loudly from the dock, wove webs of wool (the Vermont Spinsters symbol was becoming synonymous with Greenham), insisted on swearing on the Goddess, and challenged the phrase 'keeping the peace'. Each was sentenced to a week in Holloway. On Nagasaki Day in August, some Greenham women walked into the base, and ceremoniously delivered symbolic Japanese paper cranes to the commander.[45] The high jinks had started!

There were about fifteen women living at Greenham, with others arriving all the time. And it was at this point, just after the Nagasaki action, that Rebecca Johnson, a well-travelled twenty-seven-year-old politics research student who spoke Japanese, visited the camp for a week's holiday. She arrived in the middle of a major row and spent her first day chopping wood. But within two days, she recalled, 'I just suddenly realized that I wanted to go and live there. That *something* had happened. Something was there, that I found incredibly inspiring.[46] It was a good time to arrive. A Department of Transport eviction was expected shortly. Instead of just waiting for it, the Greenham women seized the initiative. On 27 August nineteen ran through the gate and occupied a sentry box *inside* the base. They were arrested for breach of the peace. 'The women', a newspaper report added, 'frustrated attempts . . . to get to them by weaving shut the base's main gates with green wool.' Then on 5 October thirteen women, trying to stop construction work at the base, were also arrested and charged with breach of the peace.[47]

The camp was now a year old. With two big court cases pending in mid November, Greenham was becoming reminiscent of the suffragettes' historic set-piece battles, with Holloway prison looming. As they waited for this symbolic confrontation with the male judiciary, the peace women were also laying exciting plans for a big international action. Exactly whose idea it first was seems unclear: so, in the absence of neat minute books, historians of anarchic popular movements like Greenham must resign themselves to the fact that there can be no *one* account of such a hectic period as late 1982.[48]

Rebecca Johnson, already a veteran of the sentry-box occupation, remembers a meeting in a caravan about the time of the camp's first birthday. Two dates were juggled – Hallowe'en and Sunday 12 December, anniversary of the original NATO decision – reflecting Greenham's complementary sides: witches and missiles. On this occasion, missiles won; and the action would be extended to Monday the 13th for a blockade. Eventually, 'Embrace the base on Sunday, close the base on Monday' was agreed upon.

About October there was a gathering in the Friends' Meeting House in Newbury; among those now involved was Margot Miller, who remembers the sense of frustration:

> Everybody sat around. And there was some woman talking about . . . vibes. . . . And it was quite an awful meeting. . . . People said, 'Oh, I've got to go at four o'clock and we haven't decided anything yet.' And there were people going out of the door. And [one woman] was sitting on the floor . . . and she was [saying], 'It's nine miles round the base. We need 16,000 women to come – I'm sure if we ask them, they'll come.' And that was just at the end of the meeting. . . . And it was [as] we went out of the door, [she] said, 'Well, if we write to everybody, and ask them to write to ten others, then maybe we'll *do* something'. . . . It was just left like that.[49]

Eventually, amid more confusion and tensions, a circular letter entitled 'Women For Life On Earth Say "No To Cruise Missiles At Greenham Common"', dated 14 October, was agreed. This historic letter said:

> The Peace Camp has been a women's initiative. Reversing traditional roles, women have been leaving home for peace, rather than men leaving home for war. . . . We cannot stand by while others are organizing to destroy life on our earth. . . . We have one year left in which to reverse the government's decision about Cruise Missiles. There is still time to stop them.
>
> We are inviting women from all over Britain, Europe and the world to come to Greenham Common on December 12 and 13 to take part in a mass action that will . . . express the spirit of peace and the politics of peace. . . .
>
> EMBRACE THE BASE ON SUNDAY . . . CLOSE THE BASE ON MONDAY
>
> . . . Women are asked to bring personal things that represent the threat of nuclear war to us and that express *our*

lives, our anger and our joy. . . . We want to decorate the entire fence with personal things. . . .

THIS IS A CHAIN LETTER WITH A DIFFERENCE. WE'LL MEET AS A LIVING CHAIN. . . . PLEASE TELL EVERY WOMAN YOU KNOW.[50]

Memories may vary about how the chain-letter process accelerated. Margot Miller's own recollection is that Helen John told her she was going down to Glastonbury to write letters, using Women and Life on Earth file cards:

> And so I said, 'Well, I've got some index cards too. All the contacts I've picked up over the years, and so on.' I'd taken addresses out of *Peace News* and kept a file. And so I took my file box down to Glastonbury. And we sat there, and there was about four or five of us, and we wrote a thousand envelopes . . . asking everyone to write to ten more people.[51]

Lynne Jones, who rashly offered to co-ordinate preparations for nonviolence and whose telephone number was on the leaflet, found that from October onwards her phone 'rang solidly all day, every day, for everything. You can forget it just ringing about nonviolent action. It rang about everything.' Diana Shelley was busy supplying a Greenham trainers' network meeting with information for a legal briefing; and Bridget Robson recalls how the Leeds WONT group:

> set up and organized in a *massive* way for December. I spent most of the autumn organizing transport for the December . . . for groups of women to actually go and take part and camp and stay the weekend, and take part in the blockades. We had six minibuses, I think. Six affinity groups. (I think CND organized actual coaches . . . for people going for the day.) But we were actually organizing nonviolence training, and getting women into affinity groups. The telephone never stopped ringing. It was a really *huge* organization.

In Wales, Ann Pettitt was again drawn directly into the Greenham orbit as one of thousands of local women photocopying the chain letter and organizing coaches; (though, speaking to local mixed peace groups, she found it 'very difficult to explain the fine line between something that was positively a *women*'s statement, and something that *wasn't against* men'). Rebecca Johnson remembers 'a palpable buzz' when she learned that her mother, not a peace activist, had received three chain letters. And in Yorkshire an 'Embrace the Base' leaflet produced by Leeds WONT soon criss-crossed the region; our Halifax CND group had already written to protest at that autumn's attempts to evict the camp; but it was not really until mid November and the court cases that news of the Greenham plans began to spread like wildfire.[52]

On 15 November, eleven women who had taken part in the sentry-box occupation appeared before Newbury magistrates. The imagination and ingenuity of their defence lent the court hearing an epic quality. Their lawyer, citing the 1967 Criminal Law Act and the 1969 Genocide Act, said the women's occupation was completely lawful as they were doing their duty as citizens in trying to prevent a crime of genocide. One of the six Welsh women in the dock said that legal means to prevent nuclear war had failed: 'Cruise missiles will mean the death of me and my children and millions more like me across the world. You cannot be a Conscientious Objector in the next war.' Rebecca Johnson added that she had visited Hiroshima and had joined the peace camp as a result of what she saw. Expert witnesses were called in. E. P. Thompson said he believed that Cruise missiles imperilled the civilization of Western Europe: planet Earth was in danger, and that amounted to genocide. The Bishop of Salisbury added that as a Christian he could not contemplate the use of nuclear weapons: it was also against all military law. Nevertheless, the eleven women were found guilty; they refused to be bound over to keep the peace and were led away chanting to begin their fortnight in Holloway.

The other court cases followed. In all, twenty-three women were imprisoned in three days! The national press began to stir. 'Tears as peace girl is jailed', commented the *Daily Express* helpfully. The *Guardian* ran a sympathetic, if pompous, editorial, 'The Greening of the Common'.[53] Even the women in prison began to get a whiff of the excitement. Johnson was amongst those in Holloway:

> I just remember people sending us in press cuttings. And I suddenly thought 'Something very big is happening'. And . . . it was coming out of prison, we were met by all these cameras, TV crews; and ITN, I think, had brought champagne so they could film us popping it. . . . Things were really moving, and people *knew* about December. So all we had to say at the prison gates was, 'If we can go to prison for this, you can go to Greenham, even if it's snowing, even if it's cold. Come and surround Greenham.'[54]

And so they did. All over the country, coach drivers unfolded road maps of Berkshire and estimated how long it would take their vehicles to lumber through Newbury. Hundreds of local organizers began to panic at the swelling demand for coach seats. My own account is just one of many: Halifax's plan for a minibus soon turned into a booking for a fifty-seven-seater coach – and the phone rang constantly. The peace movement was daily in the headlines.

Newbury Council made a new bid to evict the camp. It stood little chance. From the very beginning, Sunday 12 December was going to be a great success. At 6.30 a.m., Rebecca Johnson crawled out of her black plastic sheeting – only to discover about 200 bitterly cold women who had travelled overnight from Edinburgh and Glasgow, with candles and torches. Diana Shelley, who had arrived on Saturday and was rather horrified by the lack of organization, latched on to a woman from CND who had said: '"Oh,

God, I want someone sensible." I said, "Well, I'll work with you. You're sensible"' – and spent the rest of the day operating a walkie-talkie system around the base.

Meanwhile, more and more women were arriving. Ann Pettitt recalls that it was only when they reached the Severn Bridge that she realized what a vast number of vehicles there were; by the Newbury roundabout they were wedged into a traffic jam of coaches, minibuses and cars. 'The tears actually flowed down my face because it was just full of women. . . . It was like the greatest women's show on earth.' At Greenham, women wandered along the perimeter fence and waved from the bracken. Our Halifax coach ceremoniously crawled round the base, head-to-toe with other vehicles, until we found flat ground for Mary Brewer's wheelchair. We clambered out at Red Gate, and just had time to pose with our CND and Labour Party banners for the local paper before pinning photographs, balloons and other decorations on the fence. Mary Brewer hung up a pincushion made by one of her grandchildren, and later recalled:

I'll never forget that feeling; it'll live with me for ever . . . the lovely feeling of pinning the things on; and the feeling, as we walked round, and we clasped hands. . . . It was even better than holding your baby for the first time, after giving birth – and that is one of the loveliest feelings you can ever have. When your babe's put in your arms and you give it a cuddle. . . . Because that is a self-thing – selfish thing, really, between you and your husband, isn't it? The baby. Whereas Greenham – it was for women; it was for peace; it was for the world; it was for Britain; it was for us; it was for more.

So much was remarkable about that day. Ann Pettitt recalls that she and Carmen Kutler 'kept on reporting to each other, "Have you seen the china tea set? Someone's pinned this entire tea set!"' The planned ceremonies worked: Rebecca Johnson, who was travelling from gate to gate, remembers that at two o'clock she and the other woman just leapt out of the car, and

> ran up, and there were just a few faces we knew – of women;
> we just grabbed hands with them. And then you could *feel*
> this sound just started erupting around the base. . . . You
> knew that the base was completely surrounded by joyous,
> strong, determined women.[55]

Television news that night showed aerial shots of the Greenham base completely encircled by candles glowing in the dark. The following day, emblazoned across the entire *Daily Mirror* front page, ran: 'PEACE! The plea by 30,000 women who joined hands in the world's most powerful protest against nuclear war.' Even the *New York Times* headlined 'Women in England Rally Against Missiles'. 'Embrace the base' had encircled the world.[56]

12

An Icon for the Eighties
(1983–84)

The 'Embrace the Base' action offered the 1980s new and distinctive images. The song sung most often – 'You can't kill the spirit / She is like a mountain / Old and strong / She goes on and on and on' – captured the haunting mood of the day.[1] Television ensured that pictures of Greenham entered every British home. Among the millions watching the news that night was the wife of a lorry driver, Pauline Smith, then in hospital; she found it difficult to work out exactly what 'this "Greenham" thing' was; but, fascinated by such happy-looking women, she determined to find out more when she recovered.[2]

The iconography that sprang from 'Embrace the Base' was extremely powerful. Greenham became the evocative symbol of a popular refusal to accept nuclear missiles. But pictures of 'ordinary' women pinning photographs of their children and grandchildren to the wire were quickly overlaid by other more sharply focused images. For 12 December was followed by a series of large-scale blockades and imaginative sorties into the base, bequeathing to the 1980s unforgettable Greenham pictures: of a thick carpet of seated women stretching along a road as far as the eye could see, blocking in a bus and one helpless policeman; and of a ring of women silhouetted against the dawn, dancing on top of the Cruise silos inside the base. If the blatantly triumphant post-Falklands Margaret Thatcher offered one dominant image for the decade, then a similarly powerful alternative icon was now surely emerging: Greenham woman. It was a many-sided icon, ever shifting, a memorable mix of 'ordinary' mother-and-housewife, white-haired veteran grandmother-protester, and intrepid young base-invader – all pitted fearlessly against the government's 'resolve' to deploy weapons of mass destruction.

Monday 13 December's 'Close the Base' represented both a massive escalation of direct action at Greenham and a significant transformation of the culture of nonviolence in Britain. It revealed small informal affinity groups as an ideal *feminist* way of working. Lynne Jones was among those aware at the time of the magnitude of this attempt:

> We all [were] really excited; and we sat up in these soaking wet marquees *all* night, getting into groups. . . . And again it wasn't to me learning the law or what happens if you're arrested. The process that was important that was going on there was that women were getting to know each other. . . . We went through 'This is what I'm frightened of. This is what I'm really scared [of]. This is my name. This is where I'm coming from. Who are you?'

Of course, much of this careful preparation broke down on the day:

> Women just shifted around the base like water – where they were needed. And the affinity group they started out with in the morning had disappeared. And *forget* the legal observer! . . . Because women went on arriving all Monday.[3]

A whole new generation of women now felt confident enough together to attempt to blockade a USAF base. About 2,000 took part; many had slept overnight across the variously named gates. To permit three buses to come out, sixty Thames Valley police in the 6.30 a.m. darkness dragged thirty women away from one gate. Here, as elsewhere later in the day, women regrouped – only to be thrown aside by the police. As dawn broke, more women joined in. Rebecca Johnson, who had been blockading at Blue Gate since 6 a.m., remembers how rough some of the police were – and how vital it was that Greenham was a safe women-only space:

> A lot of women got boots in their ribs . . . and yet, when they kept going back again and again and again . . . you'd get flung to one side, and a woman would help pick you up, and you'd hug each other, and then you'd both go back. And then the next time you'd be helping another woman getting flung out, and you'd hug each other. And these were total strangers. . . . I think it made a huge difference that it was women-only because you were just picking each other up out of ditches, and hugging each other. . . . And you *wanted* to go back, but you knew you didn't *have* to. . . . Women were sitting it out on the sides at different times, getting a breather.[4]

Police policy that day was 'no arrests', but that construction work on the silos inside the base should not be disrupted. In the end, both sides claimed victory: the police because vehicles *had* got in and out; the women because work at the base *had* been delayed, and because the peaceful blockade again made headline news. 'British Police Remove Protesters From Base', noted the *New York Times*. 'The Bully and the Bomb', intoned the *Express* front page. 'Scuffles as Women Seal Off Air Base', headlined the *Guardian*, alongside a photograph of an elderly woman being 'removed' by police.[5]

For the next eighteen months, Greenham was seldom out of the news. On muddy winter mornings, women crawling bleary-eyed out of their 'benders' (instant 'tents' constructed from polythene draped over branches) were now confronted by a succession of journalists, all eager to ask exactly the same string of questions: 'How long have you been here? Where do you get your water from? How many times have you been arrested? Where do you shit? What about your family? Why is it women only? . . .' Meanwhile a series of breathtakingly inventive actions followed in quick succession. Outstanding was the silo action of New

Year's Day 1983; this aimed to refocus attention back to the preparations going on *inside* the base for Cruise's arrival later that year. The press was alerted. Reporters would be at the base at dawn. Ladders were purchased to scale the fifteen-foot perimeter fence. Over four dozen women crept out stealthily in the darkness. One of them later recorded the tension of this dramatic moment:

> The silos loom threateningly in the half-light of dawn. We knew that now, standing before the fence, we would need to be so quick. Two ladders are propped successfully against the fence, with carpet laid over the top barbed wire. . . . We start clambering over. There are headlights coming towards us from inside the base while it seems like an endless stream of women are crossing the barriers of destruction. . . . Suddenly two policemen are there, aggressively shoving the ladders and wrenching them away. . . . We begin singing and walking quickly, almost at a run towards the silos. . . .
>
> We scramble up the mud-drenched slopes towards the top of the silos. . . . For an hour we danced, sang and made women's peace symbols with the stones that lay on the surface. . . .[6]

Forty-four women subsequently appeared before the Newbury magistrates on 3 January. After consultation with the Director of Public Prosecutions (DPP) they were charged not under the Official Secrets Act (though they had penetrated into a high-security area) but merely with breach of the peace.[7] It is frustrating for peace historians to have no access yet to DPP memoranda; but it was already clear that the state chose not to bring the full panoply of the law down upon the Greenham women, as it had in 1961 against the Committee of 100's planned Wethersfield action. How had society changed in twenty-one years? Why was the state not prepared to use the Official Secrets Act against the women trespassers? Did the DPP feel that a jury trial could no longer guarantee a 'guilty' verdict? And what did that indicate about public doubts about government defence policies?

'Propaganda successes by the Greenham Common ban the bomb demonstrators and others', noted the *Express* tersely on 3 January, 'have worried the Prime Minister with a general election approaching. . . . She wants to win the nuclear argument within the next few months.'[8]

The silos case was therefore heard at the Newbury magistrates' court, far away from the Old Bailey spotlight. On 15 February about 500 supporters massed outside, chanting encouragement. The women, all but four giving the Greenham peace camp as their address, were found guilty of breach of the peace. The majority refused to be bound over and were sentenced to fourteen days' imprisonment – including a seventy-three-year-old grandmother who protested that she had witnessed two world wars, and now saw that the government was planning a third. In the court, women climbed on chairs and sang. Among other demonstrations of sympathy, fifty Swedish women held a protest outside the British Embassy in Stockholm.[9]

Even before the silos case came to court, the legal saga to establish the Greenham women's right to remain outside the base rumbled on. Twenty women got their names on the draft electoral register, to the fury of Newbury's Conservative Association. 'A piece of plastic sheeting', fumed the affronted Tory agent, 'can hardly be described as a permanent or secure home.' The prospective Conservative councillor for the Greenham ward lodged an objection. Yet on 11 January, at a day-long hearing, West Berkshire's returning officer upheld nine women's right to vote at elections; and stated that on the new register their address would be shown as 'The Peace Camp, outside the main gates, Greenham Common'. While the Conservative agent made plain his dismay, Helen John announced her intention to stand at the next election in Cardiff South against James Callaghan, the old-style Labour MP and ex-Prime Minister.[10]

Newbury District Council remained determined to rid itself of this turbulent camp. In January, at a private meeting of a few select councillors, the common land by-laws were revoked, giving the council power to apply for injunctions against 'named' trespassers; if such offences were proved, they could carry heavy sentences.[11] Writs were duly served on fifty-nine 'named' women at the camp, together with 'persons unknown'; and a High Court hearing was scheduled for 22 February. A handwritten leaflet, captioned 'Boring Old High Court', went out from the camp, inviting women to attend and:

> give the camp as your only home . . . say that you are one of the persons unknown. . . . The 'camp' seems to be the centre of the web – threads reaching everywhere – each one making up the web and creating new strands of thought in hidden corners.[12]

This appeal, with Greenham's unique combination of mystic webbery and confrontation with the state, worked. The judiciary could no longer cope with the growing number of women ready to defy the law. In addition to the 'named' defendants, at least a further ninety women presented affidavits asking to be joined in the action. Again, none of the High Court rooms could accommodate so many; the judge had to adjourn the case. 'Peace Women Swamp Court', ran the headlines.[13]

Newbury Council would not give up. Two days later, on 24 February, the Department of the Environment, at the council's request (despite protest from opposition councillors), revoked deeds allowing members of the public commonland rights. The next day six women, who had been holding a vigil outside Holloway prison, scaled scaffolding, staging a rooftop protest in support of the Greenham women still inside. During March the rash of court cases continued – with no fewer than 200 women appearing in the High Court.[14]

From New Year onwards, therefore, it became clear that 1983, with an election likely, was going to be the year of the peace movement versus the Thatcher government in a struggle for credibility over nuclear defence. While CND remained the butt of the government, Greenham now occupied the central *theatrical* arena. This struggle was dramatically staged against a variety of backdrops: the High Court, Newbury Council Chamber and magistrates' court, Holloway. With the Greenham women now a media spectacle, links between feminism and anti-nuclear militarism became the subject of intense public debate. This debate now spread beyond the more formal arena occupied by CND and the political parties and became a subject of private, domestic controversy, entering people's homes and crossing their kitchen tables. And in some households, such discussions about peace and gender politics had immediate impact as women radicalized by Greenham (mainly young and single, but a few older women as well), left home to live at the camp.

The camp at the main (Yellow) Gate grew fast, and camps at other gates – Green, Blue, Red, Orange – sprang up. Already Greenham's inspiration spread outwards. Links were made with Sicily's proposed Cruise missile site: women there wove webs across the entrance so that workers could not get in. There was a Greenham speaking tour in America, where a women's peace camp was planned for Seneca in upstate New York. Equally important, women returning home after 'Embrace the Base' set up women's peace groups in their home towns. In Brighton they produced *Lysistrata*, a women and peace magazine. In Chester, Denise Aaron's Women for Peace's newsletter published local women's Greenham stories. In Halifax there was no separate women's peace group yet, but the CND group donated £25 for the silos prisoners' action.[15] So now, in cities, towns and even villages across Britain, knots of women, many of them grass-roots CND members, were touched by the Greenham magic.

The camp could count on many levels of support in its struggle for survival; and such support challenged any government claim to a mandate to evict the camp. Particularly worrying for the government was support from Tory women in the shires and comfortable suburbs: women whom – on other issues – Thatcher might happily count among her loyal supporters.[16] It was this 'gender gap' over nuclear defence policies which became so hotly contested during spring 1983.

In *The Iron Ladies: Why Do Women Vote Tory?* Bea Campbell describes how events at Greenham touched Conservative women *as women*. Some, of course, were disgusted that such a camp was organized by women. ('It's the sordidness that upsets me', complained one. 'They've just got no responsibility about their children.') But others said: 'Before Greenham Common I didn't realize that the Americans had got their missiles here. . . . It was the fuss the Greenham women made that made me realize.' Views on the women-only peace camp might vary; but, more crucially, opinion polls revealed that considerably *more* women than men opposed Britain's Trident missile programme and, particularly, the proposed American Cruise missiles. Campbell describes how back in spring 1981, well before the walk to Greenham, 56 per cent of women (though only 43 per cent of men) opposed Cruise; by October 1982 this had risen to 64 per cent of women (and 51 per cent of men). In early January 1983, a Marplan poll revealed that opposition was still growing: 67 per cent of women (though only 55 per cent of men) disapproved of the government's decision to allow the Americans to base Cruise missiles on British soil.[17]

With another general election looming, opposition from two-thirds of women voters was worrying. Even before this poll was published, Thatcher replaced John Nott as her Defence Secretary with a bright new broom: Michael Heseltine. He was, the *Sunday Times* jokily suggested, perfect to 'dazzle the "ordinary", muddle-headed housewives who have been seduced away from the Tory ramparts by the peace movement'; and it noted a recent poll showing that the Tory lead over Labour among women voters had fallen from 10 per cent to a mere 2 per cent, 'and the indication is that disarmament is the issue that has influenced this shift'.[18]

Aided by a helpful million pound anti-CND advertising campaign, Heseltine went on the assertive, snubbing CND's request for a public debate. At his side was the trusty right-wing press, keen to caricature the Greenham women. The *Sun* divided the 'nice' women who had embraced the base and then gone home from 'militant feminist and burly lesbians' who stayed on. Equally quick off the mark, Jean Rook in the *Express* shrieked: 'The female of *this* species . . . almost deadlier than the Bomb', adding: 'I'd rather be blown sky high than survive in the grip of the feminist ringleaders.' And on 7 February Fleet Street was given the chance it wanted. Heseltine visited Newbury and the West Berkshire Conservative Association – doubtless to commiserate about electoral registers. That morning, Greenham women, arrayed in silver-foil snake costumes, had again penetrated the perimeter fence – and danced around the runway for nearly an hour before being arrested. That evening women whooped and sang as Heseltine, guarded by a hundred police, arrived for his meeting. As he was escorted in, he stumbled. Although there was no suggestion that he was pushed, the incident produced banner headlines like 'WOMEN OF FURY' and 'Peace Girls Mob Heseltine'.[19] (Less successful in the struggle to win over hearts and minds – though doubtless more honest in its tactics – was the new anti-Greenham 'Women for Defence' group, founded by *Sunday Express* diarist Lady Olga Maitland. Like the anti-suffragists earlier this century it got twisted into embarrassed knots: agreed to admit men, changed its name to 'Women and Families for Defence', elected Lord Trenchard, former Minister for Defence Procurement, to its presidency – and, despite the best of intentions, never managed to undermine either Greenham or CND.)[20]

Within the peace movement itself, arguments for and against the women-only camp at Greenham were growing heated, despite the encouraging 'gender gap' poll findings. CND *had* changed its ways of working considerably since 1958–64 when platforms of male dignitaries and formally structured meetings often seemed the order of the day. Joan Ruddock remained chair; women comprised the majority of directly elected members on the National Council. However, it was still male activists who predominantly represented CND's sixteen regions on the Council;[21] and of course, ever since the decision to exclude men a year earlier, there had been tension around the gender question among peace activists. But discussion remained fairly low-key until 'Embrace the Base' burst into the news headlines. Then the issue sprang into the centre of public debate. (Particularly striking to historians is that this discussion took place in a vacuum, as if the issues raised were *all* brand new, and as if the Olive Leaf women and the Hague Conference had never happened.[22])

Something of a war of words developed among peace activists. In the *Guardian*, 'Peace Campaign That Fuels the Sex War' correspondence was followed immediately by 'The Reasons Why Greenham Should Be a Women's World', including a letter stating:

> As long as men still insist on being at the centre of every-thing that happens in our society, we'll still need women-only demonstrations. . . . We can't deny that more women than men oppose nuclear weapons. . . . I think that the fact that, as a woman, I am excluded from military power means I'm also excluded from military fantasies.
>
> I'm entirely unseduced by violence. Too many men – even those in the peace movement – still think storming the fence is more glorious than bringing up children.[23]

The gender–peace debate remained as complex as in earlier years; and Greenham's women-only actions now gave it an added sharpness. Within the peace movement, the debate partly remained pragmatic, polarizing around two propositions: *either* women-only actions are more effective because the contrast between protesters and the nuclear state (personified by the army and police) is more stark, therefore the guarantee of nonviolence is greater and more women will respond; *or* – as many CND members argued – women-only spaces are less effective than mixed ones because, with the arrival of Cruise so imminent, the peace movement needs to unite – urgently.

This gender–peace debate within the peace movement also, of course, went beyond pragmatism and began to touch on fundamental issues. It began by asking: '*Are* women more peaceful than men?' Respondents included old-style peace activists (interestingly, many from the anarchist and libertarian left) who answered 'No' and cited, not unreasonably, the nuclear-military zeal of the Prime Minister and women's collusion in the tawdry Falklands War the previous summer. Women may not fight themselves, but – echoing Ruskin 120 years earlier – their admiration for the noble warrior helps to underpin militarism.

But there were also those who felt strongly that blaming women for male belligerence was deceitful in the extreme: it ignored far too much. As writers like Virginia Woolf had earlier stated, it ignored women's traditional exclusion from both political and military power. As Schreiner had argued, it omitted women's creating of life – and thus their fierce maternal refusal to see that life destroyed. But particularly it ignored, as Gilman had suggested, how boys are socialized to become more violent than women. Now, stemming from the 1970s Women's Liberation Movement, military and nuclear violence became linked with male violence towards women on the streets and in the home. 'Take the toys from the boys' summed it up neatly; and some more extreme feminists, holding that *all* men were actually or potentially violent, went further. Women sprayed 'WAR = RAPE, WOMEN SAY NO!' on a war memorial. Even Gilman's arguments could now take on a sharper edge when mingled with anti-patriarchal rhetoric to produce graffiti like 'War Is Menstruation Envy'.[24]

During spring 1983 these far-reaching questions were argued out among peace activists. But soon discussion about women-only spaces acquired a new urgency. With Heseltine on the offensive, the arrival of Cruise only months away, and a general election imminent, the Greenham debate grew intense as Easter approached. Feminism had had an effect on the peace movement and women were already better represented in CND than in any of the major political parties, but the separatism of Greenham was something different. Some women who had supported a 'women-led' march now opposed women-only peace actions.[25]

CND, genuinely committed to democratic decision-making, opened the pages of *Sanity* to the debate. 'Let's get on with it together', argued one National Council member, Annie Tunnicliffe. 'Over the past year, I have sometimes felt there was more sisterhood in a bus queue than in the women's peace movement.' In the next issue, a woman retaliated: 'Thousands and thousands of Greenham women have brought the nuclear issue into everyone's front room.' *Sanity*'s 'Letters Special' produced its biggest post bag for years, with the majority supporting Tunnicliffe's views. And in its 'Round Three in Women and Peace debate', the woman chair of East Anglia CND demanded: 'Now is the time to reclaim Greenham. . . . Isn't it time they buried the separatist hatchet . . . and recognized that Greenham Common does not belong to them alone?'[26]

The reply was: 'No, it isn't.' There were many reasons. But one argument was particularly powerful, both in spring 1983 and in later years: only those women *living* at the peace camp had the authority to determine what actions should take place, and whether it should remain women-only, for only they experienced the daily struggle for survival, wedged on a precarious strip of land up by the perimeter wire. This might seem like moral blackmail to the camp's critics; but this was surely to underestimate both the degree of support for the camp among CND's grass roots, and also the peace women's courage for staying put in Greenham's inhospitable mud over the last year and a half. Rebecca Johnson, who had by then been at the camp about eight months, later made this point:

> When I look back on it, I think the *struggles* are what made Greenham so powerful, so moving, and so important. Actually trying to solve those problems. We would be able to say nothing to the world about solving problems of war and problems of violence, if, in fact, we had only experienced sweetness and light. We've actually experienced the most extraordinary – I mean, police violence, vigilantes, daily evictions, often with quite a high degrees of violence, imprisonment, repeated imprisonments. . . .[27]

Such arguments were effective; and some peace activists who in less urgent times might have wanted to query separatism and the Goddess and silver-foil snakes chose not to, believing that the Greenham women needed support, not criticism. So, instead, they gently reminded the camp's detractors that extraordinary times demanded extraordinary actions – like a women-only peace camp and an almost religious faith in the need to endure hardship to save life on earth.[28]

With so many CND members recognizing the special nature of the camp, these arguments prevailed. In the event, therefore, at Easter, there was a women's blockade at Greenham. (In Halifax a dozen of us organized nonviolence training, and a petition in support of the peace camp and against Cruise, hired a minibus to take us down to this, our first blockade, and arrived by 6 a.m. at Blue Gate where we found ourselves outnumbered by a *very* heavy police presence.) On Good Friday, 70,000 people took part in CND's mixed 'human chain' linking Greenham, Aldermaston and the Royal Ordnance Factory at Burgfield – three key points along Berkshire's 'Nuclear Valley'. 'It is a great victory, and especially a victory over the government's propaganda', Joan Ruddock told the rally. Meanwhile, at Greenham, twenty-six women dressed as Easter bunnies and teddy bears entered the base and proceeded to have a picnic – until they were arrested.[29]

The strains within the peace movement over women-only actions were contained. Too many CND members could remember the damaging split over Committee of 100 tactics two decades earlier; now CND was a democratic membership organization which had structures to cope with potentially divisive issues. Women-only peace actions at Greenham and elsewhere became more firmly established as part of the peace movement.

While this debate was taking place within the *peace* movement, Greenham and the gender–peace debate also had great impact upon the *women*'s movement in Britain. This was part of a broader shift from a 1970s socialist feminism emphasizing equal rights to a stress – as we have seen – on gender difference, on opposing male violence, and on celebrating woman-centred culture. For some women, this posed no problem: their feminism was changing anyway, and they welcomed the way Greenham brought a new generation into the women's movement. Other feminists, however, remained hostile to the ideas that now seemed to be emerging from the women's peace movement. They had strong reservations about the nappies-on-the-fence imagery of 'Embrace the Base', because the feminism they grew up with was trying to get away from a constricting maternalism in which domesticity was offered as women's sole destiny. And, others argued, did not the 'ordinary' white, middle-class women so often depicted at Greenham merely silence still further women of colour – and therefore the issue of racism currently troubling many feminists? Surely, they asked, this could not *really* be what women's liberation was now about? 'The elevation of the "feminine" – mothering, nurturing, family-orientated – into a "natural" force for peace', *Spare Rib* stated, 'appears neither historically correct nor particularly feminist.' Among the letters which followed, one requested that 'someone must expose it [Greenham] for the reactionary charade that it is' – because it confused the 'symbols of life' pinned on the fence (nappies, recipes, tampons) with symbols of women's oppression.[30]

But despite such criticisms from within both the peace movement and the women's movement, energetic and imaginative celebrations of Greenham continued – and entered popular culture. From early 1983 onwards, you could wear a Greenham badge; send a Greenham picture postcard; listen to a cassette of taped Greenham music; watch a Greenham video. A moving film documentary invited women to 'Carry Greenham Home'. Songs like 'You Can't Kill the Spirit', 'Stand Up, Women, Make Your Choice' and 'Which Side Are You On?' became hauntingly recognizable. Greenham even produced a novel, *Mud*, which (rather like *Non-Combatants and Others* seventy years before) offered an affectionate dig at the women's peace movement.[31]

At the same time, a number of books focusing on Greenham rolled off the feminist presses. Virago published *Over Our Dead Bodies*; the Women's Press produced *Keeping the Peace*, which included news from Holland, Germany, America and Japan. And the Feminism and Nonviolence Study Group published *Piecing It Together* (though the group's nonviolent feminism encountered criticism from Irish and Black women. 'It is your privilege, that you can choose peaceful demonstration,' wrote Nefertiti. 'Power *does* come from the barrel of a gun, or how else did you colonize me?'[32]) Even more controversial was *Breaching the Peace*, a collection of radical feminist papers, mainly written for a workshop, 'The Women's Liberation Movement versus The Women's Peace Movement or How Dare You Presume I went to Greenham?'. It alleged that being women-only made Greenham no more *feminist* than Women's Institutes; and that peace camps diverted much-needed energy from the key enemy, patriarchy:

I see the current development of the 'women's peace movement' . . . as part of . . . the decline of the Women's Liberation Movement over the past few years. . . . Greenham
Common looks like the acceptable face of women-only
actions to me. . . . So, it's OK to link arms and hold hands
around a military base in the cause of peace, but do it on the
streets for the love of it and it's another matter, as any dyke
who's been beaten up can tell you.[33]

Breaching the Peace sent a ripple of irritation through the
women's peace movement. Some felt that it failed to recognize that Greenham women were considerably more feminist than they were being given credit for. Later, a woman
from Green Gate replied furiously with her own pamphlet,
Raging Women: In Reply to Breaching the Peace – a personal
statement which indicates the depths of feeling that
Greenham now generated.

Yes, it is possible that the peace movement could drain
energy from the feminist movement, especially in rural
areas. Do we respond by sniping at our peace sisters . . . ? If
feminism is truly relevant to the lives of wymn it will arise
where women *are*. . . . More wimin pass through Greenham
than any women's centre I've ever known. . . .
    A constant criticism in *Breaching the Peace* is that we [at the
camp] are not trying to do something for ourselves as
wymn. . . . It is empowering to be directly up against the
government, to be effectively challenging the Defence
Secretary and the Prime Minister. . . . Nowhere else but at
peace camps are womyn regularly taking this kind of action,
as well as cutting fences, entering security areas and paint-
ing on government property.[34]

True indeed. For while the feminism-versus-peace debate
might seem like so many angels on a pinhead, those at
Greenham and in the broader peace movement *were* taking

on the government. Thatcher called an election for 9 June: those standing as 'Women for Life on Earth' candidates included Rebecca Johnston in Heseltine's Henley constituency. CND had to reorientate itself quickly to the harsh realities of an election campaign. In the middle of the intense run-up to 9 June was Women's International Day for Disarmament. Plans were far more ambitious than in 1982. A 'May 24th – Women All Out for Peace' circular suggested: 'Anything can happen – we can occupy/ encircle/decorate/do die-ins/keen/blocade [*sic*] etc. at military bases, banks, armament factories and supporting industries, "nuclear" bunkers, Ministry of Defence offices etc.' Nationally, NALGO circulated all its union branch secretaries, urging members to join in.[35] In Leeds, the flourishing WONT group set up a 'Leeds Women All Out for Peace' fund; they blockaded the entrance to the Menwith Hill US telecommunications base, and 350 women joined in a city-centre mourning ceremony. In Halifax our newly formed 'Women for Peace' issued invitations to a lunchtime peace picnic in the middle of the shopping precinct, something inconceivable even one year before: 150 women and children took part.[36]

Actions in military 'service' towns were particularly daring. In the Isle of Wight, three women chained themselves to the Ventor war communications centre. In Plymouth, women organized a link across the Tamar Bridge; 500 others protested at the nearby Devonport naval base; and a small group lay across a dockyard gate and across one of Plymouth's busiest streets. Peace camps sprouted up, including three in London; and in Derby, the Rolls-Royce factory that made engine parts for Polaris was closed to deliveries as women camped outside. In London, 2,000 women marched to the Defence Ministry, which they ringed, singing peace songs. Altogether, there were no fewer than 600 local actions.[37]

But in the middle of an election, media interest in 24 May was limited compared to coverage of 'Embrace the Base' five months earlier. Nor could all this imagination and energy be translated into sufficient votes to return to Parliament a majority of MPs committed to nuclear *dis*armament. CND found itself marginalized. The Conservative Party's orchestrated attack upon 'unilateralism' swept all before it. With nuclear disarmament presented as 'defenceless' in the face of the Soviet 'threat', Labour had great difficulty arguing its defence policy. Thatcher won a landslide victory, her majority rising to 144.

For those of us believing that it was only through the government returned to power that Trident and Cruise could be halted, 9 June represented a major reverse. Yet as Joan Ruddock clearly stated in *Sanity*: 'The general election has settled nothing. A majority of people, no matter how they cast their votes, continue to oppose both the siting of American Cruise missiles in Britain and the purchase of the Trident missile system.'[38] Certainly the Greenham women, as the camp's second birthday approached, gave the government no indication whatsoever that they intended to move.

13

Fortress Greenham?

(1983–88)

The belief that the British government had received no mandate to bring in Cruise missiles at the end of 1983 – so it might still be possible to halt them – sustained peace movement enthusiasm over the coming months. This was part of a broader European campaign across the five deployment countries (Britain, West Germany, Belgium, Italy and the Netherlands) due to receive Cruise and Pershing II. Actions at Greenham, where the very first batch were to be deployed, were strongly supported and continued to inspire other women's peace encampments around the world. Particularly important were the much-harassed camp at Comiso in Sicily, where 112 Cruise missiles were due in spring 1984; the Seneca Falls Women's Encampment for Future of Peace and Justice in upstate New York, where women regularly scaled the barbed-wire fence around the army depot to draw attention to nuclear weapons there; and such distant camps as Pine Gap, an American military base in central Australia.[1]

The Greenham camp, now two years old, continued to attract new women – to support, to visit, and to live. As the thin strip of land where their tents and benders were perched grew more muddy and desolate and some women left, others took their place. Often they were very young: their growing up was shaped by Greenham and by a feminism now intimately entwined with peace and non-violence.

Nina Hall, born in 1967 near Leeds, was one such new Greenham woman. When she was twelve, a Quaker Peace Action caravan visited her comprehensive school and she quickly became involved in peace campaigns. In 1982, aged fifteen, she joined the nearby Harrogate women's

group; and she squeezed her first visit to Greenham into her
school half-term in spring 1983. Then, after a mixed blockade at the Upper Heyford base and after her O levels,
sixteen-year-old Hall took part in Greenham's July action.[2]

To coincide with American Independence Day, a week's
blockade was planned from Monday 4 to Friday 8 July;
each twenty-four hours would be designated to a different
region. Local women's peace groups, strengthened by their
24 May actions, organized nonviolence training. On the
Monday, only about 500 women blockaded. 'Police Outwit
Greenham Women', proclaimed the press. For Friday, the
day for the North of England and Midlands, Halifax
Women for Peace group booked a coach, and nineteen of us
set off at 3.30 a.m. in the pitch dark. We never arrived,
because on the outskirts of rush-hour Newbury our coach
encountered a heavy police convoy chaperoning a fleet of
construction workers' buses into the Greenham base. Immediately we all sat down in front of the approaching
vehicles, started to sing, and brought the convoy to a
temporary halt. Nine arrests followed; and we whiled away
the rest of a scorchingly hot day (along with swelling
numbers of other detained women) in the bar at Newbury
racecourse – converted, most incongruously, into a temporary police station; we were subsequently charged with
obstruction and, with all nine of us pleading guilty, bailed
to appear on 22 September.

About 1,000 women had managed to get to Greenham
that Friday. Altogether, the convoy of employees at the
base was delayed for nearly two hours and, with women
entering the base, there were sixty-six arrests.[3] Nina Hall,
who had come down by coach with the Leeds WONT group,
was at Yellow Gate [the main gate] and vividly remembers
the impression the day made upon her:

> I remember sitting in a blockade and a woman, just a few
> yards away from me, was lying down, and she was pregnant
> – about six months pregnant. She was quite thin, and so her
> pregnancy really showed, because it was just a small, nice

hump. And she was wearing dungarees and a small T-shirt. And she took her dungarees off, and let her stomach just – like show to the sun. And that was when I really decided that I had to come to Greenham again, and that women's actions were the way forward for *me*. Dunno; just sitting watching that stomach, I just made *so* many connections, between – I just remember thinking in my mind all those things I'd heard about patriarchy and male dominance and nuclear weapons being male violence. I just thought, 'It's so right. There's no way I'm ever going to doubt it ever again . . .'.[4]

On occasions like the July blockade, the Thames Valley Police would issue a bland press statement about how policing tactics had successfully kept the Greenham base working. The popular papers also tried to downplay the impact of the peace camp, sometimes smuggling in a reporter who could later reveal all: grime and rats and drugs and neglected children. The *Daily Mirror*'s 'The Grim Facts Behind a Protest for Peace' double-page spread in July serves as an example of Fleet Street's attempt to dismiss the camp:

SAD TRUTH THAT SHATTERED A DREAM

The desolate and filthy camp site was bad enough, the few women squatting round the smoky fire were a total shock. . . . A handful of peace women went off to the pub, to spend their social security benefits, as others settled by the fire to roll the first of the evening's 'joints'. . . . These women have been described as a 'bunch of lesbians'. Sadly, there's some truth in this. . . . [One woman] stood at the gates of the base camp to give birth to peace baby Jay eight weeks ago. . . . Carol from Aberdeen, safety pins piercing her cheeks, lips, nose and ears, and Jubilee clips ringing her eight fingers, browsed through a book called *Witches*. . . . Funds for the camp have dwindled. . . . If support is on the wane the women of Greenham have only themselves to blame.[5]

But if the police and the media tried to suggest that Greenham women were now little more than a minor irritation to a triumphant Thatcher government, the debate in the House of Commons a fortnight later revealed a very different picture. Michael McNair-Wilson, MP for Newbury, demanded to know, on behalf of his long-suffering constituents, 'Why the government, in the shape of the Department of Transport, are [*sic*] providing the site for those women who describe themselves as "peace women"?' Newbury District Council, he explained testily, had evicted the women on several occasions; but each High Court order cost local ratepayers about £3,000; and the evicted women were *still* 'given a safe haven on Department of Transport land'. Moreover, Thames Valley Police costs were soaring: of the £3.5 million overtime budget for 1983–84, McNair-Wilson stated, £2 million had *already* been spent in the first third of the financial year. He challenged the Under-Secretary at the Department of Transport, Lynda Chalker, 'to give me a clear-cut assurance that the women will be evicted without delay'. But the Minister was evasive: the peace camp was 'principally a matter for my Right Honourable Friend the Secretary of State for Defence'. She was empowered to remove anything constituting 'a nuisance or a danger' to the highway; but 'we have been loth to use these powers', partly – and it is here that this parliamentary debate becomes so revealing – because 'it is everybody's right in a free and civilized society . . . to make peaceful protests'; and partly because the women 'do not constitute either a danger to road safety or, except when they sit down in the road, a disruption to traffic'. Thus the Minister was 'reluctant to take more positive action . . . when such action would not only encourage confrontation and publicity, but would play into the hands of the protesters, who hunger for news media coverage'. But Greenham, the unhappy McNair-Wilson persisted, was different:

> Most other protests last for twenty-four or forty-eight hours, after which the people depart. The women at Greenham

> Common have taken up residence on land that is not theirs
> and have turned the demonstration into something different
> from anything that we have seen before.[6]

Quite so. Greenham *was* different. This parliamentary
debate revealed that the Department of Transport, in close
liaison with the Ministry of Defence, chose not to use its
powers – largely because of the adverse publicity that
would ensue. The imminent deployment of American
Cruise missiles on English soil was still unpopular; moreover, the camp had managed to retain its nonviolent image,
so scuffles between camp women and bailiffs could easily
backfire, particularly if shown on television. Any woman
wounded would quickly become a heroine. Heavy legal
charges could have a similar effect: crowds of women would
come to court and mock the judicial process. And any
woman given a charge sufficiently heavy to remove her
hearing from a magistrates' court up to trial by jury would
quite conceivably be acquitted – especially by woman
jurors. Lengthy prison sentences conjured up the spectre of
historic Holloway, rich with suffragette associations. Worst
would be real *martyrs*; for should any Greenham woman
accidentally be killed in confrontations with police or soldiers, or by the bailiffs' bulldozers, comparisons would
inevitably be made with Emily Wilding Davison, the suffragette who had died on the Derby racecourse seventy
years earlier. Such martyrdom myths might have little
direct link to peace movement history, but were none the
less extremely evocative. For opposition to Cruise still
revealed a 'gender gap', with well over half of women
opposing the missiles.[7]

With such sobering thoughts staying its hand, the
government was unable to see off the Greenham women –
so long as the camp could call upon a broad reservoir of
support. Blockading might have only a limited delaying
effect on construction work inside the base; but the camp's
symbolic importance, both in Britain and around the world,
was undiminished.

This, then, was the balance of forces in early autumn 1983. Women continued to come and go at Greenham; and as the camp approached its third winter, one arrival was Pauline Smith, now recovered and keen to find out what 'Greenham' was all about. It was not all as she had imagined:

> I think the first thing to notice was – I had these images of all these women. And when I actually arrived here – there were few women here. And I thought, 'Oh, that's a little different. However, I'm game for a laugh, as they say.' . . . I felt intrusive. Didn't feel that I belonged. I didn't quite know where they were coming from. Yes, I was in awe, I think, by then. I was in *awe* of these women. . . . And *what* could I do? What was my measly contribution to all this wonderful work that was going on? Being that I had a small child.[8]

In fact, Smith now became drawn into organizing support for Greenham in her own town, something she could fit in around her children. Support networks were now becoming very efficient: deliveries of hot meals-on-wheels and dry firewood arrived on a rota basis at the various camps dotted around the base. Regional women's peace networks, supported by a Greenham office in London, were growing.[9] In Halifax, our Women for Peace became part of that network and were also busy preparing for our court hearing. All nine of us in the Newbury dock on 23 September were, despite a sympathetic hearing, found guilty and fined. After much delay, we paid our fines by a cheque pasted to a large model of a Cruise missile – just one example of local actions keeping the issue alive in the press.[10]

Meanwhile, across Europe anti-Cruise and anti-Pershing feeling spilled on to the streets: over five million people took part in protest rallies. On 22 October CND's demonstration in Hyde Park – where speakers included Neil Kinnock, the new Labour Party leader – attracted a crowd at least 400,000 strong; in Amsterdam there were 400,000; in Rome, over 500,000; and in both Bonn and

Hamburg, 400,000.[11] The following week there was a Hallowe'en de-fencing action at Greenham; over 1,000 women arrived, many dressed as witches with pointed hats and faces painted as spiders' webs. They celebrated Hallowe'en at camp fires around the base. But in fact many of these women, already organized into affinity groups, were equipped with bolt-cutters. Among those at Orange Gate was Nina Hall:

> We'd practised getting up on each other's shoulders. And we unravelled lots [of fence, after] our bolt-cutters had been taken. And cut a *massive* section down, because we went to quite a deserted place. . . . So we cut about 200 yards down. . . . All it is is just snipping at the side of the posts, and then these big sections just fall down. . . . It was just an amazing sense of relief and freedom . . . to be able to see . . . a space where it was, and to know that you personally were responsible for taking it down. . . .

Police and soldiers were taken by surprise. As great sections of the fence tumbled to the ground, an isolated soldier inside the base opposite Hall's group tried to summon help on his radio – but so too did all the other squaddies. He kept jumping up and down, Hall recalled, repeating ' "The fucking women are cutting the fucking fence down! The fucking women are cutting the fucking fence down!" ' Soldiers panicked. Pandemonium reigned. Police with dogs used dog leads to smash the hands of women gripping the fence. More than a mile of fencing had come down. But, rather than scrambling over the rolls of barbed wire now lying entangled at their feet, the women just sat on their collapsed stretches of fencing.

In the end, 187 women were arrested on criminal damages charges and 140 pairs of bolt-cutters were confiscated. Yet some of us, watching from a safe distance, wondered whether bolt-cutters *were* nonviolent in quite the same way as, say, ladders and carpets. Was this a helpful escalation of direct action? As Greenham increasingly resembled a razor-wire fortress, did purely *symbolic* actions become more difficult to sustain?[12]

In the frenzied last few weeks of 1983, with the missiles' arrival merely a matter of *days* away, one particularly imaginative action was the 'Greenham Women Against Cruise' court case filed in America. It aimed to raise issues about Cruise – medical and psychological, military and strategic – in a court where the women were not defendants but plaintiffs. As plaintiffs, Greenham women, with a couple of US Congressmen, alleged that the missile deployment contravened both international and American constitutional law. They aimed to bring an action against the US government, with named defendants (including Ronald Reagan and his Defence Secretary, Caspar Weinberger); and to ask the court to grant an injunction halting deployment. On 9 November their evidence was filed with the New York Federal Court, and they asked the judge for an emergency hearing.[13]

The American legal system slowly mulled over the impudence of the Greenham women. (It took over a year before the US Appeal Court finally rejected the case, 'because of the lack of judicially discoverable and manageable standards'.)[14] Of more immediate impact were the twenty-four-hour peace camps set up at the invitation of Greenham Women Against Cruise, also on 9 November, one for every American base now dotted across Britain. A map was supplied, marking all 102 sites. In West Yorkshire, peace groups set off for Menwith Hill (prompting jokes about 'Menwith Big Ears'). Remarkably, twenty-four-hour peace vigils were held at *all* bases, however remote.[15]

Peace movement opposition was building to an intense crescendo. A Gallup Poll showed that although there was some movement in favour of Cruise, support was still only 41 per cent, while 48 per cent still opposed. On 14 November the missiles were flown into Greenham by US Air Force transport and quickly trundled into their new hangars, under heavy armed guard. Because delivery had been brought forward, the women were somewhat taken by surprise. For many, it was a terrible moment. 'A lot of these women worked through '81, '82, '83 more or less full-time,' commented Margot Miller, veteran of longer peace campaigns. 'Some women were physically sick; when they saw Cruise coming in they were sick – sick to their souls.'[16] But as so often happened, while some women became burnt out, others were drawn in. Among those who joined the sit-down protest at Greenham that ominous day was a Huddersfield magistrate of eleven years' standing. She was arrested – and subsequently removed from the bench on the orders of the Lord Chancellor, Lord Hailsham. Refusing to pay her fine, she spent a night in Huddersfield police cells – one of CND's small but significant number of women ex-JPs.[17]

CND announced that it would frustrate attempts to take Cruise missiles on practice exercises outside the base. Again there were tensions within the peace movement between women-only and mixed actions to mark the fourth anniversary of the NATO decision. The anger was tangible.[18] Yet, once again, the desires of the Greenham women prevailed. The 'Women – Reclaim Greenham!' action on 11 December was powerful and moving. As for 'Embrace the Base' the previous year, Halifax women booked a coach and forty of us travelled down. But, with Cruise now installed, confrontation between women and police and, particularly, soldiers was tenser. Women tried to cut the fence and some, scrambling into the base, were tugged across rolls of razor wire by inexperienced squaddies. The mood was both exhilarating and frenzied. Hundreds of women swayed against the wire, their backs to the army photographers inside the base. Later, in the dark at Blue Gate amid candles and lighted flares, mounted police were penned in by the singing, chanting crowd: the noise – and potential danger – were terrifying.[19]

More calmly, the press the next day reported: 'Cat and mouse game at Greenham. Police are caught on the hop by well-equipped fence raiders. . . . Slaphappy GIs "guard nuclear stockpile".' Over 30,000 women had been present.

Cruise might have been flown in, but neither the base nor the missiles were invulnerable.[20]

1983 was the year Greenham women and the peace movement dominated the front-page headlines. Over the next few years the authorities tried – still unsuccessfully – to see off the peace camp; the numbers of women living there declined, but it obstinately survived against all odds. This confrontation – and the struggle for credibility between the peace movement and Greenham women on one side and the government on the other – continued on through the mid 1980s. The way this unique and historic peace camp was sustained over harsh winters into a fifth, sixth, seventh, even eighth remarkable year, despite all the mud and harassment, demands a history of its own. Rather, here is an overview of the peace movement and Greenham's continued vigil since 1984.

Cruise missiles were now housed in the base, and their movements needed monitoring. Greenham women set up telephone trees. Night watches were organized, with visiting women relieving those living at the camp. Pauline Smith, for instance, became nightwatch organizer for her Oxfordshire town. Rebecca Johnson, among those who had taken the court case to America, returned to Greenham shortly after Cruise arrived. (It was a moment of choice for her: 'I just felt still it was the camp. . . . I felt that I did want to go back; and did go back to live there, and built my bender, and lived very *solidly* at the camp for the next couple of years.') She too did nightwatch, waiting in the dark for the convoy to come out. 'The first time I saw it – awful. This *huge* thing. My impression was just of noise, and incredibly loud, and just *bearing* down on you.' Gradually, the Greenham women became adroit at predicting the exercises. An impressive Cruisewatch network of people living in the dispersal area also sprang up, tracking convoys down

English country lanes and on to Salisbury Plain. They then reported these movements so that the public could know what was going on, to help nail the lie that Cruise could 'melt into the countryside'.[21]

At the same time, harassment continued. A particularly large eviction was threatened for 2 April 1984. Rebecca Johnson vividly remembers what it felt like to be living at Yellow Gate then:

> An awful lot of women started saying, 'Well, you know, this is the end of Greenham. We're going to leave.' And I just thought, 'We can't. We can't yet.' It wasn't yet time. I didn't feel it was time. . . . And *lots* of women came down for April 2nd . . . [which] did mean we weren't evicted on the 2nd. It was very clear. The bailiffs did arrive on the 2nd, but . . . they didn't arrive with enough police. And in fact the only way they managed it was in the very early hours of April 4th. They brought something like 500–600 police and 50 bailiffs, and they parked up the road, and . . . *ran*. I woke up to the sounds of police feet. . . . It was a terrifying sound. . . . It was pre-dawn. It was six o'clock in the morning. . . . It really was *very*, very frightening – just to wake up with the things being pulled from around you, and trying to save what you could. . . . And indeed, a lot of women did leave at that time.

This eviction was well publicized, but failed to close the camp.[22]

Major crises like this might drive away women who felt it was time for them to return to the comforts of normal life; yet these moments brought a fresh wave to Greenham. The camp, now two and a half years old, still inspired women to live there. Their motives remained mixed, combining a refusal to condone nuclear weapons with a preference for a women-only living space, a chance to question their sexuality, and an escape from the pressures of difficult relationships or unemployment. Meryl Antonelli, born in 1961 and living in Bradford, had visited Greenham a few times before Easter 1984:

> But it wasn't until I saw the pictures on the telly of the Yellow Gate eviction in March '84 . . . then it suddenly occurred to me, 'No, this can't go [on]. No. No, you're not doing this. I'm sorry. No way.'

A few days later, she saw the film *Carry Greenham Home*:

> And I saw how it *had* been, and how really nice those benders had been. . . . It *was* a small community. ok, fairly bizarre but – from my experience! – but there was nothing wrong with it. . . . These women were actually living in it [the countryside] and caring for the land. And then I saw the mess the bailiffs made – just *tearing* everything down. And then one woman setting light to her bender in protest. . . . And I just thought, just, 'Yeah, it's like the last bit of defiance you've got.' So I came down for three days.[23]

Antonelli hitched down to Yellow Gate – and stayed. Later she moved to Red Gate, helping to keep that small camp going during summer 1984. But when women moved away for the winter it folded, and Antonelli moved on to Violet Gate. Interviewed two years later, she was fairly resigned about how gates [i.e. camps] open and then close; and how the Greenham peace camp ebbed and flowed with the seasons:

> After an initial rush of members, summer of '84, after those pictures [of the Easter eviction] went out, we had up to about 200 women for the summer. But then it was a good summer. . . . So when the sun was here, so were the women. . . .
>
> That's the thing. Gates *open* as women arrive; and when those women go again, they close. So at the moment [May 1986], we're ticking over with a lot of visiting women, because – this goes back to the weather again . . . '84–'85

winter was quite good. There was quite a lot of women. I mean, quite regularly, numbers of forty or fifty women. But then with summer last year [1985] being so *bad*, women coming down and finding they couldn't cope, because everything gets wet. You're wet, so your sleeping bag gets wet. So when you get up in the morning, the bailiffs evict a wet tent, with a wet sleeping bag in it. And then you have to go to bed and it's even wetter. After about four days of that you think, 'Oh, my God, I'm not going on with this. Like, we support you – but in a different way.' And everybody runs away. . . . So *we* plodded on [over winter 1985–86], and kept our head down, realizing that if we *didn't*, nobody else would.[24]

Rebecca Johnson, interviewed in spring 1988 after five years at Greenham, could reflect philosophically on how the natural cycles of women moving in and out of the camp had, despite the extreme stresses, permitted it to survive such long, hard years. The 1984 pre-dawn Easter eviction:

. . . cleansed a lot of things. Because things had been getting worse and worse. I mean, the camp has really gone in cycles. And when arguments and disputes around issues like money would come to a head – and then there'd be a kind of clearing out, and the clearing out would either be like a really good action, a beautiful action; *or* it would be a major eviction. . . . Because women who were in fact getting ready – were needing to go – and that would be the signal for them: 'It's time to go'. And they would go. And new women would come, because . . . either they'd heard about the wonderful action, or they'd heard about the terrible eviction. So you'd get the new women coming at that time. So there were these cycles that happened maybe twice a year.[25]

Greenham, always an impossible utopian venture, survived, but popular support inevitably diminished once it became clear that Cruise convoys *could* leave the base fairly regularly on practice runs (though nightwatch and Cruisewatch persistently managed to cause disruption and delay). Media interest thinned. Greenham was no longer flavour of the month. The response to 'Ten million women for ten days at Greenham Common' in September 1984 was nowhere near a fraction of ten million women.[26] Evictions continued; and many women's energies shifted during the miners' strike into supporting Women Against Pit Closure. Greenham women were also making links with other campaigns – against food mountains, for a nuclear-free and independent Pacific, against nuclear power. Lambeth Women for Peace, for instance, divided its time between supporting Greenham and supporting women in Tigré, Ethiopia. But this *outward* flow of energy meant that the women keeping vigil at the base felt drained; one woman from Orange Gate expressed her feelings of betrayal in a newsletter that autumn:

> We talked about it at the fire, and I said I did the nightwatch as a trust. At the moment, I can't care less if the launchers come out. (No – that is not it. I care, but there seems to be nothing I can do to stop them when there are six of us at a gate and 100 police and fifteen vehicles driving at high speeds. So I've stopped caring because caring tears me up). . . .
>
> I'm not going to do the nightwatch any more. . . . I am going to stop making excuses for other women. . . . I am incapable of doing nightwatch when I'm getting evicted, avoiding the rain, talking to visitors, watching for changes in the base, and trying to keep warm.[27]

1985 was certainly tough. A handful of us from West Yorkshire went in the spring, and saw how gruelling it was to be evicted each morning by police, bailiffs and their municipal muncher. On 24 May there was little of the earlier popular support for Women's International Disarmament Day. In Bristol women picketed Rio Tinto Zinc (RTZ) offices, protesting against uranium mining; in Manchester, the statue of Queen Victoria was draped with banners proclaiming an independent and nuclear-free Pacific. But enthusiasm was ebbing. 'Is Greenham Dead?' mused *Spare Rib*. In Halifax, our Women for Peace group faded away.[28] Women's peace groups in big cities – Leeds WONT and the Hackney Sirens in London – remained buoyant; but the sense of 'a movement' was fading.

But if Greenham women were clinging on for dear life, the broader peace campaign remained Britain's largest active political movement. CND's national membership had risen to 110,000, and members in the 1,500 local groups brought the total of paid-up supporters to about 400,000.[29] In February 1985 Michael Heseltine, dressed in army flak jacket, led a commando-style raid on the small peace camp at Molesworth; but that did not deter about 20,000 CND protesters wading through the Molesworth mud that Easter. European Nuclear Disarmament (END) continued to provide an intellectual cutting edge challenging 'Little England' nationalism within the peace movement. Meanwhile, the Labour Party had strengthened its non-nuclear policy: its conference voted to scrap Trident and Polaris missiles, while maintaining membership of NATO, and to close the US nuclear bases in Britain. In mid 1986 the news of bases in Britain being used for America's bombing raid on Libya, followed by the Chernobyl nuclear accident in the Ukraine, caused nationwide shock waves which re-energized both CND and the anti-nuclear power campaign.

There were changes inside CND too, helping give women greater voice within the peace movement. In 1985 Joan Ruddock resigned as chair to seek a seat in the next election as a Labour candidate and to strengthen nuclear disarmament in Parliament. About the same time, Bruce Kent, who resigned as general secretary, was succeeded by Meg Beresford, a vice-chair since 1983. And at CND's 1987 conference, four out of the six officers elected were women, including Rebecca Johnson as a vice-chair. Johnson, already a member of National Council, had helped to smooth relations between CND and Greenham. This improved communication was also helped by the realization that it was often CND's grass-roots activists who helped to sustain Greenham; there was still some resentment that women-only actions divided the peace movement; but from the mid 1980s the energy gained earlier from the women's peace movement and from Greenham helped to shape CND into 'the only movement in Britain in which feminist argument and practice has become integrated into the mainstream of analysis'.[30]

So it gradually became clear that what Greenham represented had changed. It no longer held symbolic power to inspire mass actions; but when I visited again in May 1986, just before its fifth anniversary, I realized that although the scale of earlier support had ebbed, probably for ever, the camp still represented something quite remarkable: a semi-permanent women's peace presence outside a nuclear weapons base. Before the 1980s it was absolutely unthinkable that *women* should take action in this way. 'While in five years the idea of women organizing separately at a political level has not yet become acceptable', wrote Lynne Jones, visiting the camp on its fifth anniversary,

> it at least has become an established fact. . . . It is Greenham that has helped to create this sort of climate so that the women who come today no longer have to spend their time justifying themselves or fighting for political space. They can get on with what they came to do, confronting the base and the issues it raises.[31]

And it looked as if, as long as nuclear militarism remained, so would the women's peace camp. Its defiant, against-the-odds survival still endowed it with unequalled significance, a symbol of women's stubborn refusal of nuclear missiles. There might be only about thirty women still clustered in small encampments around the base; but those women refused to shift.

Looking back from the late 1980s, with Fleet Street no longer interested in women and peace, it is easy to forget what fearless adventures the Greenham women still got up to. But a few papers did continue to chronicle these historic escapades, revealing the base as vulnerable – and very ludicrous. In spring 1984 the *New Statesman* began publishing its 'Peace Protests Roll Call' which showed that · already no fewer than 1,775 women had been arrested at Greenham; by November, arrests topped 2,000.[32] In spring 1985, three women from Yellow Gate used a wash-house inside the base to do their washing; they were arrested and charged with 'theft of electricity'. And that April, Rebecca Johnson and two other women went on trial at Reading Crown Court for occupying an Air Traffic Control Tower in the base, and finding papers marked 'classified' concerning biological and chemical weapons; Johnson, who received the heaviest sentence, was jailed for a month.

From 1 April 1985 new bylaws were introduced which made it an offence to trespass inside the base, or even to pin things on the fence. Arrests at Greenham shot up: fifty-five the first day, a further seventy-eight that week, and another 370 on a mass trespass at the end of May. (The deputy clerk of Newbury Court eventually prevented the *Statesman* from receiving court listings, so 'Peace Protests Roll Call' could only guess that by May 1986 Greenham arrests had topped 4,000.[33]) Subsequently, *Sanity* began *its* 'Peace in Court' listings; the first, in November 1987, included twelve women from the Aldermaston women's peace camp charged with trespass, and four women arrested at Greenham after eggs, flour and horseshit were thrown at a returning Cruise convoy. Over the next ten months 'Peace in Court' listed sixty-two imprisonments, about 70 per cent of them women, and including a Greenham woman given three months for criminal damage to the perimeter fence.[34]

These chronicles of arrests and imprisonments suggest mass civil disobedience on a scale previously undreamt of. The women's peace movement, through imaginative non-violent actions like 'Embrace the Base', had introduced a new creative culture of radical protest into Britain, and this had rubbed off on the general peace movement. The Snowball campaign involved writing a personal nuclear disarmament statement, then symbolically snipping a strand of wire in the fence at a base. Of course, not every CND member believed that direct action was the most effective way to win the nuclear disarmament debate (and CND became increasingly professional in its approach to advertising and lobbying Parliament). But CND's energetic support for civil liberties, and its opposition to phone-taps and surveillance of members, lent the peace movement popular support at a time when the great mass demonstrations of the early 1980s were no longer possible.[35] And however much Tory backbenchers might huff and puff, the government still appeared loth to use its full powers against CND, Cruisewatch or the Greenham women – because such an attempt could easily backfire in a rash of anti-Thatcher publicity. If nuclear missiles were necessary to defend Western freedoms, then those freedoms must be seen to be upheld – including the freedom to demonstrate. Lynne Jones, who had been observing this finely balanced relationship between the government and Greenham for some years, suggested this perceptive appraisal:

> The thing about Greenham to me is . . . for me, as much as challenging the missiles, is the ability of a bunch of women to hang on to a piece of land in the face of a nuclear arms state that doesn't want them there. And it *doesn't* want them there! It's no good saying, 'Oh, well, they don't care'. They care very much. They spend an immense amount of money and energy; and yet they cannot – they're hamstrung by public opinion – by the consensus. . . .
>
> What's also happening is that . . . they don't seem to be able to find a way of using – they didn't want to use the Official Secrets Act. It's too heavy. So they invent a smaller law, April 1985 . . . the new bylaws: a hundred pounds if you go in the base, a tiny law, but – but a bit of a deterrent. So eighty women immediately go in the base; and all they [the

judiciary] do – they sit and they use the law against them that once, and after that they stopped using it. . . . Once they've realized that it isn't a deterrent, they stop using it. Which is to me an extraordinary process. . . . *Why* don't they use the Official Secrets Act? *Why* do they bring in a new law? And why does it fail? Which it has done. . . .[36]

(Of course, some Greenham women *were* worn down by successive spells in prison, and their courage cannot be underestimated. But very heavy sentencing still remained the exception: when Ann Francis, Christian peace activist, was given a year in prison for causing £120-worth of damage to the fence at Greenham she claimed that it was a 'righteous act'.[37])

In addition, the Ministry of Defence found it difficult to extricate itself from the legal muddle over military bylaws and rights at Greenham. In August 1988 the Ministry discovered that property built on the common land lacked the necessary permission, and this caused delays in several criminal damages cases; for if a building or fence was unlawfully erected, the defendants might argue, how could charges stand up? The Crown Prosecution Service, one lawyer reported, had 'got stacks of papers a yard high, and they don't seem to know what to do next'.[38]

Although a popular 'women's peace movement' had ebbed away by the late 1980s the issues raised by linking feminism and anti-militarism remained powerful. Occasionally the debates were painful, like discussion of male violence within the peace movement, prompted by alleged rapes at the Molesworth camp.[39] Greenham itself had, of course, seen off all number of threats to its continued existence. It had survived in large part because it was women-only. Yet some of the threats came from the women themselves. A few had been imperious and bossy. Because of the camp's 'open door' policy, women had arrived weighed down by heavy personal difficulties which camp women were hard put to cope with. Rebecca Johnson, who had seen her fair share of problems at Greenham, wisely reflected:

> The camp has *always* been a place of difficulty, a place of very strong-willed women of high, strong passions, who believe very strongly in things that, actually, are very different. . . .
>
> Then there was also a certain tyranny to the structureless-ness of Greenham. It was very difficult to find mechanisms for saying to someone, 'Look, you have *never* cooked. You have *never* chopped wood. . . . And you are always the first to come in with a demand for money.' . . . We tried to develop mechanisms for dealing with that, but mechanisms that were nonviolent, that were feminist and were anarchist. And inevitably sometimes those broke down. But sometimes they also worked. . . .[40]

Relations with the outside world often became fraught. These were partly personal tensions, as the intensity of living at the camp impinged upon marriages, families and friendships. There were also, of course, political tensions. The original Women for Life on Earth women would grumble that what they created had turned into something so different; communication with CND had been tense. Relations became particularly fraught when outside groups tried to take over Greenham. An early attempt was made by Trotskyist groupings, notably the Socialist Workers' Party (SWP);[41] a second, more successful (and much-publicized) attempt was by a Wages for Housework group based at the King's Cross Women's Centre in London. It attempted to raise the issue of racism within the peace movement and at Greenham; this was very important, though their intimidatory and disruptive tactics soon backfired. Johnson remembers why:

> [Greenham had] that very strong – it is a feminist and an anarchist kind of undercurrent. That the 'personal is political'. We owe a great deal to the struggles of feminists. I think

that's probably where we owe the greatest struggle. And it was that [feeling], 'We are individuals. . . . Since we have *chosen* to take personal responsibility, it means we acknowledge that we have a choice.' And that's really what defeated SWP and Wages for Housework. Because groups like that have a very tight structure, a tight command structure. The leaders tell the minions what to do, and the minions are obedient. They didn't know how to handle the way that Greenham women questioned everything. Challenged things. Greenham women weren't prepared to take orders. . . . And so when a group like SWP or Wages for Housework turned up and said, 'This is how you should believe . . .', women were just saying, 'Well, hang on a minute. We want to get to the bottom of this. We want to find out what really happened.' Of course, the *last* thing they were actually wanting was for women to get to the bottom of the truth.[42]

The issue of racism was raised at Yellow Gate in late 1987, with black and white women ranged on either side. The issue caused bitterness, and communication between Yellow Gate and the other camps remained sour long afterwards; but facing this challenge also revealed the great resources of support which the women's peace camp could still call upon.[43]

Under the Intermediate-Range Nuclear Forces (INF) Treaty, signed by Reagan and Gorbachev in December 1987, NATO agreed to get rid of its Cruise and Pershing missiles in return for the Soviet Union's scrapping its SS-20s and some other shorter-range missiles. About 2,800 missiles would be destroyed within a three-year timetable – including the ninety-six deployed at Greenham. But not *all* components of these ground-launched Cruise missiles would be dismantled: when the first pair was removed from Molesworth in September 1988, banners outside the gates demanded: 'Bye bye cruise. Now what about the warheads?' (And when the world's press paid a post-INF visit to Greenham that summer, women camping there held up similar banners.)[44] In fact, nuclear weaponry was scarcely dented by this agreement. Sea- and air-launched Cruise missiles could still proliferate, along with new nuclear bombers; indeed, defence analysts soon predicted that 'by the mid 1990s the nuclear warheads removed from Cruise missiles at Greenham and Molesworth could be back . . . [with] at least 400 *more* US nuclear weapons in Britain than there are now.'[45] And international tension in, for instance, the Libya region offered hawks in the Pentagon a perfect pretext to talk of 'testing' the US Navy's sea-launched Cruise missiles, similar to the nuclear-tipped weapons still deployed at Greenham.[46]

More than seven years since the women from Wales first arrived, the Greenham women still refused to go away – however much Fleet Street wished otherwise.[47] As late as 1988–89 the British legal system and the Thatcher government had failed to shift the dozen women still living there – and able to wander in and out of the base.[48] A women's peace movement might no longer grab headlines as it had done so successfully during 1982–84; and Greenham might no longer offer the inspirational magnet of those heady few years, but it remained a powerful symbol. It continued to inspire women to speak out for peace – and be listened to. Joan Ruddock, elected at the May 1987 general election, became one of the few well-informed MPs on nuclear disarmament issues. A 'NATO Alert Network' was formed to encourage women parliamentarians and others to lobby nuclear defence decision-makers. And Greenham continued to inspire women to link nuclear weaponry with such Third World and green issues as anti-apartheid and British Nuclear Fuel's buying Namibian uranium.

1988–89 was in some ways comparable to 1964–65 for nuclear disarmament campaigns: not only was CND no longer a mass movement, but local peace groups which had worked so energetically for eight years were now struggling.[49] It felt like the end of an era. But unlike CND's earlier 1964–65 decline, there remained an awareness of the links between nuclear, conventional and chemical warfare; and there also remained an impressive number of well-informed and concerned people who continued to monitor missile escalations. Already academic analysts were predicting for the 1990s that, 'faced with the prospect of far more US nuclear strike aircraft coming to Britain, . . . we may yet see a "third wave" for CND'.[50] And already Oxfordshire residents, living next to the noisy Upper Heyford USAF base, were beginning to protest about plans to send in an extra fifty-one F-111 aircraft equipped with both short-range missiles and air-launched Cruise missiles. 'Will Upper Heyford be the next Greenham?' wondered one angry resident.[51]

Greenham itself had provided the 1980s with some of its most memorable images – an alternative icon for the eighties, a generic name that came to symbolize women's resistance to nuclear militarism. By 1988, a women's peace movement had shrunk right back to its small dimensions of 1980; but the issues it raised continue to have far-reaching repercussions. The three strands of thinking on feminism and anti-militarism, with a history stretching to the turn of the century and even back to 1820, had inspired campaigns as different as the Olive Leaf circles, the 1915 Hague Congress, the Women's Peace Crusade and Women Oppose the Nuclear Threat. Such campaigns had powerfully shaped thinking both within the peace movement and within the women's movement. Now, after Greenham, the relationship between feminism and anti-militarism could never be quite the same again. Together it represents a powerful, unpredictable and sometimes explosive mix.

Notes

Introduction

1. *Daily Mirror*, 13 December 1982.
2. However, early in 1982 I wrote 'The Women's Peace Crusade: the History of a Forgotten Campaign', for D. Thompson (ed.), *Over Our Dead Bodies: Women Against the Bomb*, Virago, London, 1983.
3. P. Brock, *Pacifism in Europe to 1914*, Princeton University Press, NJ, 1972, mentions neither. A. C. F. Beales, *The History of Peace: A Short Account of the Organized Movements for International Peace*, G. Bell, London, 1931, pp. 82, 102, implies that Olive Leaf activity flourished only in America.
4. W. H. Posthumus-Van Der Goot, *Vrouwen Vochten Voor de Vrede*, Van Loghum Slaterus, Arnhem, 1961.
5. F. L. Carsten, *War Against War: British and German Radical Movements in the First World War*, Batsford, London, 1982, p. 170 on the Women's Peace Crusade; K. Robbins, *The Abolition of War: The 'Peace Movement' in Britain 1914–1919*, University of Wales Press, Cardiff, 1976, p. 96, introduces WIL without explanation.
6. M. Caedel, *Pacifism in Britain 1914–1945: The Defining of a Faith*, Clarendon Press, Oxford, 1980, p. 61; also P. Brock, *Twentieth-Century Pacifism*, Van Nostrand Reinhold, New York, 1970.
7. R. Strachey, *The Cause: A Short History of the Women's Movement in Great Britain*, 1928 and Virago, London 1978, pp. 288, 351; E. S. Pankhurst, *The Suffragette Movement*, 1931 and Virago, London 1977, pp. 593, 600; also E. S. Pankhurst, *The Home Front*, Hutchinson, London 1932, pp. 15–54.
8. For instance, L. Jones (ed.), *Keeping the Peace*, Women's Press, London, 1983; B. Harford and S. Hopkins (eds),

Greenham Common: Women at the Wire, Women's Press, London, 1984.

9. S. Oldfield, *Spinsters of this Parish: The Life and Times of F. M. Mayor and Mary Sheepshanks*, Virago, London, 1984; A. Wiltsher, *Most Dangerous Women: Feminist Peace Campaigners of the Great War*, Pandora, London, 1985; also J. Eglin, 'Women and Peace: from the Suffragists to the Greenham Women', in R. Taylor and N. Young (eds), *Campaigns for Peace: British Peace Movements in the Twentieth Century*, Manchester University Press, 1987.

10. However, Cambridge Women's Peace Collective, *My Country The Whole World: An Anthology of Women's Work on Peace and War*, Pandora, London, 1984, includes some early writings; A. Piper, *Herstory of the Women's Peace Movement*, Women's Peace Alliance, Nottingham (*c.* 1984, pamphlet) makes brief reference also.

11. For further discussion, see Caedel, op. cit.; Taylor and Young, op. cit.

12. L. Segal, *Is the Future Female? Troubled Thoughts on Contemporary Feminism*, Virago, London, 1987, p. 199; emphasis added.

13. L. Merryfinch, *Spare Rib*, no. 104, March 1981.

14. V. Woolf, *Three Guineas*, 1938 and Penguin, London, 1977, p. 125.

15. C. P. Gilman, *The Man-Made World, or Our Androcentric Culture*, 1911 and Johnson Reprint, New York, 1971, pp. 210–11.

16. For instance, Segal, op. cit., pp. 175–95.

17. B. von Suttner, *Lay Down Your Arms: the Autobiography of Martha von Tilling*, published in German (*Die Waffen Nieder!*) 1889 and Longmans, London, 1892; F. S. Hallowes, *Women and War: An Appeal to the Women of All Nations*, Headley Bros, London [1914].

18. *Women in a Changing World: the Dynamic Story of the International Council of Women*, Routledge & Kegan Paul, London, 1966, p. 44; A. Whittick, *Woman into Citizen*, Athenaeum with Frederick Muller, London, 1979, pp. 64–65. G. Bussey and M. Tims, *Pioneers for Peace: Women's International League for*

Peace and Freedom 1915–1965, Allen & Unwin, 1965 and WILPF, 1980, is a much more honest history.

19. Of the 24 interviews recorded, 16 have been referred to directly; see Sources.

1   The Olive Leaf Women

1.   The Society's formal title was 'the Society for the Promotion of Permanent and Universal Peace'; it supposedly still exists, but has essentially been moribund since 1914. Similar societies were formed in New York and Boston in 1815.

2.   Peace Society, 3rd *Annual Report*, 1819; also *Herald of Peace*, 1923, p. 198; other Female Auxiliaries were at Lymington and Gisborough.

3.   *Herald of Peace*, 1823, p. 195.

4.   Peace Society tract no. viii, first published in *Herald of Peace*, 1823, quoted in A. Tyrrell, '"Woman's Mission" and Pressure Group Politics in Britain (1825–60)', *Bulletin of the John Rylands University Library of Manchester*, vol. 63, no. 1, autumn 1980.

     W. H. Posthumus-Van Der Goot, *Vrouwen Vochten Voor de Vrede*, pp. 15–16, seemingly the only book to mention the Female Auxiliaries, suggests Elizabeth Clarke of Lymington might be the author.

5.   The precise beginning of Olive Leaf activity seems hazy. The standard histories say little. However, Posthumus-Van Der Goot, op. cit., pp. 41–47, describes how Elihu Burritt, the 'learned blacksmith' from Connecticut, began his European Olive Leaf propaganda about 1848; Tyrrell, op. cit., p. 218, gives a similar summary. However, exact dating remains unclear.

6.   Tyrrell, op. cit., p. 218; Posthumus-Van Der Goot, p. 47. Thanks to Alex Tyrrell for noting the 'Olive Leaf' recipes.

7.   Posthumus-Van Der Goot, op. cit., pp. 21, 26, is emphatic on this point (though adding that the Peace Society also issued personal invitations to people of exceptional merit); Tyrrell, op. cit., p. 218, also makes it clearly. (However, E. Boulding, *The Underside of History: A View of Women through Time*, Westview Press, Boulder, Colorado, 1976, p. 674,

claims that the 1848 congress not only saluted women, but also 'had them to speak'.)

8. Tyrrell, op. cit., pp. 194–202; Pease (1807–97) supported non-resistance.

9. Quoted in G. Malmgreen, 'Anne Knight and the Radical Subculture', *Quaker History*, vol. 71, no. 2, 1982, pp. 105–06.

10. 'To Richard Cobden MP', 13 August 1850.

11. 'Letter to Lord Brougham', 14 April 1849; Tyrrell, op. cit., p. 227, citing London Peace Society, *Peace Conference Committee Minutes*, 28 June 1851.

12. Brock, *Pacifism in Europe to 1914*, pp. 390–92; Beales, *The History of Peace*, pp. 85, 102, 115.

13. See L. Davidoff and C. Hall, *Family Fortunes: Men and Women of the English Middle Class 1780–1850*, Hutchinson, London, 1987.

14. *The Times*, 28 August 1854.

15. J. Ruskin, 'Of Queen's Gardens', *Sesame and Lilies*, 1865.

16. The *Englishwoman's Journal* at this time contains many references to Mill, suffrage, women's education, training and employment, but virtually none to anti-militarism.

17. J. S. Mill, *The Subjection of Women*, 1869 and Virago, London, 1983, p. 147.

18. J. Ruskin, Lecture on 'War' delivered at the Royal Military Academy, Woolwich, 1865, in *The Crown of Wild Olive*, pp. 127–28.

19. Posthumus-Van Der Goot, op. cit., pp. 36–37. I have not yet been able to trace this booklet.

20. Mill, op. cit., pp. 159, 162.

21. R. Shannon, *The Crisis of Imperialism*, 1974 and Granada, London, 1976, p. 83.

22. Brock, op. cit., p. 334 notes that by the 1852 Militia Act, imprisonment for refusing militia service became illegal; distraint on the grounds of objectors stopped in 1860, when compulsory service was suspended – at least until 1916.

2 Lay Down Your Arms

1. *Englishwoman's Review* (ER), April 1871, based on an article in the *Examiner*.

2. *ER*, July 1873. The suggestion for the peace day came from Madame Flodin, a Swede. Posthumus-Van Der Goot, op. cit., pp. 59–62.

3. The *Victoria Magazine*, 1872–73, pp. 25–36; thanks to Anne Summers for this reference.

4. *ER*, June 1875.

5. *ER*, October 1876; also R. Shannon, *Gladstone and the Bulgarian Agitation 1876*, Nelson, London, 1963, p. 45.

6. *ER*, October 1876 and November 1877.

7. *ER*, September 1876.

8. *ER*, 'The Peacemakers', May 1878. Further research would reveal a more complex picture than I can give here.

9. Posthumus-Van Der Goot, op. cit., pp. 64–68 (it seems that Fanny Lewald-Stahr had earlier read a paper to a peace congress).

10. *ER*, June 1887, June 1880, July 1881, January 1884, December 1885. The links between peace and equal rights seem strongest in education, and women elected to school boards; Eliza Sturge, member of a peace movement family, was the first woman on the Birmingham School Board.

11. *Peace and Goodwill*, no. 1, April 1882, p. 3. Posthumus-Van Der Goot, op. cit., pp. 69 ff.; also *ER*, June 1880 (Peckover had met Elihu Burritt, who founded a Wisbech Olive Leaf Circle, in 1852).

12. Posthumus-Van der Goot, op. cit., p. 77. *Peace and Goodwill* claims the following 'membership' figures: 1885, 9,000; 1888, 14,000. The precise relationship between Peckover's 'organization' and the existing Women's Auxiliary seems unclear, as is whether men were admitted as members.

13. *Peace and Goodwill*, 15 April 1885; 15 July 1885. Posthumus-Van Der Goot, op. cit., p. 108, notes that in 1890 Peckover seconded a successful resolution that women, by staying on the sidelines, were themselves responsible for the continuation of war.

14. *ER*, June 1880.

15. *Peace and Goodwill*, 15 January 1895; M. M. Shearer, *Quaker Peace Work on Merseyside*, published privately, 1979, pp. 15–21.

16.   Beales, *The History of Peace*, p. 242.

17.   The age for leaving full-time schooling was raised to eleven in 1893 and twelve in 1899.

18.   H. M. Swanwick, *I Have Been Young*, Victor Gollancz, London, 1935, pp. 80–82.

19.   ibid., pp. 117–18, 121–22, 161.

20.   J. Fisher, *That Miss Hobhouse: The Life of a Great Feminist*, Secker & Warburg, London, 1971, pp. 14, 21–23, 45–46.

21.   K. A. Rigby, *Annot Robinson: Socialist, Suffragist, Peaceworker: a Biographical Study*, MA, Manchester Polytechnic, 1986, pp. 2–5.

22.   1871, 1881 household census; Leeds Women's Suffrage Society, Report, 1899; thanks to June Hannam for information about Ford.

23.   J. Liddington and J. Norris, *One Hand Tied Behind Us: the Rise of the Women's Suffrage Movement*, Virago, London, 1978, ch. 4.

24.   Fisher, op. cit., pp. 24, 28–36.

25.   The proposal to form an 'International Woman Suffrage Movement' came from Elizabeth Cady Stanton, president of the National Women's Suffrage Association, supported by Susan B. Anthony, another leading American suffragist. Strong support for 'broadening' the appeal came from Frances Willard, temperance reformer, and May Wright Sewall, peace worker and reformer. See *Women in a Changing World: the Dynamic Story of the International Council of Women*, Routledge & Kegan Paul, London, 1966, Prologue. (The name of the British organization remained the National Union of Women Workers until 1918, when it became the National Council of Women.)

26.   C. P. Gilman, *The Living of Charlotte Perkins Gilman: an Autobiography*, D. Appleton-Century Co., New York and London, 1935, pp. 170, 259–62.

27.   D. J. Newton, *British Labour, European Socialism and the Struggle for Peace 1889–1914*, Clarendon Press, Oxford, 1985, pp. 63–67.

28.   ibid., p. 59.

29.   R. First and A. Scott, *Olive Schreiner*, Schocken, New York, 1980, pp. 228, 231.

30. *Peace and Goodwill*, 15 July 1899; *Women in a Changing World*, pp. 21–22; Gilman, op. cit., pp. 261–62.

31. *Women in a Changing World*, pp. 22, 27.

32. B. Kempf, *Suffragette for Peace: the Life of Bertha von Suttner*, Austria, 1964 and Wolff, London, 1972, pp. 7–19.

33. ibid., pp. 21–22; C. E. Playne, *Bertha von Suttner and the Struggle to Avert the World War*, Allen & Unwin, London, 1936, p. 33. Von Suttner merits a better biography than either of these!

34. B. von Suttner, *Lay Down Your Arms: the Autobiography of Martha von Tilling*, Longmans, London, 1892, pp. 47–48; the book was part of Thomas Buckle's *History of Civilization*. Helen Taylor edited Buckle's posthumous works.

35. ibid.; p. 150; also pp. 64–66, 125, 143–49.

36. ibid., pp. 255–56.

37. ibid., pp. 329–30, 424–25, 435.

38. Kempf, op. cit., pp. 23–29.

39. T. Holmes, 'Translator's Preface', pp. vi–vii; B. Suttner, op. cit.

3 *The Brunt of War*

1. R. Fry, *Emily Hobhouse*, Cape, London, 1919, pp. 60–62.

2. J. Fisher, *That Miss Hobhouse*, p. 67.

3. R. First and A. Scott, *Olive Schreiner*, pp. 235–7.

4. Fisher, op. cit., pp. 75–76, 96–99; also E. Goldman, *Living My Life*, 1931 and Dover, New York, 1970, vol. I, pp. 255–56; Tom Mann chaired the meeting.

5. Fisher, op. cit., p. 99; Fry, op. cit., pp. 66–67.

6. Fry, op. cit., pp. 67–69; the meeting was attended 'by Delegates of the Women's Liberal Federation which happened to be holding its meetings at that time'. Hobhouse began writing her autobiography before she died.

7. Fry, op. cit., pp. 69–70.

8. Fisher, op. cit., pp. 109–10.

9. Fry, op. cit., pp. 88–9.

10. First and Scott, op. cit., pp. 246–47.

11. *Co-operative News*, 1 December 1900; thanks to Gina Bridgeland for this reference.

12. Fry, op. cit., pp. 95, 98–99.

13. E. Hobhouse, *Report of a Visit to the Camps of Women and Children in the Cape and Orange River Colonies*, Friars Printing Association, London [1901], p. 5.

14. ibid., p. 9.

15. ibid., p. 4.

16. Fisher, op. cit., pp. 143–48; Fry, op. cit., p. 152.

17. E. Hobhouse, *The Brunt of War and Where It Fell*, Methuen, London, 1902, p. 163 (which also notes that a Women's League for the Promotion of International Disarmament wrote to Brodrick pleading for Boer women). Fisher, op. cit., pp. 149, 204; American criticism should be seen in the context of concentration camps in the recent Cuban War.

18. Quoted in Wiltsher, *Most Dangerous Women*, p. 63.

19. M. Fawcett, *What I Remember*, Fisher Unwin, London, 1924, pp. 149–50; R. Strachey, *Millicent Garrett Fawcett*, John Murray, London, 1931, p. 184. The organization was the Women's Liberal Unionist Committee.

20. NUWSS Executive Committee Minutes, 9 January 1902; Mrs Fawcett was absent from Easter 1901 for approximately twelve months; Strachey, op. cit., pp. 191–92.

21. Hobhouse, *The Brunt*, pp. 135–36.

22. ibid., pp. 137–39; Fry, op. cit., pp. 157–58; Fisher, op. cit., p. 196.

23. Fry, op. cit., p. 180.

24. Shannon, *The Crisis of Imperialism*, p. 334, gives the Boers' estimate of 26,000 camp deaths, and the official British estimate as 18,000. Fry, op. cit., pp. 147–78 on child mortality.

25. NUWSS Executive Committee Minutes, 3 October 1901 (letter from Mrs Chapman Catt); 17 April 1902 (Washington convention report); 5 June 1902 (NUWSS societies approve scheme for new international committee). See also *Women in a Changing World*, pp. 24–25.

25. Beales, *The History of Peace*, pp. 249, 258.

26. Hobhouse, op. cit., pp. xv–xvi.

27. ibid., p. 286.

4 Sisterhood is International

1. Quoted in Shannon, *The Crisis of Imperialism*, p. 433.

2. A. Summers, *Angels and Citizens: British Women as Military Nurses 1854–1914*, Routledge & Kegan Paul, London, 1988.

3. D. Newton, *British Labour, European Socialism and the Struggle for Peace 1889–1914*, p. 49; also pp. 161–63, 184–85, noting Will Crooks MP as an exception.

4. See G. Barraclough, *From Agadir to Armageddon: Anatomy of a Crisis*, Weidenfeld & Nicolson, London, 1982, pp. 131–32.

5. *Women in a Changing World*, p. 27, hints at how shaken ICW was by the suffrage defection to form IWSA.

6. Whittick, *Woman into Citizen*, pp. 32–37, 38–39, 51. WSPU was allowed to send a fraternal delegate, Dora Montefiore.

7. *Common Cause*, 6 July 1911, 5 October 1911; written by Ida O'Malley, NUWSS literature secretary.

8. Kempf, *Suffragette for Peace*, pp. 120–21.

9. Gilman, *The Living of Charlotte Perkins Gilman*, p. 305.

10. Thanks to Gina Bridgeland for this information.

11. Interview with Elsie Plant, recorded by Jill Liddington and Jill Norris, 1976.

12. Gilman, op. cit., pp. 78, 257, 321.

13. Gilman, *The Man-Made World*, pp. 35–41.

14. ibid., pp. 51, 132–33; also M. Hobbs, 'The Perils of "Unbridled Masculinity": Pacifist Elements in the Feminist and Socialist Thought of Charlotte Perkins Gilman', in R. Pierson (ed.), *Women and Peace: Theoretical, Historical and Practical Perspectives*, Croom Helm, London, 1987.

15. Gilman, *The Man-Made World*, pp. 210–11.

16. ibid., pp. 211–12, 215–16, 219.

17. 'The New Mothers of a New World', *Forerunner*, no. 4, 1913, quoted by Hobbs, op. cit., p. 163. See also A. J. Lane, 'Introduction', *Herland*, The Women's Press, London, 1979, pp. xii–xiii on 'Moving the Mountain' (1911); also A. J. Lane, *The Charlotte Perkins Gilman Reader*, The Women's Press, London 1981, pp. xxviii–ix, 178 ff.

18. First and Scott, *Olive Schreiner*, pp. 298, 215, 263–68 on the

problems of dating Schreiner's writing, and so links to *The Brunt of War*.

19. O. Schreiner, *Woman and Labour*, 1911 and Virago, London, 1978, pp. 33, 168–69, 170.

20. ibid., pp. 170–73, 178; First and Scott, op. cit., pp. 261, 285.

21. Interview with Gwen Coleman, recorded June 1984, pp. 25–6.

22. *Spare Rib*, no. 140, March 1984, pp. 22–23.

23. L. Nyström-Hamilton, *Ellen Key: Her Life and Work*, G. P. Putnam's, New York & London, 1913, pp. 106, 112, 146, 136; H. Ellis, 'Introduction', p. vi.

24. E. Key, *The Century of the Child*, G. P. Putnam's, New York and London, 1909, pp. 311, 316–17.

25. E. Key, *The Woman Movement*, G. P. Putnam's, New York and London, 1912, pp. 40–41, 127, 149–50, 170–71, 176–77, 182, 192, 218.

26. Beales, *The History of Peace*, pp. 242, 255, 213.

27. *Common Cause*, no. 7 – 21 December 1911.

28. Lockwood's autobiography, *An Ordinary Life: 1861–1924*, published privately (London, 1932), is based on her diaries, which were privately printed in seven parts. These in turn are based on *handwritten* diaries, but these have apparently survived only from 4 August 1914 to the end of the war (Kirklees District Archives: KC 329). Unless otherwise noted, therefore, quotation is taken from the printed diaries.

29. Lockwood *Diary*, Part IV, *Impressions*, p. 34; Victor Grayson won the by-election.

30. Lockwood, *An Ordinary Life*, p. 175; the sentence order has been slightly altered to help the sense.

31. Lockwood, *Diary*, Part V, *Before the War*, pp. 3–4, 5–6.

32. E. S. Riemer and J. C. Fout (eds), *European Women: A Documentary History 1789–1945*, Schocken Books, New York, 1980, pp. 204, 214–17.

33. *Jus Suffragii*, 15 July 1913.

34. Swanwick, *I Have Been Young*, p. 236.

35. Lockwood, *Before the War*, pp. 7, 9; Whittick, op. cit., is unhelpful here.

36. Oldfield, *Spinsters of this Parish*, pp. 159–60.

37. E.g. *Huddersfield Daily Examiner*, 7 July 1914; oddly, Lockwood says nothing of Mrs Studdard of Huddersfield, also active in IWSA.

38. H. M. Swanwick, *The Future of the Women's Movement*, G. Bell, London, 1913, pp. 12, 51–52, 187–88, 37–41.

39. ibid., pp. 40–41.

40. Playne, *Bertha von Suttner*, ch. XI.

41. *Huddersfield Examiner*, 27 June, 28 July 1914; *Huddersfield Daily Examiner*, 27, 28, 30 July 1914.

42. R. Schwimmer, unpublished typescript, p. 33, Box B-21, Schwimmer/Lloyd Papers, Rare Books & Manuscripts Division, New York Public Library; also, Edith Wynner to author, 4 January 1984.

43. Schwimmer, op. cit., pp. 4, VII, 25–26, 3.

44. *Jus Suffragii*, 1 September 1914; the 12 million claim is from Whittick, op. cit., p. 63.

45. Schwimmer, op. cit., p. 82.

46. Swanwick, *I Have Been Young*, pp. 239–41; Whittick, op. cit., pp. 63–65, manages to omit references to this rally – presumably because Corbett Ashby was, in every sense, elsewhere.

47. Interview with Coleman, p. 12.

48. Strachey, *Millicent Garrett Fawcett*, p. 276.

49. Schwimmer, op. cit., pp. 106, 95, 104–9, also Schwimmer Correspondence, Box 39, 7 August 1914 onwards.

50. Swanwick, op. cit., p. 253.

51. Lockwood, *Diary*, Sept.–Oct. 1914, 3 June 1915.

52. Lockwood, *Before the War*, pp. 29–30.

53. Quoted in H. Hanak, 'The Union of Democratic Control during the First World War', *The Bulletin of the Institute of Historical Research*, 1963, p. 169.

54. M. Swartz, *The Union of Democratic Control in British Politics During the First World War*, Clarendon Press, Oxford, 1971, pp. 11 ff., 24, 27; R. Clark, *The Life of Bertrand Russell*, 1975 and Penguin, London, 1978, p. 311.

55. Swartz, op. cit., pp. 57–58; Swanwick, op. cit., p. 254.

56. Ford to Marshall, 25 October 1914, quoted in Wiltsher, *Most Dangerous Women*, p. 63 (also pp. 28–9, 237). At various

times, the UDC executive also included Irene Cooper Willis and Mary Agnes Hamilton.

57. Interview recorded with Dame Mabel Tylecote (*née* Phythian), October 1984, pp. 4–5; September 1984, pp. 1–3; December 1984, p. 29. The date of the incident is unclear, but may have been March 1915.

58. Swartz, op. cit., p. 118.

59. Lockwood, *Before the War*, p. 13.

60. Swartz, op. cit., pp. 48, 55–56. UDC historians are unhelpful on suffrage links; however, local research suggests that they were significant – Rachel Quilter in Halifax was branch secretary of both NUWSS and UDC.

61. A. Marwick, *Britain in a Century of Total War*, Bodley Head, London, 1968, p. 86; *Towards Permanent Peace: A Record of the Women's International Congress*, British Committee of the Women's International Congress, London, 1915, p. 22.

62. V. Brittain, *Testament of Youth*, 1933 and Fontana, London, 1979, p. 139.

5   War, Motherhood and The Hague

1. V. Brittain, *Testament of Youth*, p. 104.

2. *Jus Suffragii (JS)*, 1 August 1914; Schwimmer, however, stresses that women and men are equally guilty.

3. It would be interesting to know more about the Suffragettes of WSPU and the Independent WSPU, and about suffragette rebels other than the much-cited Annie Bell.

4. *Nelson Leader*, 14 August 1914.

5. See Hobbs, 'The Perils of "Unbridled Masculinity"', in Pierson (ed.), *Women and Peace*, p. 160, for Gilman's ideas on women and defensive 'war'.

6. E. Key, *War, Peace and the Future: A Consideration of Nationalism and Internationalism, and the Relation of Women to War*, G. P. Putnam's, New York and London, 1916.

7. *Halifax Courier*, 12 September 1914.

8. *The Work of the Peace Committee of the National Council of Women of Great Britain*, pp. 1–2; the Committee first met in October 1914. *Women in a Changing World*, p. 44.

9. *Common Cause*, 19 October 1911; *Peace and Goodwill*, 15 October 1914, etc. Hallowes's many other books included *The Enemy: A Study in Heredity*, 1908.

10. Hallowes, F. S., *Women and War: An Appeal to the Women of All Nations*, Headley Bros, London [1914], pp. 6, 7, 12, 14. This pamphlet is substantially the same as the article in *JS*, 1 September 1914. Many thanks to Susan Grayzel for alerting me to Hallowes's writings.

11. *JS*, 1 September 1914.

12. *Women's Dreadnought*, 13 October 1914, quoted in S. Grayzel, *Mothers, Sisters and Outsiders: Feminist Pacifism in Britain from Olive Schreiner to Virginia Woolf*, BA, Harvard, 1986, p. 20; also *Labour Woman*, November 1913.

13. It would be interesting to know more about the background to this proposal, e.g. its links to Schwimmer's suggestion; see also Liddington, *Respectable Rebel*, p. 265.

14. F. S. Hallowes, *Mothers of Men and Militarism*, Headley Bros, London [1915], pp. 111, 47, 9, 86–87, 119.

15. ibid., pp. 48, 11–12, 56–57.

16. ibid., pp. 69–70, 117–19, 124.

17. It was, however, republished by Allen & Unwin.

18. Key, *War, Peace and the Future*, p. 144.

19. ibid., pp. 107, 100, 236, 84–85.

20. ibid., pp. 87–89, 216–17, 178–79, 240–41.

21. See R. Evans, *Comrades and Sisters: Feminism, Socialism and Pacifism in Europe 1870–1945*, Wheatsheaf Books, Sussex, 1987, ch. 5; Evans, well informed on Germany, is weak on Britain.

22. Links between suffrage and peace have been detailed in Wiltsher, *Most Dangerous Women*; however, I place less emphasis on Schwimmer's role, and more on the importance of the Liberal and maternalist traditions.

23. *JS*, 1 September 1914, 1 November 1914.

24. *JS*, 1 December 1914.

25. *JS*, 1 January 1915; I would query Wiltsher's suggestion that it was 'organized' by Hobhouse.

26. *JS*, 1 March 1915.

27. Strachey, *Millicent Garrett Fawcett*, p. 289; Lockwood, *Diary*, 4, 5 February 1915.

28. 'International Women's Congress' leaflet, 20 February 1915.

29. Swanwick to Marshall, 22 March 1915, quoted in Wiltsher, op. cit., pp. 75–76.

30. The *Anti-Oorlog Raad* was established in late 1914; from it grew the Central Organization for a Durable Peace, formed at The Hague in April 1915.

31. M. Kamester and J. Vellacott (eds), *Militarism versus Feminism: Writings on Women and War*, Virago, London, 1987, pp. 26–28.

32. *Militarism versus Feminism: An Enquiry and a Policy Demonstrating that Militarism Involves the Subjection of Women*, Allen & Unwin, London, 1915, pp. 3–4.

33. ibid., pp. 5, 9, 54, 32, 6, 39–42.

34. ibid., pp. 57, 58, 60, 63, 62, 7.

35. The role of UDC and Swanwick is confusing here; *JS* says UDC hopes the 14 April meeting will increase women's activity in UDC. About then (or shortly afterwards), Swanwick wrote *Women and War*, a UDC pamphlet; she employs all the rhetoric of feminism, but in the end argues *against* separate women's peace organizations. *I Have Been Young*, p. 258, says that she emerged from illness to 'find' The Hague – yet her name is among those wanting to go. Such inconsistencies suggest that the women's committee and UDC were jostling for space – and Swanwick's support – during those frantic days.

36. 'National Conference of Women', leaflet; *JS*, 1 April 1915.

37. *Towards Permanent Peace*, pp. 5, 13–14.

38. An *exact* chronology is elusive; this is compiled mainly from Marshall to Grey, [Dec.] 1915, Marshall papers; also H. Ward, *A Venture in Goodwill: Being the Story of the Women's International League 1915–1929*, WIL, London, 1929, pp. 1–2.

39. Bussey and Tims, *Pioneers for Peace*, p. 19.

40. *Towards Permanent Peace*, p. 6.

41. ibid., pp. 10, 7, Wiltsher, op. cit., pp. 101–02.

42. Ward, op. cit., p. 11.

43. Wiltsher, op. cit., p. 119.

44. B. W. Cook (ed.), *Crystal Eastman on Women and Revolution*, Oxford University Press, 1978, p. 240; Bussey and Tims, op. cit., p. 21.

45. Wiltsher, op. cit., ch. 6, for full details.

46. *Towards Permanent Peace*, pp. 20–21, for press reactions.

47. ibid., pp. 17, 24; WIL, *First Yearly Report*, October 1915– October 1916, p. 3.

48. Macaulay, R., *Non-combatants and others*, 1916 and Methuen, London 1986; Mrs Despard and Constance Markievicz may also have contributed to 'Sandomir'.

6 The Women's Peace Crusade

1. Liddington, *Respectable Rebel*, p. 260.

2. K. Weller, *'Don't Be A Soldier!' The Radical Anti-War Movement in North London 1914–1918*, Journeyman Press and London History Workshop Centre, London, 1985, p. 75.

3. Clark, *The Life of Bertrand Russell*, pp. 348–54; Carsten, *War Against War*, p. 68.

4. Wiltsher, *Most Dangerous Women*, p. 146.

5. J. Hinton, *The First Shop Stewards' Movement*, Allen & Unwin, London, 1973, pp. 111, 130.

6. J. J. Smyth, *Women in Struggle: A History of the Political Activity of Working-class Women in Glasgow during the First World War*, MA, Glasgow, 1980, pp. 10, 17.

7. 1911 Census, Glasgow: only 5.5 per cent of married women and 26.5 per cent of widows were classified as occupied. Housing: 13.8 per cent lived in one-roomed, and 48.7 per cent in two-roomed, 'houses'.

8. Smyth, op. cit., pp. 8–11, quoting Annie Maxton.

9. W. W. Knox (ed.), *Scottish Labour Leaders 1918–1939: A Biographical Dictionary*, Edinburgh, 1983, entry by Helen Corr, p. 89.

10. S. Fleming and G. Dallas, 'Jessie', *Spare Rib*, no. 32, February 1975, p. 11.

11. Helen Crawfurd to 'Phil', 17 February 1954 (letter written two months before Crawfurd died, aged seventy-seven; punctuation slightly altered to make it clearer). Very many

thanks to Audrey Canning for letting me see copies of her Crawfurd material; sources marked * are from her notes.

12. Knox, op. cit., entry by Corr, p. 82.

13. Quoted in Smyth, op. cit., p. 14.

14. Hinton, op. cit., pp. 125–27; also Smyth, op. cit., pp. 28–33.

15. Crawfurd's last contribution to *Forward* was 22 August 1914; thanks to Anne Wiltsher for her help here.

16. WIL, *Annual Report* 1915–16, p. 4; *Forward*, 18 December 1915*.

17. It would be interesting to know of any links with Dorothea Hollins.

18. Quoted in Wiltsher, op. cit., p. 147; presumably the same Mrs S. Cahill who signed the open *Jus Suffragii* letter eighteen months earlier.

19. *Forward*, 3 June 1916, 17 June 1916, 8 July 1916, 15 July 1916*.

20. Fleming and Dallas, op. cit., p. 12.

21. *Forward*, 5 August 1915; *Glasgow Herald*, 18, 24 July 1916*.

22. WIL *Annual Report* (*An Rep*), 1915–16, pp. 4–5; *Bradford Pioneer*, 24 November 1916, also suggests local Crusade activity that winter.

23. Quoted in Wiltsher, op. cit., p. 152.

24. Smyth, op. cit., pp. 41–42. Other WPC activists were Miss Walker, Mrs Ferguson, Mrs Mossman, and Alice Peachley of the Women's Humanity League.

25. WIL *An Rep*, 1915–16 p. 4; 1916–17, p. 4; Clark, op. cit., pp. 37–76.

26. Interview with Tylecote, October 1984, p. 7; Tylecote, pocket diary, 1916.

27. HO 45 10741/263275/61.

28. WIL *An Rep*, 1915–16, pp. 4–23.

29. ibid., pp. 7–8, 17; *An Rep*, 1916–17, p. 15.

30. Liddington, op. cit., p. 274; Weller, op. cit., pp. 74–75.

31. HO 45/10814 312987; HO 45/10743 263275/264, 274.

32. S. Rowbotham, *Friends of Alice Wheeldon*, Pluto, London, 1986, pp. 6, 39.

33. ibid., pp. 51–52, 55, 80.

34. WIL *An Rep*, 1916–17, p. 17; Lockwood, *Diary*, 1917; A.

Linklater, *An Unhusbanded Life: Charlotte Despard: Suffragette, Socialist and Sinn Feiner*, Hutchinson, London, 1980, p. 193.

35. *Forward*, 12 May 1917, 16 June 1917*.

36. WIL *Monthly News Sheet*, August 1917; *Daily Herald*, 14 July 1917; *Labour Leader*, 12 July 1917; Swanwick put the crowd at 8,000.

37. Liddington, op. cit., p. 275; *Labour Leader*, 19 July 1917; there are already signs of tension between Crawfurd and the ILP women, and between WIL and the more revolutionary WPC.

38. WIL *Monthly News Sheet*, September 1917; *Labour Leader*, 26 July 1917; the larger figure suggested by Wiltsher for the Birmingham meeting seems misleading.

39. Liddington, op. cit., pp. 277–79.

40. *Labour Leader*, 16 August 1917; interview with Tylecote, October 1984, p. 6.

41. *Labour Leader*, 16, 30 August 1917.

42. *Bradford Pioneer*, 14 September 1917; *Labour Leader*, 6, 13 September 1917; a Mrs Sandiforth was active in Bradford.

43. Lockwood, *Diary*, 18 September 1917.

44. *Labour Leader*, 6, 20 September 1917; Liddington, op. cit., pp. 279–80.

45. *Labour Leader*, 27 September, 25 October, 1 November 1917; also Linklater, op. cit., p. 197.

46. Lockwood, *Diary*, 17 November 1917.

47. WIL *Monthly News Sheet*, December 1917.

48. Quoted in Wiltsher, op. cit., p. 193; *Labour Leader*, 8, 15 November 1917.

49. *Forward*, 8 December 1917; *Glasgow Herald*, 14 December 1917, 10 January 1918; the *Bulletin*, 23 January, 20 March 1918*; also W. Gallacher, *Revolt on the Clyde*, Lawrence & Wishart, London, 1936, pp. 177–79.

50. WIL *Monthly News Sheet*, November 1917; HO 45/10744/263275.

51. S. Butt, 'Cranquettes and Cassandras: a view of the women's peace movement in Britain during the First World War', dissertation, York, 1987. For a different appraisal of wartime peace initiatives, see J. Hinton, *Protests and Visions:*

Peace Politics in 20th Century Britain, Radius, London, 1989.

7 Wars will cease when . . .

1. Brittain, *Testament of Youth*, p. 458.
2. *Spare Rib*, no. 23, p. 8.
3. Rowbotham, *Friends of Alice Wheeldon*, pp. 80–82.
4. Liddington, *Respectable Rebel*, p. 300.
5. *Scottish Labour Leaders*, pp. 90, 84.
6. Membership was apparently around 150,000 and rising.
7. Wood Green, Women's Section Minute Books, 17 September 1924; 10, 24 June 1925. However, they were not all pacifist; the Section's exact title is unclear.
8. M. Caedel, 'The Peace Movement between the Wars: Problems of Definition', in Taylor and Young (eds), *Campaigns for Peace*, p. 80; *Guardian*, 11 March 1968.
9. Brittain, op. cit., pp. 553, 555–56, 564.
10. Lockwood, *Diary*, Part XIII, pp. 15–16, 28–9.
11. Caedel, *Pacifism in Britain*, pp. 61, 155, 319.
12. Brock, *Twentieth-Century Pacifism*.
13. Ward, *A Venture in Goodwill*.
14. Introduction, endnotes 8–10, 18.
15. WIL *An Rep*, 1917–18, pp. 3–4. There were 3,687 branch members; the rest were 'Central' members.
16. WIL *An Rep*, 1918–19, pp. 8, 9, 12–13.
17. Linklater, *An Unhusbanded Life*, p. 207.
18. F. Wilson, *Rebel Daughter of a County House*, Allen & Unwin, London, 1967, pp. 173–74.
19. Oldfield, *Spinsters of this Parish*, pp. 214 ff.
20. Fisher, *That Miss Hobhouse*, pp. 261–62; Wilson, op. cit., p. 184.
21. WIL *An Rep*, 1918–19, pp. 17, 21; Wilson, op. cit., p. 175.
22. Bussey and Tims, *Pioneers for Peace*, p. 30.
23. Ward, op. cit., p. 36.
24. Swanwick, *I Have Been Young*, pp. 318–19.
25. WIL *An Rep*, 1918–19, p. 4.
26. WILPF *An Rep*, 1920–22, pp. 13–14; Ward, op. cit., p. 31.

27. Interview with Tylecote, October 1984, p. 14; some aspects of the blockade may since have become myth.

28. For pressure from the American patriotic right on WILPF see J. Lemons, *The Woman Citizen: Social Feminism in the 1920s*, University of Illinois Press, Urbana, 1973, ch. 8, 'The Spider Web'.

29. WILPF *An Rep*, 1923, pp. 7–11; Bussey and Tims, op. cit., p. 77.

30. Interview with Tylecote, December 1984, pp. 13, 19.

31. Total membership and number of branches: 1919: *c.* 4,000 (43), 1920: 3,043 (31), 1923: *c.* 3,500 (24), 1924: 3,000 (25) (precise figures not supplied every year).

32. WILPF *An Rep*, 1920–22, p. 11; 1922, pp. 26–27; 1924, p. 23. It was at 55 Gower Street.

33. In 1925 the Chelsea branch proposed that WILPF should merge with other groups; this was heavily defeated.

34. WILPF *An Rep*, 1923, p. 4; 1924, pp. 19–20.

35. *Woman in a Changing World*, p. 55; also pp. 97–99 for a *furious* argument within IWSA, when Nina Boyle demanded 'Are we feminists, or are we pacifists?' and Corbett Ashby attempted to respond.

36. Bussey and Tims, op. cit., pp. 74–75; WILPF had debated the merits of the League as early as 1919; the prevailing view was that WILPF *should* work with it.

37. Also Cicely Hamilton, 'The Peacemaker as Firebrand', *Time and Tide*, 15 September 1922; she represents the libertarian extreme of equal-rights feminism.

38. Anonymous, *Ancilla's Share: An Indictment of Sex Antagonism*, Hutchinson, London, pp. 267–68.

39. ibid., pp. 282, 274, 300, 308.

40. ibid., pp. 287–88, ch. XXIX; Robbins shares some of Gilman's racism; see pp. xxx–xxxiv.

41. Quoted in N. Black, 'The Mothers' International: the Women's Co-operative Guild and Feminist Pacifism', *Women's Studies International Forum*, 1984, p. 471.

42. Quoted in M. O'Brien, *Women and Peace Movements in Britain 1914–1939*, MA, London, 1983, p. 19.

43. Swanwick, op. cit., p. 317.

44.   WILPF *An Rep*, 1925, pp. 3–4.
45.   WILPF produced a floridly unhelpful resolution on the strike.
46.   Ward, op. cit., p. 49.
47.   Liddington, *Respectable Rebel*, pp. 406–07.
48.   Liddington, 'The Women's Peace Crusade', in *Over Our Dead Bodies*, p. 195.
49.   WILPF *An Rep*, 1926, p. 4.
50.   WILPF *An Rep*, 1927, p. 6.
51.   WILPF *An Rep*, 1927, p. 7; Ward, op. cit., pp. 64–65. NCW was involved. (Exactly why the 'Crusade' name was selected again is unclear. Probably WILPF found it helpful to have a broad-based campaigning organization; but as it was based at 55 Gower Street, it is unclear how independent of WILPF it really was.)
52.   Leaflet, *Women's Peace Crusade*; *Evening Standard*, 9 May 1929.
53.   *Women in a Changing World*, pp. 60–64; Whittick, *Woman into Citizen*, p. 109.
54.   Bussey and Tims, op. cit., p. 101.
55.   *Vox Populi*, Vox Populi Committee, Geneva (pamphlet); Whittick, op. cit., p. 110.
56.   Bussey and Tims, op. cit., p. 115.
57.   Quoted in B. Harrison, *Prudent Revolutionaries: Portraits of British Feminists between the Wars*, Clarendon Press, Oxford, 1987, p. 195.

8   Pacifism – or Anti-Fascism?

1.   M. Caedel, 'The Peace Movement between the Wars: Problems of Definition', in Taylor and Young (eds), *Campaigns for Peace*, pp. 88–89.
2.   For instance, Brock, *Twentieth-Century Pacifism*.
3.   M. Caedel, *Pacifism in Britain*, pp. 233–34.
4.   Liddington, *Respectable Rebel*, ch. 21.
5.   WILPF *An Rep*, 1933, pp. 14–15.
6.   M. Caedel, 'The First British Referendum: the Peace Ballot, 1934–5', *English History Review*, October 1980, pp. 818, 828; also, 'The Work of the Peace Committee of the National Council of Women of Great Britain', [*c.* 1935]; WILPF *An Rep*, 1934, pp. 6–7.

7. Bussey and Tims, *Pioneers for Peace*, p. 39.

8. Oldfield, *Spinsters of this Parish*, pp. 261–63.

9. 'The Peace Army. A Sermon by A. Maude Royden . . .', preached 28 February 1932, pp. 1–2, 5; also M. Caedel, *Pacifism in Britain*, pp. 93–97. It seems highly probable that Royden was inspired by Hollins's 1914 proposal.

10. WILPF *An Rep*, 1933, p. 23; report of meeting March 1934.

11. Bussey and Tims, op. cit., p. 126; WILPF *An Rep*, 1934, pp. 12, 16.

12. WILPF *An Rep*, 1933, p. 14; *Manchester Guardian*, 11 March 1968.

13. Liddington, op. cit., pp. 410 ff.

14. Bussey and Tims, op. cit., pp. 139–40; WILPF *An Rep*, 1936, pp. 6–7.

15. M. Caedel, 'The Peace Movement', op. cit., pp. 80 (1931: 406, 868), 90 (1939: 193, 266).

16. V. Brittain, *Testament of Experience: an Autobiographical Story of the Years 1925–1950*, 1957 and Virago, London, 1979, p. 14.

17. ibid., pp. 118, 167–68.

18. Y. Bennett, *Vera Brittain: Women and Peace*, PPU, London, 1987, p. 13.

19. J. Gaffin and D. Thoms, *Caring and Sharing: The Centenary History of the Co-operative Women's Guild*, Co-operative Union, Manchester, 1983, p. 268.

20. *Of Whole Heart Cometh Hope: Centenary Memories of the Co-operative Women's Guild*, Age Exchange, London, *c.* 1983, p. 39.

21. Interview with Emma Chatterton, March 1987, p. 1.

22. Interview with Chatterton, p. 2; she became national Guild president 1966–67.

23. *Of Whole Heart*, p. 38.

24. Hampstead Garden Suburb Guild Branch, Minute Book (HGS), 2 February 1933–16 November 1933.

25. HGS, 5 July, 13 September, 1 November 1934.

26. HGS, 16 May, 18 August 1935; *Of Whole Heart*, pp. 31 ff.; many thanks to Gill Scott for her scholarly comments.

27. HGS, 19 September–10 October 1935; 6 February, 21 May 1936.

28. HGS, 16 July 1936; 26 May 1938; Gaffin and Thoms, op. cit., p. 115; this account is disingenuous, and *Of Whole Heart* is more honest here.

29. HGS, 13 April 1938–30 March 1939.

30. V. Leff, *Dare to Speak*, typescript, 1978, pp. 22, 25; the author died in 1980. Many thanks to Sonya Leff for her generosity.

31. ibid., pp. 64–65, 83.

32. ibid., pp. 100–01.

33. ibid., pp. 103–04.

34. ibid., pp. 108–09.

35. WILPF *An Rep*, 1937, pp. 5, 6, 14. There *was* a small WILPF revival, but it was too little, too late. WILPF had 25 branches, and 11 in north Wales; there were still some local and national affiliations, but WILPF's 'Friends of Peace and Disarmament' had been disbanded.

36. H. M. Swanwick, *The Roots of Peace*, 1938, pp. 186, 189.

37. V. Woolf, 'Introductory Letter', *Life as We Have Known It*, 1931 and Virago, London, 1977, p. xxiii.

38. P. Rose, *Woman of Letters: A Life of Virginia Woolf*, 1978 and Pandora, London, 1986, p. 202.

39. V. Woolf, *Three Guineas*, 1938 and Penguin, London, 1977, pp. 25, 43, 121.

40. ibid., pp. 122–25. (There are echoes in *Ancilla's Share*. Robbins, a friend of Woolf's mother, had kept in touch with Woolf.)

41. ibid., p. 118; Q. Bell, *Virginia Woolf: a Biography*, vol. II, 1972 and Granada, London, 1976, pp. 204–05.

42. Gaffin and Thoms, op. cit., pp. 111, 118; this account is not candid.

43. *The Guildswoman*, May 1939, quoted in Gaffin and Thoms, op. cit., pp. 111–12.

44. WILPF *An Rep*, 1938, pp. 4, 8–9, 13–14.

45. Caedel, *Pacifism in Britain*, p. 294.

46. WILPF *An Rep*, 1939, p. 6; 1940, p. 3.

9   Hiroshima to Aldermaston

1. *The Dora Russell Reader: 57 years of writing and journalism, 1925–1982*, Pandora, London, 1983, pp. 128–29.

2. J. Lindsay, *The Moment of Choice: A Novel of the British Way*, Bodley Head, London, 1955, pp. 35, 79 ff.

3. D. Russell, *The Tamarisk Tree: vol. 3: The Challenge to the Cold War*, Virago, London, 1985, pp. 144, 151 ff.; WIDF was formed in 1945; its roots go back to the World Committee of Women Against War and Fascism.

4. S. Rowbotham, *Woman's Consciousness, Man's World*, Pelican, London, 1973, pp. 3, 12.

5. D. Spender, *There's Always Been A Women's Movement This Century*, Pandora, London, 1983, p. 6.

6. E. Wilson, *Only Halfway to Paradise: Women in Postwar Britain: 1945–1968*, Tavistock, London, 1980, pp. 185–87.

7. Gaffin and Thoms, *Caring and Sharing*, p. 268: 59,666 (1950); 46,495 (1960).

8. Bussey and Tims, *Pioneers for Peace*, pp. 189–98; a very fair account.

9. Russell, op. cit., pp. 118–19; for a similar story of the Married Women's Association, see pp. 119–23.

10. J. Hersey, *Hiroshima*, in *New Yorker*, August 1946; Penguin, London, 1946, pp. 108–09.

11. M. Gowing, *Britain and Atomic Energy, 1939–1945*, London, 1964, pp. 21–22; in January 1947, General 75 Committee was reconvened as a new General 163, including only Attlee, Bevin, Morrison, Alexander, Addison and Wilmot. See also Gowing, pp. 212–13 for the 1948 disguised 'leak' to the Commons.

12. R. Taylor, *Against the Bomb: The British Peace Movement 1958–1965*, Clarendon Press, Oxford, 1988, pp. 118–21.

13. C. Driver, *The Disarmers: A Study in Protest*, Hodder & Stoughton, London, 1964, pp. 25–27.

14. In Yorkshire, about 15 members of the Spenborough Labour Party were expelled; some were involved with Communist Party members in publishing *Yorkshire Voice of Peace*, which attacked the expulsions, demanding 'Ban That Bomb!'

15. Bussey and Tims, op. cit., p. 211. Interview with Sheila Jones, recorded November 1985.

16. Driver, op. cit., p. 31; he has marginalized Communist Party members' involvement in CND generally.

17. See Taylor, *Against the Bomb*, pp. 5–6; also R. Taylor, *The British Nuclear Disarmament Movement of 1958 to 1965 and its Legacy to the Left*, Ph.D, Leeds, 1983, pp. 29–31.

18. Before the war, there were active Guild branches in both Hampstead Garden Suburb *and* Golders Green, but the Guild lost 245 branches between 1939 and 1950, apparently including these. After the war, they seem to have amalgamated. Thanks to Richenda Barbour for all her kindness.

19. Interview recorded with Richenda Barbour, May 1986, pp. 14–15.

20. Golders Green Women's Co-operative Guild, Minute Book (GG), 14 December 1954; 8, 23 February 1955.

21. GG, 26 January, 2 February 1955; the conference was organized with the Scientific Workers' Association.

22. *Guardian*, 2 January 1986, 'Nuclear Power News Timed to Shield H-bomb Plans'.

23. GG (upside down, at back), 22 February 1955.

24. GG, 2, 9 March 1955; Leff fell ill and went to hospital on 30 March 1955.

25. Leff, *Dare to Speak*, pp. 242–43; the preceding section suggests that the topic was originally raised by a local comrade lamenting suspicions against the British Peace Committee.

26. *Hampstead and Highgate Express* (*H&HE*), 25 March 1955.

27. GG, 30 March 1955; Golders Green Preparative Meeting of the Society of Friends, 3 April 1955; thanks to Arthur Goss for this reference.

28. *H&HE*, 24 March, 1 April 1955.

29. *H&HE*, 8 April 1955; four Japanese women had been invited to Britain by the Socialist Medical Association.

30. Interview with Barbour, p. 24.

31. GG Friends, 8 May 1955; *H&HE*, 27 May 1955.

32. GG (committee), 18 May 1955; (branch), 25 May 1955; (comm), 2 June 1955; Leff was now out of hospital.

33. *H&HE*, 17 June 1955; GG, 15 June 1955, noting Fishwick gave out leaflets on voluntary euthanasia.

34. Leff, op. cit., p. 243; Leff, writing 23 years later, has elided separate incidents.

35. Driver, op. cit., p. 31; corroborative evidence (e.g. about the

suffragette claim) seems elusive; I have not yet traced an obituary. Leff, op. cit., p. 244.

36. GG Friends, 10 July 1955; GG WCG circular letter, 24 June 1955; at least four copies surviving in Arthur Goss's NCANWT collection.

37. Circular letter from Fishwick, 23 July 1955; interview recorded with Arthur Goss, by Dick Taylor, January 1978; *H&HE*, 5 August 1955.

38. Leff, op. cit., pp. 246–47; GG Friends, 11 September, 9 October 1955; GG, 21 September, 5 October 1955; *H&HE*, 7 October 1955.

39. Taylor, *Against the Bomb*, pp. 7 ff.

40. Interview with Sheila Jones, November 1985.

41. For instance, documents in NCANWT collection, 6 May 1956, and list of GGJCANW Activities.

42. Circular letter, Fishwick, Council for the Abolition of Nuclear Weapons, November 1956, enclosed within GG WCG Minute Book.

43. For details of NCANWT's confused start, see Taylor, op. cit., pp. 7–8; Ianthe Carswell became joint secretary with Jones.

44. By early 1957, NCANWT had three dozen sponsors; six were women – Dame Edith Evans, Dr Winifred de Kok, Barbara Hepworth CBE, Dame Rose Macaulay, Flora Robson CBE, and Professor Barbara Wootton.

45. According to D. Boulton, unpublished MSS account of origins of NCANWT, 'The Liberals', p. 7.

46. *Guardian*, 2 February 1988, 'Superpower Cloud over Weapons Testing'.

47. NCANWT, 'Women's Protest March', leaflet; interview with Jones, November 1985.

48. *Times*, 9 May 1957 (House of Lords' discussion on gamma radiation and sterility).

49. *Times*, *Manchester Guardian* and *Daily Worker*, 13 May 1957; a group of Watford Guildswomen who had been lobbying the Commons also marched (with Renée Short).

50. *H&HE*, 7 June 1957; P. Duff, *Left, Left, Left*, Allison & Busby, London, 1971, p. 120.

51. Boulton, op. cit.

52. Taylor, op. cit., pp. 15–17.

53. Bolton, op. cit.

54. Duff, op. cit., pp. 132, 153.

55. Duff obituary, *Spare Rib*, no. 107. Fishwick caught pneumonia and died, according to Driver, two days before CND's Central Hall launch. Leff, of course, survived until 1980; but her Aldermaston memories focus on her growing children rather than on herself.

56. See note 68 below.

57. Russell, op. cit., p. 248; she was secretary of a small International Committee of Mothers, linked to WIDF.

58. Taylor, op. cit., pp. 31, 79.

59. Taylor, *The British Disarmament Movement*, p. 874, quoting the *Daily Mail*, 6 November 1961. Driver, op. cit., p. 127, suggests that this led to the formation of 'Women Against the Bomb', but I have little evidence of this.

60. *Guardian*, 7 March 1962.

61. Driver, op. cit., pp. 127–28.

62. *Guardian*, 8 March 1962.

63. Taylor, *Against the Bomb*, pp. 79–80. The deputation: Jacquetta Hawkes, Diana Collins, Marghanita Laski, Dr Antoinette Pirie, Professor Dorothy Hodgkin, Dr Janet Aitken, Dame Alice Meynell, Dr Dorothy Needham, Mary Stocks.

64. *Call to Women*, no. 56, Sep.–Oct. 1967.

65. *Call to Women*, no. 9, June 1963. The Liaison Committee was started by Dorothy Alton, but its precise foundation date seems unclear.

66. However, in Holloway Pat Arrowsmith wrote her prophetic novel, *Jericho*, based on a peace camp (though that phrase was not then used) at Aldermaston in 1958.

67. Interview with Barbour, p. 37.

68. F. Parkin, *Middle Class Radicalism: The Social Bases of the British Campaign for Nuclear Disarmament*, Manchester University Press, 1968, pp. 146–51, 181 n. 1. The parents of 445 youth supporters of CND surveyed after participation in the 1965 Easter march reveal that 11 per cent of mothers (but only 8 per cent of fathers) were 'active supporters' of CND; 42

per cent of mothers (but only 33 per cent of fathers) approved, but were not active; while only 19 per cent of mothers (but 22 per cent of fathers) *dis*approved. Research on the role of women in particular local CND groups would be helpful here.

10 Feminism, Eco-feminism, Nuclear Power and Cruise

1. R. Taylor and C. Pritchard, *The Protest Makers: the British Nuclear Disarmament Movement of 1958–1965, Twenty Years On*, Pergamon Press, Oxford, 1980, pp. 22, 32. Of 403 respondents, only 141 (35 per cent) were women, perhaps due to the method of contacting informants. About 56 people (14 per cent) were involved in WLM.

2. Interview recorded with Diana Shelley, December 1984, pp. 4–5, 7, 19, 25–27.

3. ibid., p. 28.

4. A. Coote and B. Campbell, *Sweet Freedom: The Struggle for Women's Liberation*, Pan, London, 1982, pp. 147–48 (and ch. 1 for a summary of demands).

5. D. Widgery, *The Left in Britain 1956–68*, Penguin, London, 1976, p. 113.

6. Parkin, *Middle Class Radicalism*; Driver, *The Disarmers*; see ch. 9.

7. Though note S. Hemmings, *A Wealth of Experience: The Lives of Older Women*, Pandora, London, 1985, pp. 74–75.

8. Coote and Campbell, op. cit., first edn (1982).

9. G. Chester and A. Rigby (eds), *Articles of Peace: Celebrating Fifty Years of Peace News*, Prism, Bridport, 1986.

10. *Call to Women*, no. 93, Feb.–Mar. 1971; thanks to Margot Miller for access to her papers.

11. Interview recorded with Margot Miller, May 1985, pp. 1–3.

12. ibid., pp. 4–7; *Call to Women*, no. 94, Apr.–May 1971.

13. *Guardian*, 4 August 1975, reprinted in *Call to Women*, Aug.–Oct. 1975.

14. *Guardian*, 12 April 1976, reprinted in *Call to Women*, May–June 1976.

15. J. Minnion and P. Bolsover, *The CND Story*, Allison & Busby, London, 1983, pp. 72–3. WILPF's membership was just over 400: WILPF *Annual Report*, 1977–78.

16. Coote and Campbell, op. cit., pp. 26, 303–05; the 1982 edn does not refer to nuclear or conventional militarism.

17. L. Comer, *The Myth of Motherhood*, Spokesman, Nottingham, n.d., pp. 3, 4, 9.

18. *Spare Rib*, no. 53, December 1976.

19. Interview with Shelley, p. 34. Pat Arrowsmith, also ex-C100 and in BWINIC, was jailed in 1974 for nine months for distributing BWINIC leaflets.

20. Interview with Shelley, p. 41; the other woman was Sophie Laws.

21. Interview recorded with Gay Jones, April 1985, pp. 2, 5, 6, 16.

22. ibid., pp. 19–20; the US women were Betsy Beyler and Marty Zinn.

23. ibid., pp. 21–22; also *P Snooze*, 16 May 1975.

24. Interview with Jones, pp. 23–25.

25. *Women in the Nonviolent Movement: Les Femmes Engagées dans la Nonviolence: Frauen der Gewaltfreien Bewegung*, IFOR–WRI International Gathering: 13–18 July 1976, pp. 11–12.

26. ibid., pp. 11, 15.

27. Interview with Jones, p. 23.

28. ibid., p. 26; others included Gail Chester, Jenny Jacobs, Lesley Merryfinch, Jo Somerset, Jill Sutcliffe, and, later, Diana Shelley.

29. Interview with Jones, pp. 29–30.

30. J. Mayerding and B. Smith (eds), *We Are All Part of One Another: A Barbara Deming Reader*, New Society Publishers, Philadelphia, 1984; 'On Revolution and Equilibrium' (1968), pp. 175–78.

31. ibid., 'Remembering Who We Are' (1977), pp. 279, 285–86.

32. Segal, *Is the Future Female?*, ch. 1.

33. Interview with Shelley, p. 37; interview with Gay Jones, p. 28.

34. *Shrew: Neither Victim Nor Assassin: Feminism and Nonviolence*, summer 1978, p. 3.

35. *Guardian*, 17 June 1989.

36. *Guardian*, 2 January 1988 (also 2 January 1989).

37. *Shrew*, pp. 26–27.

38. ibid., pp. 30–31.

39. The neutron bomb was designed to kill people, with minimum damage to buildings, etc.

40. Information from Sarah Perrigo (though exact date is unclear).

41. *Spare Rib*, no. 70, May 1978; no. 80, March 1979; no. 81, April 1979.

42. *SCRAM* (Scottish Campaign to Resist the Nuclear Menace) *Journal*, no. 50, Oct.–Nov. 1985, p. 12.

43. *Spare Rib*, no. 91, February 1980, pp. 6, 40–41.

44. Quoted in A. Beales, *Against All Wars: Fifty Years of Peace News 1936–1986*, Peace News, 1986, p. 48.

45. E. P. Thompson, 'The State of the Nation', *New Society*, 13 December 1979, reprinted in *Writing by Candlelight*, Merlin Press, London, 1980, pp. 248–50.

46. *Peace and Freedom*, no. 97, February 1980.

47. *Sanity*, Oct.–Nov. 1980.

48. Interview recorded with Meg Beresford, August 1985, pp. 9–11.

49. Minnion and Bolsover, op. cit., p. 96; interview recorded with Lynne Jones, August 1985, pp. 7–9; Halifax Nuclear Disarmament (HNDG) *Bulletin*, no. 1.

50. For instance, J. Harber and M. Beresford, 'The New Movement for Nuclear Disarmament', Beyond the Fragments Conference, Leeds, August 1980.

51. For instance, C. Merchant, *The Death of Nature: Women, Ecology and the Scientific Revolution*, USA, 1980 and GB, 1982; S. Griffin, *Woman and Nature: The Roaring Inside Her*, USA, 1978 and GB, 1984.

52. Y. King, 'All is Connectedness', in Jones (ed.), *Keeping the Peace*, pp. 41, 45.

53. Interview recorded with Bridget Robson, March 1985, pp. 9–10.

54. *Spare Rib*, no. 94, May 1980; no. 97, August 1980.

55. Interview with Gay Jones, p. 37; interview with Shelley, p. 45.

56. *Spare Rib*, no. 98, September 1980; interview with Robson, pp. 11–13. Among the early names were 'Women Against Warmongering' and 'Women Versus War'.

57. Leeds WONT petition, *c.* August 1980; it was never sent to Mrs Thatcher; *Spare Rib*, no. 99, October 1980.

58. Interview with Lynne Jones, pp. 10–11.

59. See Jones (ed.), *Keeping the Peace*, pp. 42–43.

60. ibid., pp. 45–51; interview with Lynne Jones, p. 13.

61. *Sanity*, Apr.–May 1981, cover, p. 11.

62. *Sanity*, Feb.–Mar. 1981, pp. 7–10; Oxford Mothers for Nuclear Disarmament, an offspring of Campaign Atom, was another local group.

63. Interview with Miller, pp. 10–11.

11   The Pebble that Started the Avalanche

1.   Thanks to Alan Betteridge for information on closure periods.

2.   The exception, Rebecca Johnson, was interviewed in 1988, shortly after she stopped living at Greenham.

3.   The Pettitt papers were deposited with Glamorgan Record Office, Cardiff, in 1986. I completed a 33-page Preliminary Listing of these papers; as the Record Office has not yet been able to undertake a complete calendar, the notation from this Listing is referred to here.

4.   Interview recorded with Ann Pettitt, Llanpumsaint, August 1985, pp. 2–4.

5.   She expressed her criticisms in 'Feminism For Her Own Good', which stirred up considerable controversy.

6.   Interview with Pettitt, pp. 12, 15.

7.   B1, p. 3; interview, p. 16.

8.   F1, pp. 2, 3; interview, pp. 17, 18.

9.   K2, minute book, untitled, of CANC, 13 May [1981]–8 December [1982].

10. C19, 17 March 1983, pp. 1–3.

11. Interview, pp. 18, 22.

12. A9, B23, p. 1, B5, leaflet, and A5, 20 June 1981; also interview, p. 23.

13. A17, 9 July 1981–A46, 4 August 1981.

14. Interview with Pettitt, pp. 27–28; interview with Lynne Jones, pp. 28–29; also *Women for Life on Earth* Newsletter, autumn 1982.

15. A8, typed press release. For replies to *Sunday Times*, see A50–A64.

16. B2, B9, A92; afterwards the distance was given as 120 and even 125 miles.

17. C19, pp. 11, 13; interview with Pettitt, p. 30.

18. H2, H7, H5, H9, pp. 1–2 (File H mainly comprises memoirs of the WfLOE marchers); *Arcade*, 13 November 1981.

19. Interview, pp. 32–33.

20. H2; H9, pp. 2–3.

21. C19, p. 14; H9, pp. 5–6; *Undercurrents*, no. 48, p. 8; B27, pp. 3A–4A.

22. Interview, p. 34.

23. The details of exactly how the suggestion originated are cloudy; compare, for instance, H5 (which gives a realistic account of the tension) and B. Harford and S. Hopkins (eds), *Greenham Common: Women at the Wire*, The Women's Press, London, 1984, p. 14.

24. Interview, pp. 35–36, 31–32.

25. H5, p. 6; B27; interview with Pettitt, pp. 36–37; interview with Shelley, pp. 52–53.

26. C19, p. 15a; interview with Pettitt, p. 39; Harford and Hopkins, op. cit., p. 15, for details of keening, etc.

27. A94, 'Women's Action for Disarmament', open letter.

28. A110, telegrams; H9, p. 7; A112, 11 September 1981.

29. C19, p. 15a; interview with Pettitt, pp. 41–44.

30. A109, 17 September 1981; A116, 23 September 1981–A127, 16 October 1981; A144, 6 November 1981, includes correspondence with: editor of 'Weeker I World', Lord Chalfont, BBC Secretariat and John Nott.

31. Interview with Shelley, p. 54; interview with Gay Jones, pp. 39–41; H9, p. 8; B24; interview with Pettitt, p. 47.

32. *Observer*, 13 September 1981; *Leveller*, 2–15 October 1981;

Arcade, 13–16 November 1981; *Sanity*, Oct.–Nov. 1981; *Spare Rib*, November 1981; and others.

33. B25, circular letter (9 October 1981), citing a report in the Newbury paper.

34. END *Journal*, spring 1982.

35. *Rebecca*, December 1981; *Guardian*, 16 November 1981; *Sanity*, Feb.–Mar. 1982; A140, A142, A156.

36. *Standard*, 2 December 1981; *Observer*, 22 November 1981.

37. HNDG Mins, 9 December 1981.

38. Women's Peace Alliance (WPA), *Newsletter*, n.d. (*c*. November 1981); interview with Robson, p. 16.

39. Harford and Hopkins, op. cit., pp. 31–34, for one account.

40. Jones (ed.), *Keeping the Peace*, p. 83.

41. *Guardian*, 22, 23 March 1982; Jones, op. cit., pp. 89–93.

42. *Sanity*, Apr.–May 1982.

43. Margot Miller papers; WPA *Newsletter*, May 1982.

44. *Guardian*, 15, 28 May 1982.

45. Harford and Hopkins, op. cit., pp. 47–53, 60; details of the origami cranes action differ.

46. Interview with Rebecca Johnson, March 1988, p. 7.

47. *Guardian*, 28 August, 6 October 1982; 30 September 1982.

48. Accounts include Harford and Hopkins, op. cit., p. 61; interview with Lynne Jones, pp. 38–40.

49. Interview with Miller, p. 14.

50. Letter, addressed 'Dear women', from Greenham Common Women's Peace Camp.

51. Interview with Miller, pp. 14–15; compare Harford and Hopkins, op. cit., p. 65; Glastonbury was the home of Stephanie Leland of WALOE.

52. Interviews with Lynne Jones, p. 40; Pettitt, pp. 50–51; Johnson, pp. 15–16; Shelley, p. 58; Robson, p. 17.

53. *Guardian*, 16, 17, 18 December 1982; *Times*, 17 November 1982; *Daily Express*, 17, 18 November 1982.

54. Interview with Johnson, pp. 16–19.

55. Interviews with Johnson, pp. 20–22; Shelley, p. 58; Pettitt, pp. 52–53; interview recorded with Mary Brewer, September 1985.

56. *Daily Mirror*, 13 December 1982; *New York Times*, 13 December 1982; also *Daily Express*, 13 December 1982.

12   An Icon for the Eighties

1. Songbook, *Women Come Together, Greenham Common, Dec. 12 1982*; this song was to be sung at 2, 3, 4, 5 and 6 o'clock.

2. Interview with Pauline Smith [pseudonym], recorded September 1986, p. 2.

3. Interview with Lynne Jones, pp. 41–43.

4. *Guardian*, 14 December 1982; interview with Johnson, pp. 24–25.

5. *New York Times, Daily Express* and *Guardian*, 14 December 1982.

6. Harford and Hopkins (eds), *Women at the Wire*, pp. 96–97, 100–01.

7. *Guardian*, 3 January 1983.

8. *Daily Express*, 3 January 1983. Driver, *The Disarmers*, pp. 124–25, 164; Helen Allegranza's sentence was 12 months; another comparison is with the 1978 'ABC trial'.

9. *Guardian*, 16, 17 February 1983; Harford and Hopkins, op. cit., pp. 104–06, for details of expert witnesses.

10. *Guardian*, 14 December 1982, 12 January 1983; 11 women failed to appear.

11. According to Harford and Hopkins, op. cit., p. 113; also *Guardian*, 15 December 1982.

12. 'February 22nd: Boring Old High Court: Ocean of Women', [1983].

13. *Guardian*, 23 February 1981; there was a second action, in which 21 women (19 of them on the electoral register) were named in injunction proceedings.

14. *Guardian*, 25, 26 February 1983.

15. *Lysistrata*, no. 1, winter 1982; Chester Women for Peace, *News*, January 1983; HNDG Mins, 5, 19 January 1983.

16. *Sunday Times*, 19 December 1982, 23 January 1983.

17. B. Campbell, *The Iron Ladies: Why Do Women Vote Tory?*, Virago, London, 1987, pp. 126, 130; also *Guardian*, 18, 21 January 1983 ('Over the Greenham Fence and into the Poll Findings').

18. *Sunday Times*, 16, 23 January 1983.

19. *Sun*, 14 December 1982; *Express*, 15 December 1982, 8 February 1983.

20. *The Defence Campaigner*, Women and Families for Defence, summer [1984].

21. Minutes of CND National Council, 16 January 1983; overall, men outnumbered women on Council by three to two, with some CND regions being represented by men only.

22. There were, of course, exceptions; Thalia Campbell (*Ynni*, May 1983) noted, 'I know that some of the committed older women share my feelings of frustration and isolation by the attitudes of some women who have just "seen the light" and joined the movement. They lack humility, a historical perspective . . .'. See also Introduction, notes 9, 10.

23. *Guardian*, 13, 15 December 1982.

24. *Lysistrata*, no. 3, spring 1984, no. 1, winter 1982.

25. For instance, *Western Mail*, 15 April 1983, interview with Pettitt.

26. *Sanity*, March 1983, pp. 10–11; April 1983, pp. 36–37; May 1983, pp. 14–15, 27.

27. Interview with Johnson, p. 56.

28. Comparison with the suffragettes' use of mysticism and imagery is interesting here.

29. 30–31 March 1983; papers in possession of author; *Halifax Courier*, 31 March 1983; *Guardian*, 2 April 1983.

30. *Spare Rib*, no. 127, February 1983, p. 18; 130, May 1983, p. 23; 132, July 1983, p. 36. For a coherent appraisal of these complex questions, see K. Soper, 'Taking the Toys from the Boys?' *END* Journal, Oct.–Nov. 1986.

31. N. Edwards, *Mud*, The Women's Press, London, 1986, especially chs 5, 12; *Carry Greenham Home* by film-makers Beeban Kidron and Amanda Richardson.

32. Feminism and Nonviolence Study Group, *Piecing It Together*, 1983, pp. 9, 33. *Spare Rib*, no. 132, July 1983; this coincided with a row at *Spare Rib* over racism and Zionism.

33. *Breaching the Peace*, Onlywomen Press, London, 1983, pp. 7–8.

34. J. Freer, (C. Lee), *Raging Women: In Reply to Breaching the*

Peace, n.d., privately published, pp. 4–5, 7, 17; spelling as given.

35. Circular, 'May 24th – Women All Out for Peace', n.d.; Circular letter, NALGO, 4 April 1983.

36. *Spare Rib*, July 1983; *Halifax Courier*, 25 May 1983.

37. *Guardian*, 25 May 1983; on Plymouth, interview with Gay Jones, p. 45.

38. *Sanity*, July 1983; also J. Harber, 'Tory fudge sweetens Bomb', *END Journal*, Aug.–Sept. 1983.

13 Fortress Greenham?

1. *END Journal*, Oct.–Nov. 1983; WPA *Newsletter*, no. 11, October 1983.

2. Interview recorded with Nina Hall, August 1986, pp. 1–4.

3. *Guardian*, 5, 9, 13 July 1983; *Halifax Courier*, 9 July 1983.

4. Interview with Hall, p. 4.

5. *Daily Mirror*, 11 July 1983.

6. *Hansard*, 25 July 1983, cols 967–75.

7. Campbell, *The Iron Ladies*, p. 131 (November 1983: 57 per cent women, 43 per cent men).

8. Interview with Smith, p. 3.

9. Circular letter, 'Greenham Support Groups Meeting, Manchester Sept. 10/11', London Office, 11 August 1983; handwritten list, 'Regional Contacts for Women's Peace Movement'.

10. *Huddersfield Examiner*, 17 September 1983; *Halifax Courier*, 24 September, 29 October 1983; 23 February 1984.

11. *END Journal*, Dec. 1983–Jan. 1984; there were also demonstrations in Canada, the USA, etc.

12. Interview with Hall, pp. 5–6; *Guardian*, 31 October 1983.

13. Press Release, 'Greenham Women Against Cruise', 23 October 1983.

14. *Guardian*, 23 November 1983; *Sanity*, April 1985, p. 45.

15. *Guardian*, 10 November 1983.

16. *Guardian*, 15, 21 November 1983; interview with Miller, p. 18.

17. *Daily Telegraph* and *Yorkshire Post*, 6 March 1984; also *Sanity*, November 1985, p. 35.

18. For instance, F11–F25, Pettitt papers.

19. Author's own notes.

20. *Guardian*, 12, 13, 20 December 1983.

21. Circular letter, 'Dear Sisters', n.d.; interview with Smith, p. 3; interview with Johnson, pp. 39–40; *Sanity*, July 1985 on Cruisewatch.

22. Interview with Johnson, pp. 41–42; *Guardian*, 2, 5–7 April 1984.

23. Interview with Meryl Antonelli, May 1986, pp. 1–2.

24. ibid., pp. 3–5.

25. Interview with Johnson, pp. 12–13, 42.

26. WPA Newsletter, October 1984; *Guardian*, 30 August 1985, 'Greenham Women's Tenacity Surprises US Missile Chief'.

27. Newsletter, *Green And Common Womyn's Peace Camp*, Autumn 1984; *Guardian*, 9 September 1985.

28. WPA Newsletter, October 1985; *Spare Rib*, no. 155, June 1985; *New Statesman*, 16 August 1985.

29. *Sanity*, January 1985, p. 4.

30. *New Statesman*, 25 November 1988 (also 17 May, 5 July 1985); *Sanity*, July 1985, March 1987, January 1988. The other women elected at the 1987 conference were Elena Lievan and Marjorie Thompson as vice-chairs, and Linda Churnside as treasurer; Bruce Kent was subsequently elected CND chair.

31. *New Statesman*, 5 September 1986.

32. ibid., 'Peace Protests Roll Call', 3, 9, compiled by Janey Hulme.

33. ibid., 14, 3 May 1985; 16, 28 June 1985; 20, 25 October 1985; 27, 23 May 1987. It should be easier for historians to acquire precise figures next century.

34. 'Peace in Court', *Sanity*, November 1987–August 1988; many were Snowball arrests; the woman was Sarah Hipperson.

35. For instance, the cases of Sarah Tisdall, Clive Ponting and Cathy Massiter; also *Sanity*, August 1986.

36. Interview with Lynne Jones, pp. 45–46, recorded August 1985.

37. *Sanity*, June 1985.

38. *Guardian*, 8 August 1988; also *Sanity*, August 1987, December 1988.

39. *Sanity*, Oct. 1986–June 1987; particularly helpful is 'Sexism in the Peace Movement', *Sanity*, June 1987.

40. Interview with Johnson, pp. 39, 52.

41. *Spare Rib*, May 1983, p. 23.

42. Interview with Johnson, pp. 53–54.

43. Press coverage included *Guardian*, 23 November 1987; letters 28 November 1987–17 January 1988; interview with Wilmette Brown, 23 December 1987; *Marxism Today*, November 1987; *Sanity*, November 1987.

44. *Guardian*, 9 June, 8 September 1988.

45. *New Statesman*, 21 October 1988.

46. *Guardian*, 6 January 1989.

47. However, the *Guardian*, for instance, continued to mark Greenham's anniversaries each September and December (e.g. 7, 9 December 1987).

48. *Time Out*, 10–17 August 1988; thanks to Sarah Baxter for her help here; and information from Doreen Ward, November 1988.

49. 1988 membership figures: national members – 72,500; local membership estimated at 185,000, giving a total of approximately 257,500, CND *Annual Conference Report 1988*, p. 18. (See page 278 above for comparison with 1984 figures.)

50. *New Statesman*, 21 October 1988.

51. *New Statesman*, 19 May 1989.

Sources

(Major sources only are referred to here; others are listed in the appropriate endnote.)

Oral Testimony

24 interviews were recorded; of these, reference has been made to:

June 1984	Gwen Coleman (Chapman), 1890–1985	Henley-on-Thames
Sept.–Dec. 1984	Dame Mabel Tylecote (Phythian), 1896–1987	Manchester
Dec. 1984	Diana Shelley, b. 1943	London
Mar. 1985	Bridget Robson, b. 1949	Leeds
Apr. 1985	Gay Jones, b. 1949	Plymouth
May 1985	Margot Miller, b. 1939	Shilton, Oxon
Aug. 1985	Ann Pettitt, b. 1947	Llanpumsaint, Dyfed
Aug. 1985	Lynne Jones, b. 1952	Redruth, Cornwall
Aug. 1985	Meg Beresford, b. 1937	London
Sept. 1985	Mary Brewer, b. 1924	Sowerby Bridge, Halifax
May 1986	Richenda Barbour, b. 1926	Golders Green, London
May 1986	Meryl Antonelli, b. 1961	Violet Gate, Greenham
Aug. 1986	Nina Hall, b. 1967	Leeds
Sept. 1986	[Pauline Smith: pseud.], b. 1946	Red Gate, Greenham
Mar. 1987	Emma Chatterton, b. 1915	Clayton, Bradford
Mar. 1988	Rebecca Johnson, b. 1954	London

Copies of these tapes, with their transcripts and summaries, are deposited with Calderdale District Archives, Halifax Library.

Women and Peace Histories

Malmgreen, G., 'Anne Knight and the Radical Subculture', *Quaker History*, vol. 71, no. 2, 1982

Pierson, R. R. (ed.), *Women and Peace: Theoretical, Historical and Practical Perspectives*, Croom Helm, London, 1987

Posthumus-Van Der Goot, Dr W. H., *Vrouwen Vochten Voor de Vrede* (Women Fought for Peace), Van Loghum Slaterus, Arnhem, 1961

Tyrrell, A., '"Woman's Mission" and Pressure Group Politics in Britain (1825–60)', *Bulletin of the John Rylands University Library of Manchester*, vol. 63, no. 1

Wiltsher, A., *Most Dangerous Women: Feminist Peace Campaigners of the Great War*, Pandora, London, 1985

General Peace Histories

Beales, A. C. F., *The History of Peace: A Short Account of the Organized Movements for International Peace*, G. Bell, London 1931

Boulton, D., unpublished MS account of origins of NCANWT, NCANWT Archive

Brock, P., *Pacifism in Europe to 1914*, Princeton University Press, New Jersey, 1972

Caedel, M., *Pacifism in Britain 1914–1945: The Defining of a Faith*, Clarendon Press, Oxford, 1980

Driver, C., *The Disarmers: A Study in Protest*, Hodder & Stoughton, London, 1964

Minnion, J. and Bolsover, P. (eds), *The CND Story*, Allison & Busby, London, 1983

Newton, D. J., *British Labour, European Socialism and the Struggle for Peace 1889–1914*, Clarendon Press, Oxford, 1985

Parkin, F., *Middle Class Radicalism: The Social Bases of the British Campaign for Nuclear Disarmament*, Manchester University Press, Manchester, 1968

Swartz, M., *The Union of Democratic Control in British Politics During the First World War*, Clarendon Press, Oxford, 1971

Taylor, R., *Against the Bomb: The British Peace Movement 1958–1965*, Clarendon Press, Oxford, 1988

Taylor, R. and Pritchard, C., *The Protest Makers: The British*

Nuclear Disarmament Movement of 1958–1965, Twenty Years On, Pergamon Press, Oxford, 1980.

Taylor, R. and Young, N. (eds), *Campaigns for Peace: British Peace Movements in the Twentieth Century*, Manchester University Press, Manchester, 1987

Peace Polemics

Anon [Robbins, E.], *Ancilla's Share: An Indictment of Sex Antagonism*, Hutchinson, London, 1924

Breaching the Peace, Onlywomen Press, London, 1983

Feminism and Nonviolence Study Group, *Piecing It Together: Feminism and Nonviolence*, Devon, 1983

Hallowes, F. S., *Women and War: An Appeal to the Women of all Nations*, Headley Bros, London, [1914]

Hallowes, F. S., *Mothers of Men and Militarism*, Headley Bros, London, [1915]

Harford, B. and Hopkins, S. (eds), *Greenham Common: Women at the Wire*, The Women's Press, London, 1984

Hobhouse, E., *Report of a Visit to the Camps of Women and Children in the Cape and Orange River Colonies*, Friars Printing Association, London, 1901

Hobhouse, E., *The Brunt of War and Where It Fell*, Methuen, London, 1902

Kamester, M. and Vellacott, J. (eds), *Militarism versus Feminism: Writings on Women and War*, Virago, London, 1987

Key, E., *War, Peace and the Future: A Consideration of Nationalism and Internationalism, and the Relation of Women to War*, G. P. Putnam's, New York & London, 1916

Jones, L. (ed.), *Keeping the Peace*, The Women's Press, London, 1983

Mayerding, J. and Smith, R. (eds), *We Are All Part Of One Another: A Barbara Deming Reader*, New Society Publishers, Philadelphia, 1984

Militarism versus Feminism: An Enquiry and a Policy Demonstrating that Militarism involves the Subjection of Women, Allen & Unwin, London, 1915

Neither Victim Nor Assassin: Feminism and Nonviolence, Shrew (special issue), 1978

Thompson, D. (ed.), *Over Our Dead Bodies: Women Against the Bomb*, Virago, London, 1983

Towards Permanent Peace: a Record of the Women's International Congress held at The Hague, April 28th–May 1st, 1915, British Committee of the Women's International Congress, London, 1915

Women in the Nonviolent Movement: Les Femmes Engagées dans la Nonviolence: Frauen der Gewaltfreien Bewegung, IFOR–WRI International Gathering, [1976]

Woolf, V., *Three Guineas*, 1938 and Penguin, London, 1977

Biographies and Autobiographies

Brittain, V., *Testament of Youth*, 1933 and Fontana, London, 1979

Brittain, V., *Testament of Experience: an Autobiographical Story of the Years 1925–1950*, 1957 and Virago, London, 1979

Duff, P., *Left, Left, Left*, Allison & Busby, London, 1971

Fisher, J., *That Miss Hobhouse: The Life of a Great Feminist*, Secker & Warburg, London, 1971

Fry, R., *Emily Hobhouse*, Cape, London, 1919

Gilman, C. P., *The Living of Charlotte Perkins Gilman: an Autobiography*, D. Appleton-Century Co., New York & London, 1935

Kempf, B., *Suffragette for Peace: the Life of Bertha von Suttner*, Austria, 1964 and Wolff, London, 1972

Knox, W. W. (ed.), *Scottish Labour Leaders 1918–1939: A Biographical Dictionary*, Edinburgh, 1983

Leff, V., *Dare To Speak*, unpublished typescript, 1978

Liddington, J., *The Life and Times of a Respectable Rebel: Selina Cooper 1864–1946*, Virago, London, 1984

Lockwood, F., *An Ordinary Life: 1861–1924*, published privately, London, 1932

Nyström-Hamilton, L., *Ellen Key: Her Life and Work*, C. P. Putnam's, New York & London, 1913

Oldfield, S., *Spinsters of This Parish: The Life & Times of F. M. Mayor and Mary Sheepshanks*, Virago, London, 1984

Russell, D., *The Tamarisk Tree: vol. 3: The Challenge to the Cold War*, Virago, London, 1985

Swanwick, H. M., *I Have Been Young*, Victor Gollancz, London, 1935

Novels

Arrowsmith, P., *Jericho*, 1965 and Heretic Books, London, 1985

Edwards, N., *Mud*, The Women's Press, London, 1986

Lindsay, J., *The Moment of Choice: A Novel of the British Way*, Bodley Head, London, 1955

Macaulay, R., *Non-Combatants and Others*, 1916; Methuen, London, 1986

Suttner, B. von, *Lay Down Your Arms: the Autobiography of Martha von Tilling*, 1889 and Longmans, London, 1892

Accounts of Women's Movement and Organizations

Bussey, G. and Tims, M., *Pioneers for Peace: Women's International League for Peace and Freedom 1915–1965*, Allen & Unwin, 1965; WILPF British Section, London, 1980

Campbell, B., *The Iron Ladies: Why do Women Vote Tory?* Virago, London, 1987

Coote, A. and Campbell, B., *Sweet Freedom: The Struggle for Women's Liberation*, Pan, London, 1982

Gaffin, J. and Thoms, D., *Caring & Sharing: The Centenary History of the Co-operative Women's Guild*, Co-operative Union, Manchester, 1983

Gilman, C. P., *The Man-Made World, or Our Androcentric Culture*, Fisher Unwin, London, 1911

Key, E., *The Woman Movement*, G. P. Putnam's, New York & London, 1912

Of Whole Heart Cometh Hope: Centenary Memories of the Co-operative Women's Guild, Age Exchange Theatre Company, London, 1983

Schreiner, O., *Woman and Labour*, 1911 and Virago, London, 1978

Segal, L., *Is the Future Female? Troubled Thoughts on Contemporary Feminism*, Virago, London, 1987

Swanwick, H. M., *The Future of the Women's Movement*, G. Bell & Sons, London, 1913

Ward, H., *A Venture in Goodwill: Being the Story of the Women's International League 1915–1929*, Women's International League, London, 1929

Whittick, A., *Woman into Citizen*, Athenaeum with Frederick Muller, London, 1979

Wilson, E., *Only Halfway to Paradise: Women in Postwar Britain: 1945–1968*, Tavistock, London, 1980

Women in a Changing World: the dynamic story of the International Council of Women, Routledge & Kegan Paul, London, 1966

General

Mill, J. S., *The Subjection of Women*, 1869 and Virago, London, 1983

Ruskin, J., Lecture on 'War', delivered at the Royal Military Academy, Woolwich, 1865, *The Crown of Wild Olive*

Shannon, R., *The Crisis of Imperialism 1865–1915*, 1974 and Paladin, London, 1976

Summers, A., *Angels and Citizens: British Women as Military Nurses 1854–1914*, Routledge & Kegan Paul, London, 1988

Journals and Newsletters

Call to Women
Common Cause
Englishwoman's Journal (later *Review*)
Halifax Courier
Halifax Nuclear Disarmament Group *Newsletter*
Hampstead and Highgate Express
Huddersfield Daily Examiner
Labour Leader
Leeds WONT *Newsletter*
Lysistrata
(Manchester) Guardian
New Statesman
Jus Suffragii
Peace and Goodwill
Sanity
Spare Rib
Women's Peace Alliance *Newsletter*

Personal Papers, Annual Reports and Minute Books

Ann Pettitt Papers, Gwasanaeth Archifau Morgannwg (Glamorgan Archive Service), County Hall, Cardiff

Fawcett Library, pamphlet boxes 327 etc.

Halifax Nuclear Disarmament Group, minute books, Calderdale District Archives

Hampstead Garden Suburb (Golders Green) Branch Women's Co-operative Guild, minute books, Co-operative Women's Guild headquarters

Florence Lockwood, manuscript diaries 1914–18, West Yorkshire Archive Service, Kirklees Library

Margot Miller, personal papers

National Council for the Abolition of Nuclear Weapons Tests (Arthur Goss papers), now deposited with CND

Public Record Office, Home Office papers, HO 45/10741–10814, etc.

Rosika Schwimmer papers, Schwimmer/Lloyd papers, Rare Books and Manuscripts Division, New York Public Library, Astor Lenox and Tilden Foundations

Scottish Gallacher Memorial Library, papers

Dame Mabel Tylecote, pocket diaries

Women's International League for Peace and Freedom (WILPF), British Section, Annual Reports

Unpublished Theses

Grayzel, S., *Mothers, Sisters and Outsiders: Feminist Pacifism in Britain from Olive Schreiner to Virginia Woolf*, BA, Harvard, 1986

Smyth, J. J., *Women in Struggle: A Study of the Political Activity of Working-class Women in Glasgow during the First World War*, MA, Glasgow, 1980

Taylor, R., *The British Nuclear Disarmament Movement of 1958 to 1965 and its Legacy to the Left*, Ph.D, Leeds, 1983

Index